LIFE
AT FULL
THROTTLE

LIFE AT FULL THROTTLE

From Wardroom to Boardroom

by

ADMIRAL SIR JOHN TREACHER

Pen & Sword
MARITIME

First published in Great Britain 2004 by
Pen & Sword Maritime
an imprint of
Pen & Sword Books Ltd
47 Church Street
Barnsley
South Yorkshire
S70 2AS

ISBN 1 84415 134 4

A CIP catalogue record for this book is available from the
British Library

Typeset in Plantin by
Phoenix Typesetting, Auldgirth, Dumfriesshire

Printed and bound in England by
CPI UK

Pen & Sword Books Ltd incorporates the imprints of Pen & Sword
Aviation, Pen & Sword Maritime, Pen & Sword Military, Wharncliffe
Local History, Pen & Sword Select, Pen & Sword Military Classics and
Leo Cooper.

For a complete list of Pen & Sword titles please contact
PEN & SWORD BOOKS LIMITED
47 Church Street, Barnsley, South Yorkshire, S70 2AS, England
E-mail: enquiries@pen-and-sword.co.uk
Website: www.pen-and-sword.co.uk

CONTENTS

To my wife Kirstie and my children
Jonathan, Alison, Toby and Mhairi,
and all those who served with me at sea and in the air.

INTRODUCTION AND ACKNOWLEDGMENTS

It was not until my third 'retirement' that I thought seriously about leaving some trace of my activities, although my family had from time to time suggested that a number of the events in which I had taken part were indeed worth recording.

Apart from my thirty-five years of naval service which saw many fundamental changes in naval equipment and operations, my family ties with North and South America, the Far East and Australia, and my subsequent twenty-seven years in business have provided some interesting and even unique experiences. However, I had never been a diarist by inclination. Not for me the 'Assassin's Cloak'. But I had been required during my war service as a midshipman to keep a journal which has proved useful in providing detail for that period and I have referred to my flying log books. For the rest, I have relied mostly on memory and hence there are few verbatim reports and, I trust, less chance of mis-quoting those I have encountered.

These recollections do not belong only to me. They belong to all those with whom I have worked, most notably in the Navy where every single member of a ship's company plays a vital part. They were mostly aged between eighteen and thirty, in the smallest inshore mine-sweeper or the biggest aircraft carriers where daily operations were particularly complex and testing. In *Eagle* there were about three thousand of them and when the ship visited Gibraltar the male population in that age group doubled.

At the end no account of times past compares with what one has perhaps contrived for the future and the four children from my two marriages, who are not only siblings but really good friends, will be my legacy. They have so far produced seven grandchildren and still counting.

I am indebted to those who have assisted and contributed to the completion of this task: to Graham Mottram, Director of the Fleet Air Arm Museum, to Commander Macdonald, Director of the Fleet Air Arm Officers' Association, to Alan Leahy, Geoff Higgs and Denis Higton for helping with dates and names associated with flying operations, to Tugg Wilson for permission to reproduce some of his work, to Rodney Sturdee for some verse, and the *Daily Mail* and *Evening Standard* for the reproduction of cartoons and photographs.

Above all I am indebted to Kirstie, who encouraged me, not just at the beginning but in the continuing of the task, proof-reading without obvious signs of boredom and always with good humour, and my younger son, Toby, whose magic touch has kept my ageing word processor alive well beyond its normal life span.

None of this would have been possible without the advice and patience of Henry Wilson who risked becoming my publisher and Tom Hartman who tried to ensure that the syntax was without sin.

PROLOGUE

Admiralty House – Northwood, 28 March 1977

Breakfast in the nursery; usually the only chance to see my two young children every day. Deliberately I had no reading matter, certainly no newspapers. However, on this morning there was a carefully folded page with a headline that read 'NAVY CHIEF RESIGNS'. Harry Chapman Pincher had telephoned me the previous evening and, although I had tried to put him off the scent, his well-tuned antennae clearly detected a senior resignation in the air and this had to be newsworthy. But this wasn't his by-line.

Petty Officer Rice, who had served with me on and off over the past ten years, was hovering in the background and obviously expected, and deserved, an answer. 'Yes,' I said, 'It's true.'

The formal announcement was due to be made public the next day and I intended to inform the whole military staff, National and NATO, later that morning. The awkward moment was ended by the arrival of the children.

I had written to the First Sea Lord some months before, saying that I did not wish to be considered for another appointment. I was aware that, just like a sudden death or incapacity, a totally unexpected wish to leave the Service expressed by one of the very few four-star officers would inevitably cause some juggling with other planned appointments and I wanted to allow time for this due process: but I also asked to be released as soon as possible.

It can always be argued, and some took this view at the time, that it was the duty of those who had been entrusted with high command and had gained the experience which should enable them to exercise it with good judgment should no longer make personal decisions about their own future.

In times of war, of course, that view must prevail, but in peacetime surely not. The armed forces are blessed with the ability to recruit, develop and retain a cadre of officers at every level, most of whom are equally experienced and capable of filling a more senior post at very short notice. I was well aware of the abundance of talent in my own service at the time.

At the age of 52 I had served nearly 35 years in the Navy, many of them devoted to the Fleet Air Arm. I had, perhaps uniquely, commanded a front-line squadron, served as Commander Air in one of the three biggest aircraft carriers and on the staff of the Flag Officer Flying Training, as well as being Director of Naval Air Warfare on the Naval Staff, Captain of the Carrier HMS *Eagle,* Flag Officer Carriers and Amphibious Ships and Flag Officer Naval Air Command before becoming Vice Chief of the Naval Staff and Commander-in-Chief of the Fleet. I had seen the preservation of the carriers and the acceptance of the Sea Harrier.

I believed I had fifteen to twenty working years ahead of me with a young family to support. If a change of direction was to take place it had to be now. Many of my fellow officers found my decision difficult to understand, as did Her Majesty the Queen when I made my farewell call. 'My son tells me you shouldn't be leaving,' she said.

My decision was wholly supported by my wife, who, while accepting the domination of the grey mistresses which demanded so much of my time, had always looked forward to having a larger share herself. In the event some of my business activities were to be almost more demanding.

The only other person in whom I confided was my splendid secretary, Michael Hudson, who confessed he was also planning to leave whenever I did and was currently studying to become a Chartered Secretary.

What follows attempts to trace my four score years, all of which I have enjoyed immensely and for which I am forever indebted to an abundance of good fortune, the skill of two eminent heart surgeons, the selfless care and attention of my mother in my early years and the forbearance of my family.

GLOSSARY

ACAS	Assistant Chief of the Air Staff
ACCHAN	Allied C-in-C Channel
ACLANT	Allied C-in-C Atlantic
AD-W	Attack Aircraft (Warning) made by Douglas
AEW	Airborne Early Warning
AFT	Advanced Flying Training
AMGOT	Allied Military Government of Occupied Territory
ASW	Anti-Submarine Warfare
BAC	British Aircraft Corporation
CAS	Chief of the Air Staff
CBI	Confederation of British Industry
CDS	Chief of the Defence Staff
CEO	Chief Executive Officer
CNS	Chief of Naval Staff
CPE	Chief Polaris Executive
DLCO	Deck Landing Control Officer
DNAW	Director of Naval Air Warfare
DOPC	Defence and Overseas Policy Committee
EASTLANT	NATO Eastern Atlantic Command
ETA	Estimated Time of Arrival
FAA	Fleet Air Arm

FAETULANT	Fleet Airborne Electronic Training Unit Atlantic
FLAPS	Front Line Armament Practices
FOCAS	Flag Officer Carriers and Amphibious Ships
FOFT	Flag Officer Flying Training
FONAC	Flag Officer Naval S Air Command
FOST	Flag Officer Sea Training
FRC	Fleet Requirements Committee
HMCS	Her Majesty's Canadian Ship
HMS	Her Majesty's Ship
MNC	Major NATO Commander
NA3SL	Naval Assistant to Third Sea Lord
NATO	North Atlantic Treaty Organization
OFT	Operational Flying Training
ORI	Operational Readiness Inspection
OTC	Officer in Tactical Command
PERT	Project Evaluation Review Technique
SACEUR	Supreme Allied Commander Europe
SACLANT	Supreme Allied Commander Atlantic
SAR	Search and Rescue
SBAC	Society of British Aerospace Companies
STANAVFORLANT	Standing Naval Force Atlantic
STU	Service Trials Unit
USMC	US Marine Corps
USS	United States Ship
WRNS	Women's Royal Naval Service

1

START UP

SOUTH AMERICA

Concepción – Chile 23 September 1924

Treacher. To Gladys Mary Treacher (Née Page) at the German Clinic a son John, a brother for Barbara.

My mother was 34 years old when I was born in the German Clinic in Concepción. She had nursed in Flanders without a break for the four years of the Great War; the years when Britain was bled white by the terrible attrition of the trenches where the slaughter made no distinction of rank and the very junior seldom survived more than a few months. Here the losses of young officers were out of all proportion and heirs to families and fortunes, however modest, were devastating.

This was a country which my mother knew mostly from seeing the flower of its youth die in the wards or on the operating theatres in which she worked. The British were not alone. The same fate befell the young Canadians with whom she had grown up and who had sailed across from Canada to support the mother country.

In 1919 she married and immediately sailed for Chile where her husband had obtained a job with Williamson Balfour, a well-established English trading house. He was six years her junior. In the Argentine when war broke out it was two years before he could get passage to England and by then the worst of the slaughter was over.

My sister had been born three years earlier in the same German Clinic and the immeasurable tolerance, patience and absolute determination my mother displayed throughout her life must have been sorely tested by her enforced dependence on German medical support after her appalling experience tending the wounded and dying and particularly those who had been gassed during the war.

My father, Frank Charles Treacher, was no stranger to South America having been born and brought up in the Argentine, and my mother, born and brought up in Canada, was no stranger to remote areas. But Chile was altogether different. A narrow strip of land squeezed between the high Andes and the Pacific ocean with a thousand-mile coastline, stretching from the arid desert in the north to the glaciers in the south, it had won independence from Spain only some one hundred years before.

Chile owed its freedom to two people. One was Bernardo O'Higgins, the illegitimate son of an obscure Irishman who had worked his way up to become Viceroy of Peru. O'Higgins, small and with no redeeming physical features, led the Chileans to victory in a series of fierce battles against the Spanish forces in southern Chile to become leader of the new Republic.

The other, Admiral Lord Cochrane, son of a Scottish Earl, had established his reputation as one of Britain's greatest sea captains and victor of a number of the most spectacular battles of the Napoleonic wars. Known worldwide as the Sea Wolf, and considered by many as the model for Captain Aubrey in Patrick O'Brien's famous books, he managed to lead his life ashore in much the same fashion, incurring such serious wrath in high places that in 1817, concluding there was no future command for him in the Royal Navy, and his financial situation now perilous, he undertook to head the Chilean Navy.

In fact he had been bought. He was to become a mercenary, engaged by an emissary of the new republic of Chile which desperately needed a daring naval commander to rid the long coastline of the domination of the Spanish navy which had continued after the army's defeat on land. Cochrane quickly overcame the Spanish Pacific Fleet with Chilean forces less than one sixth of the size and indeed his exploits were to exceed anything he had achieved before.

Chile a hundred years later was at ease with itself. It had avoided the turbulent political unrest and military regimes that had beset many of the other fledgling republics in South and Central America and enjoyed a stable economy based mainly on its natural resources of nitrates and copper. It had welcomed expatriates from Britain,

Germany and France, who lived peacefully together, forming small communities in the major cities where they manned the volunteer fire engines among other civic duties.

Concepción was one of these, situated close to the Chilean naval base at Talcahuano. From Concepción we moved to Valparaiso and then to Valdivia [named, strangely, after the hated conquistador, Pedro de Valdivia] which was to be devastated by earthquake and flood in 1960, where we lived close to the beach at Niebla opposite the Port of Coral. Here we swam in the freezing Pacific waters and ran out onto the black volcanic sand which was not only hot enough to burn the soles of our feet but also produced hard-boiled eggs for the picnic lunches. Finally, we lived in Temuco near the shore of the lake of Pucón and in the shadow of the magnificent conical volcano of Villarrica.

Life in Chile, disjointed and often primitive as it was, must have seemed a haven of tranquility after the war years, but was to be destroyed by the collapse of the Chilean currency in the wake of the 1929 Wall Street crash. For our family this meant the inability to afford the cost of sending children to school in England and hence the choice of either remaining in Chile for a lifetime or returning to England and starting again.

My father chose the latter option and we sailed, literally with all our worldly goods, from Valparaiso in November 1929 in the Dutch steamship *Bodegraven*. The ship stopped at Antofagasta, Iquique and Lima before passing through the Panama canal.

After the canal came a slow journey across the Atlantic, enlivened by the daily routine on the fo'c's'le where we watched the animals being given fresh air and hosed down and sometimes slaughtered for the larder. There was no refrigeration on board.

We landed in Rotterdam with twenty-seven assorted pieces of luggage. It was raining. Then on to the ferry to Harwich and finally to join my grandparents in the village of Clopton for Christmas.

SOUTHERN ENGLAND

My maternal grandfather, John Walter Bowden Page, on leaving Oxford took Holy Orders and soon afterwards settled in Canada, taking up his duties in the Province of Manitoba. In 1888 he married Ada Jesse Adams, the eldest of eight children of a retired Indian Army officer who had become a senior executive in the Hudson Bay Company. My mother, their only child, was born in 1890 in Kenora, near Winnipeg.

Grandfather Page was a man of immense moral and physical courage whose various feats of single-handed bravery in tending his parishioners during the bitter winters of mid-Western Canada were modestly recorded by the Humane Society of Kenora and inscribed on the case of a gold hunter watch and the head of an ebony cane presented on 6 October 1906.

By this time an Archdeacon, he returned to England and took a country living in the village of Clopton in Suffolk. When war broke out he was asked to serve as Chaplain with the First Canadian Infantry Division and crossed to France in 1914, remaining with them there until the end of the war. He was accompanied by his daughter, now an army nurse.

The Rectory at Clopton was to be our first home on our return to England. His was a wonderfully benign presence and this infected all those around him. I was thirteen when he died and I missed him greatly.

Sadly, my grandmother was as introspective and egocentric as he was thoughtful and generous. She outlived her son-in-law by six years. We were all very fortunate that my mother took after her father.

My sister and I settled into a happy routine at the rectory, sharing a governess with the two youngest daughters of the Round-Turner family who lived in the neighbouring village of Grundisburgh. The father, a friend of my mother's family, was a captain in the Navy and had commanded a squadron of ships which had paid a courtesy visit to Valparaiso while we were living there. In 1933, when he was the Admiral at Chatham Dockyard, he gave me my first sight of the Navy. Although he had two sons in the Service our paths never crossed, but some fifty years later I sat next to a young lady at dinner whose mother had been one of the Round-Turner girls. She said her mother thought I had been a real bruiser. There's no answer when a pretty girl says that.

For my father, times were much more difficult. Jobs were in short supply and, after several moves, my parents decided to invest the remains of their capital in a London house which, divided into flats would, they thought, give us somewhere to live and a rental income from the tenants. We ended up in the basement.

I went to school at Colet Court from the age of eight. Colet Court had a splendid mix of pupils from many different lands and differing backgrounds: from the sons of Earls and of Emperor Haile Selassie to prosperous English merchants and impecunious recent immigrants from Europe.

Although the twenties and thirties have been described by some of my contemporaries as innocent decades of childhood, the happy pre-war time of benign summers, cricket in the meadows and tea in the pavilion, this hardly fitted the reality of a London day school where what was happening in the world outside was never far away and the financial uncertainty in our family a daily drama. Nevertheless we never felt deprived, enjoyed summer holidays in Suffolk, staying with the grandparents now in Ipswich, and bicycling daily to the beach at Felixstowe.

In London we frequently saw three of my mother's aunts who were, in contrast to my grandmother, a jolly lot. The spinster Aunt Mabel effortlessly ran a small flat for her one-armed sister Judy who sat contentedly in a large armchair knitting furiously with one hand while the other needle was held firmly by the stump of her other arm. This had been amputated by her father to save her life when she had been bitten by a poisonous snake as a child on the North-West Frontier of India.

Aunt Judy, despite this handicap and losing her husband in action during the First World War, was always full of fun and an easy favourite. The dramatic action in which she had lost her arm never ceased to fascinate me as I pictured her father, in full dress uniform, drawing his sword and severing her bone in one clean stroke.

After the girls came a much younger brother who stayed in Canada and the USA singing operas for a living. His two children gravitated to Hollywood where Claire became a star of the silent screen, while her brother Gerald wrote scripts. No one talked much about them until Claire wrote to say she was not happy in the new talkies and had decided to marry an Australian landowner, Scobie MacKinnon. They would be passing through England on honeymoon, which they did in style.

A family outing took us to Southampton to see them off in the *Queen Mary* and, beautiful as she was, Claire was well matched by her Clark Gable look-alike husband. The press cameras did not know which way to turn. Scobie had graduated from and rowed for Oxford and his father had been one of the founders of the Flemington Race Course in Melbourne where the race run immediately before the Cup on Melbourne Cup Day is still called the MacKinnon Stakes. I was thrilled to have been their guest on Cup Day many years later.

Meanwhile brother Gerald Drayson Adams stayed in Hollywood, wrote scripts, won an Oscar, married a French Canadian and lived comfortably in the Hollywood Hills and a large beach house at Malibu. 'Frenchie' kept cats, lots of cats. They had no children but were great hosts.

Both my paternal grandparents had died before I was born. Charles Skipper Treacher was born in 1847, the son of the Rev. Joseph Skipper Treacher, Chaplain of Merton College Oxford. He married Florence Hickman, daughter of Devereux Henry Hickman, in 1881 and died in 1920. He took his bride to the Argentine and they had five children, two sons and three daughters – my father was in fourth place. Grandfather Charles was both rancher and banker during the decades when these activities were important to the growth of the Argentine economy, at that time impressively strong.

My father's younger sister, Vivien Farmer, lived in London with her two daughters. We saw them regularly and I am still in close touch with the younger of the two girls. Vivien's husband, a major in the Royal Marines, had been killed in Russia in 1919.

The two elder sisters departed for Canada after the Great War, and before we returned from Chile. Our paths never crossed. But after marriage and divorce they reverted to their maiden names, so there are some other Treacher cousins still in Vancouver, Los Angeles and Mississippi who correspond and we see on their periodic visits to the UK.

At this time I also had my first introduction to the Collins side of the family, one of my father's aunts having married Sir William Collins, a distinguished eye-surgeon and one-time Chairman of the London County Council. It was not until nearly fifty years later that Leslie

Collins, a nephew, asked me to accept some Treacher memorabilia which had come from Sir William. These included a portrait of John Treacher, City merchant and Councillor, born in 1756. He married Elizabeth Sharpe who bore him thirteen children and one, Samuel Sharpe Treacher, had joined the Navy. So I could claim to a previous naval connection.

Lieutenant Samuel Treacher served in South American waters for several years and in 1808 was in command of a schooner *Dolore*, taken from the Spanish off the River Plate the year before. Treacher's career sadly came to an abrupt end when his ship, HMS *Holly*, parted her cables in a violent storm and ran onto the rocks under the Mount of San Sebastian in Spain at four o'clock in the morning of 29 January 1814 and was wrecked. Samuel and three other men, including the surgeon, Mr Crane, were washed overboard. Lieutenant Treacher was 'no more seen' as the Ship's Clerk reported in a letter to his parents.

Addressed to Mr Treacher Senr
12 Paternoster Row
London   *Her Majesty's Ship* Porcupine
                                 30th January 1814

Sir

I am sorry to inform you of the loss of
His Majesty's Schooner Holly in the Harbour of
Sn. Sebastian's at 4 o'clock yesterday morning which
I have no doubt but you will be very sorry to hear
Especially when I explain the loss we have sustained.
Your dear son Saml. Sharpe Treacher is no more.
We parted our cables drum upon the Rocks under
the Mount of St Sebastian's a heavy /sea/ running at
the time washed my dear friend Lt Treacher
(with Mr J Cram Assistant Surgeon & two men)-
overboard & was never more seen. I with the rest of
the officers most bitterly lament their loss and I with
the rest of the officers and men escaped in our
shirts. The tide setting out drifted every thing to sea
no bodies yet found – If you wish any
explanation respecting his accounts I should
find myself pleased to the highest degree in

giving you every information in my power.
We are at present on board His Majesty's Ship
Porcupine expecting to be sent to England in
the first vessel that goes.

> *I am Dr Sir with greatest*
> *Respect your most*
> *Humble servant*
> *CPt. Clerk★*

I also received the original letter, together with some ship's log books – events written in perfect script on linen – and a watercolour of his ship painted by him.

Soon after we arrived in London my father's brother Harold came to live near us. Older than my father by ten years, he chose to start his working life in Malaya where his uncle, William Hood Treacher, was making a name for himself as one of the great colonial administrators. Harold, however was not to take the gentle path of the civil servant: he made for the plantations where his capacity for beer drinking was apparently matched only by his consumption of whisky in the flesh-pots of Kuala Lumpur and Singapore. It was generally accepted in the family that if he had not come home in 1914 to go to war with the King's Own Scottish Borderers he would have been thrown out of Malaya.

No doubt his uncle was glad to see the back of this roistering nephew as his own career moved smoothly ahead with appointment as Governor of North Borneo and a Knighthood. He had pioneered education and was the driving force behind the founding of the Victoria Institution in 1893. A grander building was opened in 1929 and the Japanese in Malaya signed the document of surrender in the school hall on 12 September 1945. In 1947 the ship's bell from the battleship HMS *Malaya*, built in 1913 and paid for by the people of Malaya, was presented to the school and now hangs above the entrance porch.

Sir William also left behind his name on the main street in Kuala Lumpur – now renamed as Jalang Ishmail – and the girl's school subsequently founded by his wife rejoiced in the name of The Lady Treacher Girls' School.

★ See facsimile of the original letter on p. 248.

8

Harold appeared in London in the early thirties, unrepentant, often unemployed but full of enthusiasm and mischief. He often took me to football matches, introducing me to Chelsea games at Stamford Bridge. Although my interests soon turned to the rugby field I retained an enormous affection for my only uncle and used to drink the occasional pint with him at his local pub in Wimbledon whenever I was in London until he died, having outlived his much younger brother by several years.

The summer term 1938 brought my five years at Colet Court to an end. One of my friends from early days, who I called 'Jimmy' Parsons, was among those who came on to St Paul's but left after one year. We have stayed in touch ever since and he is better known today as Nicholas.

SCHOOLING

London

While there had been a gradual increase in talk about war my first introduction to the reality of what was happening in the outside world had come when in 1935 Mussolini invaded Abyssinia which was then ruled by the Emperor Haile Salassie, both of whose sons were at Colet Court. We all felt directly involved.

September 1938 was the month of the Munich crisis and it was quite a shock as I prepared for my first term at St Paul's to find that we were called in ahead of time to dig air raid shelter trenches in the playing fields. Tension rose as Hitler threatened to invade Czechoslovakia and Prime Minister Neville Chamberlain made his well-documented three flights to Munich.

When Chamberlain signed the agreement with Hitler abandoning Czechoslovakia in return for a promise that Hitler would make no further territorial claims, England appeared to accept Chamberlain's words about 'a quarrel in a far-away country between people of whom we know nothing'. It was 'peace in our time' in exchange for 'forty thousand square kilometers of the Sudetenland'. My mother was overjoyed. My father had fewer illusions.

But it was not exactly to be school as usual. A new interest was the OTC, the Officer Training Corps, and we were inspected in the summer of 1939 by Major General Wavell who at that time commanded the London District. One day a week we had to appear at school in OTC uniform, very much 1918 style with breeches and puttees above our Army boots. As we walked down to the school from Hammersmith Broadway station we were often met with cries of 'Thank God we've got a Navy'.

I was not headed for the classical education for which St Paul's was and still is renowned. I joined the alternative science and mathematics stream as I intended to join the Navy. Sport was a tremendous interest, with matches against other schools, and life was too full for there to be any time spent on wondering what next year might bring.

The school, however, was facing a crisis of its own. The previous High Master had resigned suddenly in the summer of 1938 and the brilliant Walter Oakeshott, still in his mid-thirties and currently at Winchester, had been selected as his replacement. The Governors [the majority of whom were appointed by the Mercers Company] were now informed that, if war came, the pupils would have to leave London and the school buildings would be requisitioned. This posed a very serious threat to the whole future of St Paul's because, if it were to close for the duration of the war, it might never open again.

For the newly appointed High Master this was unthinkable. The search for a new home began. Three criteria had to be met: one, there should be suitable buildings available, two, the area should be amenable to billeting pupils with local families and third, there should be close by an established school which could make essential facilities available.

A choice was made by March. The location was to be the village of Crowthorne in Berkshire, the school buildings would be at Easthampstead Park and the supporting school was Wellington College, also in Crowthorne.

The Country

The summer holidays were very unsettled. We did not make our annual visit to Ipswich because the increasing threat of war caused coastal areas, particularly in East Anglia, to be considered too dangerous. Following the declaration of war the move to Crowthorne began well in advance of the normal date for term to start. Familiarization with Easthampstead Park and billeting of the pupils with families in Crowthorne, plus having to 'make good' the old science laboratories kindly provided by Wellington College, became an all-absorbing task for the first few weeks.

We soon discovered that Crowthorne was also the home of a prison for the criminally insane called Broadmoor and made lots of schoolboy jokes about it in the early days. None of us was made aware that it had housed an American army surgeon guilty of murder who had become one of the most significant contributors to the production of the Oxford English Dictionary.

Despite the potential for administrative chaos and a collapse of the curriculum, everything settled down remarkably smoothly. Dress regulations were relaxed, the black jacket and striped trousers of London being replaced by a sports jacket and grey flannels and the bicycle became a central feature. The patience of the villagers was extraordinary and the behaviour of the boys in general was good. The actual number of boys was much higher than originally planned for and this put a huge strain on accommodation. It soon became essential for some large houses to be acquired by the school and run by the masters.

The forbearance of Wellington College was also a major factor in the success of the move and good relations between the two schools at all levels were vital. Oakeshott was a great personal friend of the headmaster of Wellington, Robert Longden, and this provided a solid foundation. We were all shocked when Mr Longden was killed by a stray bomb one night about a year after we arrived.

The spring of 1940 saw the invasion of Norway in April, followed by the blitzkrieg attack on central Europe. Holland surrendered within three days and the attack on France through Belgium and Luxembourg resulted in the Belgian forces surrendering at the end of May. Then came Dunkirk as the Germans swept on almost unopposed into France to enter Paris – undefended and declared an open city by the French Government to avoid being bombed or shelled – to take the surrender of the French on 22 June.

Churchill had taken over from Chamberlain as Prime Minister on 10 May, while France was suing for peace and collapsing into the arms of the German army. Talk of imminent invasion was widespread. The real danger of an airborne invasion was clearly in the minds of the Government when they created a new home defence force called the Local Defence Volunteers, later to become the Home Guard and immortalized in one of the BBC TV's most successful post-war comedy series. The Home Guard was open to boys from sixteen and to men up to sixty-five, armed with whatever weapons of whatever vintage which could be mustered. England now stood alone.

The Home Guard claimed to be the first citizen's army since Napoleon posed a threat of invasion in 1803. By the time those of us in the OTC and in our seventeenth year were enlisted we were properly armed and uniformed and I don't think any of us who did regular night duty guarding ammunition depots thought there was much to joke about. We were given instruction by regular battle-hardened NCOs at Aldershot, mainly on how to prevent ourselves from being garrotted by a German parachutist while patrolling the depot. Most of the time we were scared stiff.

Nevertheless we seemed able to live our lives in compartments. There were lessons to attend and exams to be taken and plenty of sport, and it was still possible to spend a day on the cricket field without another care in the world.

I was now old enough to ride a motor bicycle and my godmother made ownership possible with a cheque for ten pounds. This was enough to purchase a third-hand 250cc side-valve Royal Enfield which was sufficiently docile to pass the parental panic test yet good enough to catapult me into the small and exclusive group of boys permitted to ride one to school.

My School Certificate results were sufficient to give me what was needed to move on to work for Higher Certificate in my last year at school while preparing to sit the Civil Service examination for entry to the Navy in May 1942.

My parents were living in Weybridge at this time, my sister had joined the WRNS, better known as the Wrens, and my father was still spending three nights a week in London as a Fire Warden. Meanwhile, Hitler's troops were storming their way to the gates of Moscow, much too easily it seemed to us.

I was now running one of the new 'Houses' in Crowthorne village, on behalf of the Bursar, the splendid Mr Priest, who was a natural House Master. He was excellent with the boys and was gifted with a sure touch on the tricky balance between discipline enforced by the House Captains, School Monitors and the staff.

For academic work my tutor was Mr Bird to whom I owe an

enormous debt for his help and encouragement in tackling the Civil Service examination and the special interview which counted almost as much in terms of achieving success. There were only two other boys taking the same route, one Richard Stock, who wanted to join the Navy and whose older brother had done so some three years before, and Graham Hennessy, who was heading for the Royal Marines.

I recall we had rather a good summer on the cricket field. The school routines were running very smoothly and the OTC inspection by an Old Pauline, General Montgomery, went reasonably well, although he was not particularly pleased to learn that the parade Sergeant was about to join the Navy. I had by this time also volunteered to join the RNVR as an Ordinary Seaman under what was then called the 'Y-scheme'. In fact this meant little other than your track record was on file and you might be spotted for earlier advancement. It would come into play if I had failed my exams.

So my last school term ended with uncertainty about which path would be open to joining the Navy, but that, one way or another, I would be in uniform before the end of August. I made the most of the time available. Weybridge was a sociable area with the excellent facilities of the St George's Hill Club for tennis and squash and lots of pretty girls about. I found that having wheels – even if only two – was a considerable advantage and certainly no hindrance to taking a partner to a dance.

By the end of July it was decided that I should not wait beyond mid-August for news of the exam results. If nothing had been heard by then I would join up under the Y -Scheme and this duly took place. I reported to HMS *Collingwood*, a new-entry establishment near Portsmouth in Hampshire, where I was issued with my kit and was just beginning to understand how to deal with a sailor's collar when I was sent for by the Commanding Officer, Captain Sedgewick.

Having been ushered into the great man's presence – it was the first time I had set eyes on him or he on me – I stood at attention in front of his desk. He eyed me silently for what seemed an eternity and then looked down at his desk. Eventually he looked up again.

'Young man,' he said at last, 'I am commanded by the Admiralty to inform you that you have been successful in your examination for entry into the Royal Navy and you are to be sent on leave. You will receive further instructions in due course.'

★   ★   ★

13

I have no recollection of my departure from *Collingwood*. There followed a few more days at home before reporting to the Naval College at Dartmouth.

By this time my godmother Dorothy Taylor was living with us in Weybridge while her husband remained trapped by the war in Ecuador and her only son, Aubrey, had just joined the RAF as a Bomber Command air crew. He was much the same age as my sister and they were close friends. He was killed over Germany on his fifth bombing mission the following year.

2

WAR YEARS

THE MEDITERRANEAN

Dartmouth 1942

The train from Paddington to Kingswear, followed by a ferry across the River Dart, brought the thirty new cadets to the Frobisher wing of the Royal Naval College at Dartmouth. The Frobishers enjoyed a splendidly British compromise in that they were treated as adult students in classroom work and sport and in being allowed to smoke and drink under carefully controlled conditions, but they were required to sleep in hammocks and otherwise conform to the discipline and routine of junior sailors. This included meeting rather harsher standards than imposed elsewhere in new-entry establishments, punishment at the top end of the scale for failure to carry out one's duties to the full satisfaction of the staff and very restricted opportunities to leave the grounds of the college. Those who recall 'requestmen and defaulters' will know what I mean.

This was all very well for the teenagers, but we also had among us cadets and some junior officers from The Royal Netherlands and Royal Norwegian and Greek navies who were all in their twenties and found this regime more than irksome. Fortunately the Frobisher Commanding Officer, Lieutenant Commander Pedder, was a wise old bird well able to make sensible exceptions which, while coming nowhere near what the foreign cadets expected, was enough to keep the lid on without undermining the authority of the staff.

Classroom work was devoted to celestial navigation, ship construction, meteorology, engineering and great emphasis was placed on learning about weapons with their associated control systems.

★ ★ ★

There was plenty of scope for boat work and it was when my particular group were on the river, handling a service cutter under oars, that
the college was attacked by a flight of four Focke-Wulf 190 fighter
bombers. Several bombs landed on or close to the college and some
damage was caused. The only casualty was an unfortunate Wren Petty
Officer.

In our boat we were straffed a couple of times, the coxswain [the
renowned Chief Petty Officer Savage and well-named] having
ordered us all to lie under the thwarts in the boat. There was not
room for even half of us. I shared my crouched position with a
Norwegian, Bjiane Eia, who remained a lifelong friend. He had a
distinguished career in the Royal Norwegian Navy and for three years
was the Defence Attaché in London as a Commodore. He also had
the distinction of serving as a member of parliament while an active
officer on the Naval Staff in Oslo. He said it helped to be able to
discuss naval matters with the Prime Minister while they were sharing
a sauna!

That this attack could be carried out so easily by mere fighter
bombers resulted in the college being transplanted to Eaton Hall in
Cheshire. So for the second time I was uprooted from a purpose-built
establishment to a makeshift alternative to complete my training.

HMS *Nelson*

With Colin Balfour, who had become a close friend, I was appointed
to HMS *Nelson*, (Captain the Hon. Guy Russell) which was at a buoy
in Plymouth Sound when we joined.

Nelson had been laid down in 1922 as a ship of 46,000 tons with a
main armament of twelve 16-inch guns in four turrets. However, to
comply with the Washington Treaty, her overall size was limited
to 35,000 tons and one of the gun turrets removed. This resulted in
an ungainly ship with three turrets forward of the bridge and none aft.

Our first two days were spent in hectic familiarization with where we
were to sleep – a hammock slung in the Gunroom Flat (the area allocated to midshipmen) – to eat – in the Gunroom itself – and to work.

Within forty-eight hours we had sailed for a ten-day work-up when
I had my first introduction to my action station as Midshipman of B
Turret with its three massive 16-inch guns. This huge structure, on
its own as big as a destroyer, handled the massive shells, themselves
close to four feet long, and their propellant which was made up of

16

three bags of cordite each weighing over 200 pounds. This was not machinery tolerant of stray human parts, as missing fingers among some of the sailors testified.

We then sailed for Gibraltar where my harbour duty was in charge of the First Motor Boat. This was a thirty-six-foot twin-screw diesel-engined boat normally used for taking officers to and from the ship on duty and when going ashore. I worked alternate days with another midshipman, days which usually began before 0800 and seldom ended before 2 am.

From Gibraltar we set out, as Flagship of Force H, with Vice Admiral Algernon (Sampan) Willis embarked, for Mers el Kebir, near Oran on the North African coast, where we anchored in company with a vast Anglo-American fleet, including tankers and numerous troopships. This was an area of high risk of attack by human torpedo and in my fast motor boat we carried out patrols around the fleet all night, armed with heavy machine guns and light depth charges. The next morning this armada set forth for Sicily.

The Sicily Landings

With heavy naval gunfire support, landings began on the coast of Sicily at 0245 on 10 July by British and Canadian troops – including Royal Marines – under General Montgomery and with the US First Army under General Patton. Among the supporting ships the destroyer HMS *Eskimo* was hit by Stuka dive bombers and put out of action. She was taken in tow to Malta by HMS *Tartar*. Meanwhile one Italian submarine had been sunk and another captured.

On land rapid progress was made and by day three more than 150,000 troops and 700 tanks had been landed and two-thirds of the island was in Allied hands. This had been the largest amphibious landing in the war so far, with over 1600 craft involved.

As the campaign continued some of the supporting ships were able to withdraw and *Nelson* proceeded to Malta which had by this time seen the worst of the bombing and was considered a 'good run ashore' by the sailors. *Nelson* had among its ship's company a number of long-service ratings, many in their thirties and contrasting strongly with the teenage wartime recruits. They were experienced seamen who knew how to work hard as well as play hard when ashore and still keep out of trouble. Drink was your friend or your enemy depending on whether you were on shore for a good time or on shore patrol trying to control or defuse the excesses of your shipmates. For me it was also an introduction on how to handle those unable to handle themselves as they arrived back on deck in the early hours. They were laid out in rows on the deck and hosed down from the fire main to make sure they did not choke on their own vomit.

On 25 July Mussolini was overthrown, the King of Italy assumed command of the armed forces and Marshal Badoglio was appointed Prime Minister. We heard that Italian troops in Sicily were throwing away their arms and it seemed as if Italy was starting to crack up.

Mainland Italy

We were soon off the west coast of Italy, ready to support the seaborne assault in the bay of Salerno south of Naples and behind the German lines. Commenting on the news that Italy had accepted our terms for unconditional surrender, the Captain reminded us that there were still sixteen German divisions and 700 aircraft in Italy and many U-boats in the area, so we should not expect any let-up in activity.

The landing of the Fifth Army at Salerno – operation Avalanche – took place in the early hours of 26th against stiff German resistance. Air support was provided from the carriers and artillery by the destroyers and cruisers, backed up by *Nelson, Valiant* and *Warspite*.

As part of the surrender terms three major Italian battleships, *Roma, Italia* and *Vittorio Veneto,* were instructed to sail from Spezia that night and pass to the west of Corsica. They should have carried on south again passing to the west of Sardinia, but for unknown reasons turned to pass north of Sardinia and ran straight into German air attack with the new glider bombs, the *Roma* being sunk with heavy losses, including the Italian Commander-in-Chief himself.

The next morning *Warspite* and *Valiant* escorted the Italian ships to Malta. They were joined there by the battleships *Andrea Doria* and *Caio Duilio.* There was no room for this number of ships in Malta and all but two of them were rapidly moved to Alexandria, and ultimately to the Great Bitter Lakes.

By the 13 July we were back in Malta where Admiral Willis formally received the surrender of the Italian Fleet from the Italian C-in-C on board *Nelson*.

Our stay was cut short and we sailed the next day to return to

Salerno where the situation was precarious as the Fifth Army fought desperately to maintain their foothold while Montgomery's Eighth Army was driving up from the south. More strikes by the Luftwaffe, again using the new glider bombs, put the US Cruiser *Savannah*, operating very close to us, and HMS *Uganda* out of action. Despite heavy casualties, both ships were able to limp back to Malta.

Italian Surrender

We returned to Malta and on 29 July *Nelson* was host to the major UK/US/Italian meeting when the 'long-term' surrender document would be signed. Those attending were headed by General Eisenhower, the Allied Commander-in-Chief, and Admiral Cunningham, C-in-C Mediterranean Fleet, plus a formidable supporting cast which included General Alexander and the US General, Bedell-Smith, the British Minister to North Africa, Harold Macmillan, the American Minister, Robert Murphy, and Air Marshal Tedder. Heading the Italian group was Marshal Badoglio who, as Head of State, was to sign the surrender document.

Careful stage management was essential and fundamental to that was the need to keep close tabs on each and every one of them, not least to make sure they did not lose their way around the ship. The Navy does this by attaching a personal 'doggie' to each visitor: I was assigned to look after General Eisenhower and relieved to be addressed as 'young man' rather than the customary 'mister'.

I ran a number of errands for the General, almost all of which were as a messenger to other members of his staff located elsewhere in the ship. Perhaps not the best example of how top commanders operate but a fascinating close-up view. I got quite used to 'Hey mister, where the fuck is he now?' from those I was trying to round up.

Return to England

Having spent most of the past three months as an air defence control officer it was time to rotate midshipmen's duties and I was appointed 'tankey' to the navigating officer, (the 'Pilot') Lieutenant Commander Jasper Synott. This was not something to which I looked forward but it turned out to be fascinating, professionally rewarding and enjoyable. The only guidance I was given by my predecessor, who was leaving the ship, was to 'take care pilot doesn't set fire to the ship'.

19

This was a reference to his pipe-smoking habit of knocking his ashes out into the waste paper bin under the chart table without regard to them still smouldering. If you failed to anticipate it, the first warning came from smoke and flames usually detected by the Captain.

On our subsequent passage back to the UK the ship was routed far into the Atlantic to avoid a strong submarine threat and due to low cloud and mist no sights were possible and navigation was entirely by DR – Dead Reckoning. This was complicated by the constant alterations to course dictated by suspected submarine contacts, while the effects of wind and currents all had to be allowed for. When we were able to fix our position after nearly five days and over 1500 miles, the error was just over twelve miles.

Early in December our Captain was relieved by Captain Maxwell-Hyslop. We were all very sad to see Captain Russell leave and I felt this particularly, having been in such close contact with him on a daily basis at sea on the bridge. From *Nelson* he went as Flag Captain to the Commander-in-Chief Home Fleet, Admiral Sir Bruce Fraser, in HMS *Duke of York* and was soon to be engaged in a major battle.

On Boxing Day *Nelson* was at anchor in Scapa Flow when the ship was rapidly prepared for sea on hearing that Vice Admiral Burnett in HMS *Belfast,* leading a force of two more cruisers and four destroyers providing cover against surface attack for a north-bound convoy to Russia, was in contact with the German battleship *Scharnhorst.* The C-in-C, Admiral Fraser, in the battleship *Duke of York* was some way south, but made twenty-five knots in heavy seas to join the cruisers soon after dark.

In a fierce night action the *Scharnhorst* was sunk by a combination of accurate gunfire from *Duke of York* and the cruisers and torpedo attacks by destroyers which had reduced her speed. The action, known as the Battle of North Cape, was all over before *Nelson* could put to sea!

Early in the new year *Nelson* sailed from Scapa Flow for a period alongside in the dockyard at Rosyth, a popular location close to Edinburgh. Here the midshipmen were able to catch up on their studies uninterrupted by calls to action. This period was marred by the sad news that Balfour's older brother Anthony, who was in the Scots Guards, had been killed shortly after the landings at Anzio in Italy.

There was much talk about the forthcoming assault on Europe, expected to take place in May or June and Balfour and I soon received a new appointment to the cruiser HMS *Glasgow*.

NORMANDY to ARCHANGEL

HMS *Glasgow*

Colin Balfour and I joined HMS *Glasgow* (Captain C.P.Clarke) in April 1944 while she was running from Greenock for regular exercises with the US Army off the Isle of Aran. This involved live firings at targets indicated from spotting aircraft by grid reference. Rumours were rife that this was a practice for the real thing – the assault on Europe, Operation Overlord – which was understood to be coming in the summer and would depend heavily on gunfire support from many ships, including *Glasgow*.

The ship was in great spirits after her very successful encounter soon after Christmas with a strong force of eleven German destroyers in the Bay of Biscay. HMS *Enterprise* was in company and between them the two ships sank three German destroyers and disabled four others before the Germans escaped.

We were shortly to embark an American Shore Fire Control Party (SFCP) headed by a lieutenant from the US Navy who would land with the assault troops and, being in radio contact with the ship, advise on targets to be engaged. This was the first indication that we would be supporting the American beaches. When I asked him why he had volunteered for this duty he said he intended to enter politics after the war and wanted to have been among the first ashore on this historic occasion. (Sadly, he survived only two days.) We then began taking part in live exercises and the SFCP were duly impressed by our ability to strike designated targets while steaming and manoeuvring at speed.

On 26 April *Glasgow* proceeded south to Plymouth and joined HMS *Black Prince* which, with three destroyers (including two Royal Canadian Navy ships HMCS *Haida* and HMCS *Athabascan*), had been in action in the channel the previous night against German warships of the Elbling class, one of which was sunk and one severely damaged. Two nights later the two Canadian destroyers encountered more German Elblings off the coast of Brittany and, after driving one ashore, HMCS *Athabascan* was torpedoed and sunk.

*   *   *

For the Royal Navy the Normandy landings (Operation Neptune) marked the end of all their endeavours since 1939. Sea lines of communication with the USA had been kept open and the hard-fought battle with the U-boats in the Atlantic had been virtually won, while the Russians were supported in their heroic battles by the equally heroic battles fought against not only the U-boats but against the savage storms and ice to bring essential weapons to Murmansk. The German battleships *Graf Spee*, *Bismarck* and *Scharnhorst* had been sunk and the *Tirpitz,* lying crippled in a Norwegian Fjord, could pose no serious threat to the landings and made this 'masterpiece of planning' possible to execute. The only threat remaining was the weather.

For the next ten days *Glasgow* exercised day and night, great attention being given to essential damage control practice, so vital to ensure that the ship could continue to operate and survive with various levels of damage. The Captain had warned that the ship would continue in action until she had lost more than 50% of her fighting ability.

On departure from Plymouth on 26 May we headed north for Belfast Lough where we anchored close to the USS *Texas* and *Nevada*. We were now in company with all the ships who would be with us on D-Day.

On 31 May the ship was 'sealed'. No shore leave was allowed nor any communication from the ship. A briefing of all officers took place in front of a detailed relief map of the landing area which clearly showed the areas assigned. There were three British and Canadian areas to the east (code-named Sword, Juno and Gold), and two US beaches to the west (code-named Omaha and Utah). Omaha covered the area from St Honorine to Vierville-sur-Mer.

Glasgow was assigned to Omaha beach, perhaps the most critical for two reasons, first because the steep cliffs just behind the beach made any assault more difficult for both infantry and tanks and also because any failure in this area could split the assaulting forces and make counter-attack more effective.

The Naval units were divided into two task forces with the Eastern Force under Admiral Vian in HMS *Scylla* and the Western Force under Admiral Hall in the USS *Ancon*. This Task Force, designated number 124, was divided into two Task Units, one for Utah beach (USS *Nevada, Quincy, Tuscaloosa,* HMS *Enterprise, Hawkins* and

Black Prince), the other for Omaha beach (USS *Texas* with Admiral Bryant, USS *Arkansas*, HMS *Glasgow* – Captain Clarke second-in-command for this operation) and many supporting USN and RN destroyers.

We still did not know the date for D-Day, but the Western Bombardment Group was ordered to proceed on 3 June via designated channels to assigned rendezvous positions. The USS *Tuscaloosa*, followed by HMS *Glasgow, Bellona, Enterprise, Black Prince, Hawkins* and USS *Quincy*, with the US destroyers *Butler, Hernden, Schubrick* and *Murphy*, set sail. Four large convoys were passed during the night and about 0700 on 4 June we joined up with the battleships. Tomorrow would be D-Day. We had passed the Lizard soon after dawn, steaming east, when the Captain announced that we would shortly be turning through 180 degrees as the operation had been postponed!

Operation Neptune, the greatest amphibious landing ever attempted and the essential prelude to the re-conquest of Europe, had been frustrated by the weather which was expected to deteriorate beyond acceptable limits. With the release of tension came the uncertainty about the length of the delay. Would it be twenty-four hours or fourteen days?

The operation plan called for our Task Unit to assemble south of the Isle of Wight on D-1 and, escorted by minesweepers of the Fourth Flotilla (Commander Cochrane) and the Thirty-First (Commander Stoors RCN) and six destroyers with *Glasgow* leading, to be in position at H-5 hours and to commence bombardment at H-40 minutes, our initial targets to be the beach exit at Les Moulins and a heavy shore battery at Pointe du Hoc.

Air attacks were timed to start at H-4 and continue non-stop until H hour when the Second Rangers were due to land east of Pointe du Hoc to take out the shore battery at the top of the cliff. The main assault would be undertaken by the First and Twenty-Ninth Infantry divisions and the Second and Fifth Rangers who would land between H hour and H+2. We had been working with them all during the past weeks and felt closely involved.

The number of ships taking part was about 1800 in the Eastern Task Force and 1000 in the Western. Nearly all of them started loading on 3 June and most had completed when the weather deteriorated as a depression moved in across the Atlantic bringing rising winds, high seas and the decision to postpone. This was an incredibly difficult time for all. Adrenalin was high and the assault troops at peak states of readiness.

I noted in my journal that, as the weather worsened, visibility dropped rapidly and fog buoys were streamed. This was the first gale in the area for two months. What timing!

The gale force winds drove the rain horizontally and the prospect of a postponement longer than forty-eight hours would have meant fourteen days before the tides would again be right. Then the forecasters detected a break in the weather and General Eisenhower made the firm decision to land on 6 June. As it happened, between 19 and 21 June the channel was hit by one of the worst storms in its history and any landing at that time would have ended in disaster.

Omaha Beach

At 0415 Admiral Ramsay, who had planned and was now executing the whole operation, sent the following signal:

> It is a privilege to take part in the greatest Amphibious Operation in History; the hopes and prayers of the free world and all the enslaved people of Europe will be with us. We cannot fail them. I count on every man to do his utmost to ensure the success of this great enterprise which is the climax of the war in Europe. Good luck to you all and God speed.

This was certainly deeply felt by the entire ship's company and as the Chaplain said prayers just after we went to action stations he included one written by the Captain that day:

> Lord bless this enterprise to restore peace and freedom to the peoples of Europe. We give thanks for the privilege of taking part in it. We are a mighty company, but having done all we can, the fate of this operation is in Thy hands.
>
> For ourselves in the *Glasgow* we offer our lives and ask Thy blessings on our endeavours. Give to each of us quiet confidence, courage and endurance, that our ship will give her best.
>
> Finally, if some of us should be taken, we ask for the comfort and care of those who have loved and depended upon us.

There was not a man on board who did not think we would suffer heavy casualties, but with the confidence of youth, most felt it would not be them and adrenalin did the rest. At my action station there was a lot of chatter to start with, but it soon dried up and our thoughts turned to the troops who would have to hit the beach.

At 0130 we had passed the transport area and moved slowly inshore immediately behind the sweepers. The next few hours were the worst. We knew the waters had been heavily mined and, although the sweepers had been through, there was never any certainty about clearance and it seemed that the relentless air attacks which started soon after midnight must have alerted the Germans to the fact that this was not just another night. We expected a rapid and violent response.

By H–40 minutes it was light enough to see the landing craft streaming past us towards the shore, first with the infantry and then the tanks, some specially equipped to blast their way through the shallow water and beach obstacles. The *Arkansas* opened fire from behind us as we attacked our assigned targets. There was no immediate counter-fire from shore batteries but the landing craft were having a hard time, many being wrecked before hitting the beach and nearly all the tanks suffered the same fate, only a half dozen out of over forty succeeding. Most of the troops – some 1500 in the first wave – had to wade ashore.

Opposition on the ground was much heavier than expected, the Germans having moved an additional Division up to the coastal defence area, something which was not known to our intelligence. This was a Division toughened by service on the Eastern front and they proved formidable opponents.

Omaha had a very hard time securing its beachhead, losing nearly 3000 men and 50 tanks on the first day. Many armchair critics have suggested that the landing craft were launched too far from the beach, but the loss of a troopship struck by a mine would have been catastrophic. Two destroyers and several minesweepers were sunk this way.

The story of Omaha beach has been told and written up time and again, also featuring in *The Longest Day* and more recently *Saving Private Ryan*. Although well off the beach, we felt very much part of the battle and at times engaged our own targets in direct fire. As we continued providing gunfire support on an ever-increasing scale, by day three we had used more than half our ammunition.

We may at times have doubted the value of our support, but Colonel Mason, Chief of Staff of the First Division, said that the German defences would have been impregnable without the naval gunfire. After five days the ship returned to Portsmouth to replenish ammunition and stores before returning to the beachhead.

Nearly three weeks after D-Day the major port of Cherbourg still remained in German hands and a squadron of American ships and *Glasgow* were ordered to support an assault on this stronghold which held heavy batteries for defence against seaborne attack. Just as the force assembled the predicted storm swept through the area causing havoc in the landing area and delaying this assault by four days.

The bombardment took place on 26 June and, while the object was finally achieved, it was not before *Glasgow* had been subjected to heavy and very accurate shelling by the big guns of the shore batteries. The ship was straddled almost continuously and was hit twice, amidships and in the aft fire-control position, forcing the ship to withdraw for a short period to assess damage before returning to the firing line. We were now in the thick of the action as bombardment continued into the late afternoon.

Following reports that the aims of the Army commander had been achieved (the entire peninsula surrendered on 29 June when 30,000 prisoners were taken) *Glasgow* was ordered to Portland for landing the wounded and re-ammunitioning. In the event the ship did not return to the Normandy beaches but sailed westabout round Scotland and down the east coast to the Tyne where she entered Palmer's Yard, Hebburn, for damage repairs and a major refit.

HMS *Keppel*

The next appointments for Balfour and me were to escort destroyers based on the Clyde and working the Russian convoys, he to HMS *Bulldog* and I to HMS *Keppel*, a Great War veteran of 1,400 tons with two 4.7 inch guns, a pair of oerlikons for close air defence and a hefty anti-submarine armoury of the ahead-throwing weapon Hedgehog and multiple depth-charge throwers and rails on the stern.

Keppel was commanded by Commander I. J. Tyson, RNR, an experienced Western Approaches commanding officer with a number of U-boat kills to his credit. Tyson commanded the 5th Escort Group on a relatively standard pattern of operations, taking a convoy each month from the assembly point in Loch Ewe to the bay of Polyarno near Murmansk, north round the coast from Archangel.

★   ★   ★

The Arctic convoys began in August 1941 and these desolate and dangerous voyages continued for four years. Forty convoys were dispatched to Russia on what was probably the most hazardous and certainly the most uncomfortable convoy route of them all. Ice, furious storms, constant light in the summer and permanent darkness in the winter accompanied by the never-ending threat of air and U-boat attack, plus, always in the background, the menace of surface attack from the heavy units of the German fleet lurking in the Norwegian fjords: a two thousand-mile corridor with sea room restricted to the west and north by ice and to the south and east by the Norwegian coast. Each delivery of arms to the Russians was an epic achievement.

For the journey north, which took about ten days as convoy speed was seldom more than nine knots, the merchant ships were laden with tanks, ammunition, aircraft and other military stores. On arrival the escorts spent three to four days in the anchorage at Polyarno, to seaward of Murmansk, where the merchant ships unloaded. Murmansk, a port built with British aid for the supply of stores for the Tsar's Army, and Polyarno were two of the bleakest, most poverty-stricken corners of Stalin's Russia, showing only too clearly the surly presence of Soviet authority. It was no place for a run ashore. But some ships did go alongside and one officer reported that 'although we had, not without some difficulty and much danger, brought them warships and a vast quantity of supplies, we lay alongside for three days and not one courtesy call was paid. Are we allies?'

After collecting the ships for escort home and a similar but perhaps marginally less fearful journey we returned to Gourock on the Clyde where the ship had seven or eight days to clean up and carry out minor maintenance while half the ship's company were sent on leave for a week. Despite the punishing programme, there were seldom any sailors who failed to return to the ship on time.

By the time I joined *Keppel*, with the Battle of the Atlantic to all intents and purposes won, the Luftwaffe and the U-boats, driven from their bases on the French coast, concentrated on the arctic route where re-supply of the Soviet forces remained critical. During the convoy before I joined, *Keppel*, in company with HMS *Kite*, was patrolling astern of the convoy to guard against U-boats attempting to approach from the rear when *Kite* was hit by two torpedoes and sank in minutes. *Keppel* immediately went to her rescue but was only able to save seven

27

men, of whom three survived. There was a very sombre mood on board when I arrived.

With U-boat attack the primary threat, only the depth-charge crews lived and worked at the stern of the ship. As this was where all the cabins were located, officers slept on camp beds in various forward passageways while at sea. This was also sensible as the only access fore and aft was along the open midship deck which was regularly swept by the waves.

Watch-keeping was four hours on and four hours off, all on an open bridge, often in rain or sleet and always bitterly cold. The duffle coat was standard wear with a lifebelt underneath and a 'bene' inhaler just in case we ever felt drowsy. It seems surprising to many that an enhancing drug was issued as a matter of course, but I can swear that no one became addicted!

The weather during my time was invariably atrocious. I thought I had my sea legs but they could not withstand the full impact of ploughing straight into a force eight gale immediately on leaving the anchorage. My stomach took a day to settle down on each leg, but thereafter I could eat greasy bacon with anyone and the first twenty-four hours seemed to pass quickly enough as duties had to be carried out regardless.

Conditions below decks could only be described as foul. There was no natural light in this steel box. The air was stale, clothing damp and the fug of sweat, smoke and sometimes vomit ever-present, but at least it was warmer than being on deck.

There were always some ciphers to be decoded by the off-watch officers. Great store was set by wireless intercepts, made more difficult by the recent introduction of 'squash' transmissions by the Germans, whereby signals were compressed into very short bursts. Shore intelligence was vital and this usually came on highly secure 'one time' code pads.

Radar had become a major factor in detecting schnorkels and surfaced submarines at night and the tactics developed by perhaps the most relentless U-boat hunter of them all, Captain Johnnie Walker, had proved highly successful.

For those who experienced these conditions for years on end, the Battle of the Atlantic and Arctic convoys were perhaps the greatest test of all. Many, including some of the most successful Captains, did not survive; like Johnnie Walker they just died of exhaustion. I only spent four months at sea with them, but it was long enough to feel the stress and to watch men who had fought on without complaint, accepting what they believed in, paying the price with their lives and never whingeing.

The Arctic convoys were instituted to support the Soviet resistance to Hitler which was fundamental to the ultimate success of any assault on Europe by the Allies. So, despite the terrible losses being sustained in the Atlantic, that vital sea lane to ensure Britain's survival, resources were diverted to the Arctic route. In addition, these convoys added greatly to the burden of meeting the Admiralty's overall strategic plan and for the Commander-in-Chief who was responsible for routing and protecting them.

Overall over four million tons of supplies flowed through to Russia, including 5,000 tanks and 7,000 aircraft, for the loss of ninety merchant ships and 7.5% of the stores. The Navy lost two cruisers and sixteen destroyers and corvettes. The last ship to be lost in the European theatre was lost in the Arctic.

AIMING FOR THE PACIFIC

Training Courses

On completion of nearly two years at sea and subject to having passed their Seamanship Examination Boards, midshipmen were promoted to sub-lieutenant and posted ashore for three months to undergo courses in all the specializations open to them after promotion to lieutenant and the award of full watch-keeping certification.

The infrequent spells of leave during the past two years brought home to me the reality of the appalling damage and loss of life caused to the civilian population, quite apart from the discomfort and frustration of sleeping in shelters, underground railway platforms or, as my parents did, lying on the floor under a metal frame designed to keep them safe from falling masonry at the house in Ealing to which they had now moved.

Now we spent nearly three months ashore on courses and the mass bombing attacks had been replaced by the V1 and V2 missile and flying bomb (doodle-bug) raids, the latter being perhaps the most unnerving. I spent every weekend in London and soon came to understand why many thought these were the most demoralizing. The stream of flying bombs persisted, so there were seldom any 'all clear' periods and the tension induced during the seconds between the engine noise stopping and the bomb landing wore people down.

However, that did not stop us going to night clubs when on leave, despite the destruction of the Café de Paris where my father's secretary very nearly lost her life. There was a vibrant night club scene in London and price controls made a night out affordable even to a midshipman. A modest expenditure for four hours (midnight to 4 am) in a dimly lit cellar with an excellent band [Harry Roy at the Milroy, Raimundo at the Coconut Grove and John Adams at the 400 if my memory can be trusted] and of course the love of the night in one's arms.

The attraction of some social life ashore [courses took place mainly in Portsmouth but included a short spell at Greenwich] tempted one to burn the candle at both ends. However, there was an incentive to pass out with high marks in terms of extra seniority on promotion to lieutenant. This was a rather too longterm carrot to have immediate appeal, but it may have done something to reduce the number of those who were unable to keep awake in a stuffy lecture room after lunch.

Towards the end of these courses we were asked to state preferences for one's immediate next appointment. In my case, having decided to become an airman, I was required to earn my watch-keeping certificate as quickly as possible. I was also anxious to serve in the Far East. The war in Europe was clearly coming to an end and I felt I had seen enough of the North Atlantic and the Mediterranean and therefore asked for an appointment to a small ship going to join the Pacific war.

This was the last time Colin Balfour and I served together. He became a distinguished gunnery officer, First Lieutenant of HMY *Britannia*, and Captain of HMS *Finisterre*, before leaving the Navy to look after family affairs on the death of his father. We have remained close friends and his son, Jamie, a godson, is now a Brigadier in the Green Jackets.

HMS *Mermaid*

HMS *Mermaid* had been refitted, following her arduous running on Arctic convoys, for her designated role as an anti-aircraft frigate but retaining a full Anti-Submarine (ASW) capability, and was to be my home for the next eighteen months. Her captain was Lieutenant Commander John Mosse who had made a reputation as a U-Boat killer.

As the junior sub-lieutenant I took on the traditional duty of Captain's Secretary and also as Fo'c'sle Officer with responsibility for all anchor and cable work as well as acting as Divisional Officer for the Fo'c'sle Division of seamen.

The ship was preparing to join the British Pacific Fleet and, shortly after I joined, Lieutenant Commander John Kimpton assumed command from Mosse; a more extrovert character, he had also commanded escorts in the Atlantic. After work-up in UK waters we sailed for the Mediterranean en route to the Far East but did not get beyond the Suez Canal before the atomic bombs brought the Pacific war to an abrupt conclusion.

Overriding priority was now given to bringing all reserve personnel home as soon as possible and to steer the majority to demobilization. *Mermaid's* officers were reservists, with the exception of the Captain, the First Lieutenant and me. One of the first to leave us was Henry Danskin, the Navigating Officer, a wonderful Yorkshireman who had served the whole war at sea and mainly in the North Atlantic. By this time I had become a full lieutenant and took over from Danskin as navigator.

In Europe the occupation forces were gradually being pulled back and AMGOT – The Allied Military Government of Occupied Territory – or Aged Military Gentlemen On Trial – as they became known, took over the huge task of administering almost the whole of Europe.

Mermaid was deployed to Tunisia to take part in the VE day celebrations – I had to lead our Platoon in the Victory parade – then dispatched to Alexandria where I and another officer were given a Tank Landing Craft each to sail back to Malta. A brief but satisfying first command. On return to Malta the ship was ordered to Aden as escort to a floating dock on tow by tugs and en route to Singapore.

After passing through the Suez Canal we made a fast passage to Aden where, needless to say, we discovered the voyage of the floating dock had been cancelled. However, we enjoyed a leisurely return

31

journey north through the Red Sea calling first at Kamaran Island off the coast of Saudi Arabia. There a lone British Resident Officer was responsible for the operation of the quarantine harbour where all ships bearing pilgrims making their way to Mecca were required to clear medical screening.

We were his first visitors since the start of the war and the Resident rather defensively said, 'You think I am mad'. I had hoped our expressions would not give us away but, temporarily at a loss for words, he went on, 'I was mad when I came here'.

In fact, he became more coherent as soon as he discovered we could be of some real assistance. First, a very pregnant woman needing urgent medical attention allowed our Sick Berth Attendant to give a realistic impression of a doctor as he welcomed this challenge as considerably more attractive than the regular treatment of venereal disease. Secondly, the island's diesel generator had given up the ghost some six months previously and life had become almost unbearable. Our engineering staff were happily able to bring it back to life.

A call at Massawa allowed most of the ship's company to take the train up the mountain to Asmara for three days' leave and blessed relief from the heat rash which was part of life in a floating metal box in tropical temperatures and long before the delights of air conditioning.

Then across to the Saudi coast and north to Jeddah for the first courtesy call by any HM ship since the war began; a very difficult landfall with few marks and uncertain depths. A gift of thirty live sheep caused some embarrassment as we carried no qualified butcher on board, but honour dictated that we receive the gift with suitably gracious thanks. In the event one of the chefs proved a dab hand with the knife and the sailors appreciated the fresh meat.

This had been an interesting time, but I was becoming frustrated by no news of an appointment to flying. Back in Malta, we found the island was coming alive and a captive Italian destroyer was made available as a ferry taking UK servicemen to Catania in Sicily and a leave camp at nearby Taormina at the foot of Mount Etna. This was an enchanting location and hugely popular. Little wonder it should become a major tourist resort in later years.

Mermaid made duty visits to Greece and then up the Adriatic to Trieste and Venice where we were to spend the Christmas of

32

1945. Trieste was an Army town virtually garrisoned by 56th London Division which included the 3rd Battalion, Scots Guards. One of their officers, Donald Deane, who had survived the bitter fighting up the Italian coast from Salerno, was a close friend from school days and he was well connected with the local social scene and some particularly attractive girls from Yugoslavia. Indeed one of them was to marry his Company Commander, Anthony Tuke, who later became Chairman of Barclays Bank.

It was in Trieste that the frigate HMS *St Austell Bay* joined us and I first met Henry Lambert who was a reserve sub-lieutenant. Captain of Winchester and an exhibitionist at New College, he became a good friend and we have remained close ever since. A keen Reserve Officer after the war he rose to become a lieutenant-commander, but this did not stop him becoming Chairman of Barclays Bank International and the Royal and Sun Alliance. His only daughter is my godchild.

In Venice, where we were secured practically opposite Harry's Bar, the UK enjoyed the rights to the Royal box at the Fenice Theatre. We would travel by boat in full mess dress and perhaps failed to appreciate just how lucky we were. My first opera was Verdi's *Nabucco* and it has remained my favourite to this day.

My general unrest did not go unnoticed by the Captain who was tough enough to keep me right up to the mark, but human enough to understand the frustration. However, a happy event was the appointment to the ship of Peter Shand Kydd. He had trained as a midget submarine crewman just in time to miss the action and had been sent to *Mermaid* to see out his time as a reserve officer.

Peter was a kindred spirit and has remained a lifelong friend; he is godfather to my eldest daughter. He did much to jazz up the social scene after our return to Malta where a delightful group of young ladies emerged to make the time pass pleasantly and not until he left us all too soon did I realize what I suspect was the true reason for his appointment. By this time the major units of the Italian Fleet had been incarcerated in the Great Bitter Lakes – in the centre of the Suez Canal – and Peter, a talented linguist, was destined to be one of the very few British liaison officers. In fact he was alone in one of the battleships with nearly a thousand sex-starved Italians and he had to barricade himself in his cabin and sleep with a revolver under his pillow. I missed him badly, and so did the girls in Malta.

★   ★   ★

Eventually the Admiralty appeared to recall I had volunteered for flying over a year before and I was soon on the next troop train back to England from Trieste.

3

IN AND OUT OF
THE COCKPIT

TRAINING TO KOREA

Flying Training

Having returned home in some haste and great discomfort overland I
found there was no immediate place for me on a flying training course.
I joined a group of fellow hopefuls who were soon dispatched on a
series of pre-flight training courses until the new flying training
programme which was to replace those hitherto carried out in the
USA and Canada had been introduced.

Among our familiarization courses was one at Londonderry in
Northern Ireland where combined sea and air anti-submarine exercises were carried out in the North West approaches. The Coastal
Command four-engined Lancaster long-range patrol aircraft [a
version of the famous night bomber] were based at RAF Ballykelly
and disaster struck when one flew into the sea at night taking six of
our course with it. I think we were all prepared for some casualties
during flight training, but we were devastated to lose a third of the
course before we had started.

We were a motley group ranging from sub-lieutenants to quite
senior lieutenants, more than a few of whom were qualified Observers
with considerable wartime operational carrier experience. Over
Christmas leave one of the other lieutenants, Martin Boissier, and I
took off for Zermatt, ski-ing under the eagle eye of Bill Bracken, the
only Olympic skier in the UK. The seventy-five pound maximum
foreign exchange allowance was barely adequate, but apres-ski was
relatively inexpensive.

We finally reported for basic flying training at RAF Booker in the first week of April 1947. This was a small grass field, situated at High Wycombe, perfectly adequate for the Tiger Moths which we were to fly.

The instructors were all RAF; mine was Flight Sergeant Croisdale. They were all highly qualified and also excellent tutors. Half of every day was spent under flying instruction and the other half in the classroom where we had to get our brains back into gear and our minds out of the cockpit.

It was a benign English summer which saw most of us go solo within about five hours, complete our aerobatic and general handling tests and brave our first night landings beside a single line of goose-neck flares. By the end of June we were all pronounced ready to move on to Advanced Flying Training (AFT). Croisdale was quite right when he said that never again would I enjoy pure flying so much.

Next came RAF Ouston, near Newcastle, the base for AFT. However much we could have wished to be training in sunny Florida at least we became quickly introduced to serious clouds and rain and flying on instruments. We were airborne in the redoubtable Harvard within a week of leaving our Tiger Moths, giving excellent continuity. This was where the real work began; using an aircraft as a weapon platform and understanding the limits of its capability.

Graduation from AFT came at the end of the year and brought the award of wings. This meant next stop Seafire at the Royal Naval Air Station at Lossiemouth commanded by Captain Caspar John, son of Augustus, and a distinguished naval fighter pilot. He was a legendary figure who enjoyed a bohemian life style when not in uniform, but was a strong disciplinarian in all things naval and particularly when flying.

Lossiemouth enjoys one of the best weather factors in the British Isles, situated right on the coast of the Moray Firth, but the living accommodation was primitive and the Captain's house was a Nissen hut.

Although most of us were bicycle-bound there were a few with four wheels like Jim Pinsent (whose nephew Matthew later proved rather good at rowing) and Ric Rickard whose green-label Bentley was much in demand. There were good opportunities for golf, but no local night life, which was just as well.

A long-time friend of my mother, who, with her husband, had been incarcerated in Changi jail, Singapore, by the Japanese for four years only to see him jump overboard to his death when on their way home after their release from prison, had remarried one Boyd Anderson who happened to live in Lossiemouth. They were a splendid couple and most generous hosts to those of us at the air station.

The somewhat eccentric Boyd, who was Captain of the Golf Club, had built his house on the edge of the links. It had a periscope from a U-boat installed for scanning the Moray Firth, a camera obscura in the corner of a long bar looking out to sea and opening onto an indoor swimming pool. Jet black martinis were a required tipple and an invitation to swing from one end of the pool to the other by rings suspended from the roof was given to all newcomers. The distance from ring to ring made a transit seem eminently achievable. Actually it was impossible and hapless novices found themselves hanging over the water until muscles gave out and immersion followed to the delight of all onlookers who had been there before.

Fitness was very much on the agenda with attendance at regular training sessions mandatory. Those who had skied with Bill Bracken in Zermatt found he had set up in the Cairngorms where he had trained ski troops during the war and now invited us to join him. He had arranged accommodation in an hotel in Newtonmore and buses to take skiers to and from the ski area.

However, there were no lifts and the snow was packed tightly between boulders and heather, neither of which were skier-friendly, and the weather was awful. Nevertheless, Bill's enthusiasm was infectious and the boys soon got used not only to carrying their skis up every hundred feet they would ski down, but they carried the girls' skis too. Sandwich lunches were eaten sitting on the rocks and when the time came to catch the bus home we were all totally knackered. Revival came with rum and hot milk provided by a pub en route to the hotel.

An appeal to the CO that skiers should be excused routine PT was rejected until we persuaded him to join us on the mountain and he was quickly converted.

The flying regime was equally tough and extra caution was being exercised during first flights following an accident which had occurred recently when French Naval pilots came to Lossiemouth to convert to and collect some earlier model Seafires Mk 3 with which to re-start their naval air arm. One pilot took off for his first solo watched by his instructor, his squadron commander and the RN squadron commander. On clearing the end of the runway he pulled the nose up and began a barrel roll, emulating the victory rolls of the Spitfire pilots returning to base after successful encounters with the Luftwaffe. But this young man had neither the experience nor the skill and ended up in a smoking wreck on the ground.

The French C.O., on seeing this, took a long pull on his Gaulois and ground the stub under his foot. Turning to his counterpart he said, 'I told Pierre not to do zat!' Not unnaturally these words remained with the Lossiemouth squadrons for some years, to be used whenever a pilot made a mistake, however trivial.

Sadly we too had a number of fatal flying accidents and these were compounded by a tragic sailing accident at Findhorn which cost three lives.

Among our married men, wives began to wonder why, now the war was over, lives still had to be lost in this way. One or two of our course decided to call it a day.

Nevertheless a solid core carried on to complete our Operational Training which included weaponry on the nearby ranges and then a move on to the satellite airfield next door at Millfield for practice deck landings.

Then came the flight south to Lee-on-Solent in early July whence we departed to make our first deck landings on board the aircraft carrier HMS *Implacable* about 50 miles off the coast. With one exception we all completed satisfactorily and were now judged ready to be appointed to operational squadrons.

Front Line Squadron

Completion of deck landing qualification may have meant pilots were ready for appointment to operational squadrons but it was to be over six months before most of us found homes. In the meantime I spent several weeks on ferry duties, which had the advantage of becoming qualified on a number of different aircraft requiring delivery between constructor's airfields or overhaul facilities and operational stations.

However, the majority of my time was spent in 768 Squadron based at Eglinton, near Londonderry in Northern Ireland. This was the training squadron for pilots appointed to carriers as Deck Landing Control Officers (DLCO). To gain the necessary experience the student DLCO had to be exposed to a very large number of aircraft making a carrier style – steep descent, continuous tight turn and very low speed – approach. Hence the need for a number of us to fly these circuits – round and round like clockwork mice: which of course was what we were called.

Under the skilled tutelage of the C.O., Lieutenant Commander Donald MacQueen, himself a very experienced DLCO, we played our part by varying our approaches and generally giving the students views of a full range of errors needing urgent action.

Finally in March 1949 my appointment came through to join 800 Squadron, part of the 13th Carrier Air Group from HMS *Triumph* (Captain Hutton). The ship was in a maintenance period at the time and the squadron had disembarked to RNAS Donibristle close to the dockyard at Rosyth on the Firth of Forth. This was a repair and over-haul facility rather than an operational airfield, but it served its purpose which was to see the squadron re-equipped with Seafire Mark 47 aircraft, the last of the line, powered by the up-rated Rolls Royce Griffon Engine with the unique two contra-rotating propellers It was also unique among all Seafire marks in that for the first time the wing-fold mechanism was power-operated.

The Squadron was commanded by Lieutenant Commander Richard Pridham –Whippel. The other squadron in the air group was No 827, equipped with Fairey Firefly Mark 2, commanded by Lieutenant Commander Pat Jackson and the Search and Rescue (SAR) aircraft was an old Vickers Osprey amphibian. The Air Group Commander was Lieutenant Commander Stanley Orr, a wartime ace with many kills to his name.

We arrived at Malta in early May expecting a two-year deployment with the Mediterranean fleet. Wives moved into local accommodation and the general mood was of anticipation of a pre-war style pattern of exercises at sea and a generous amount of time in Malta. And so it seemed. There were good weapon ranges and training facilities and the air group was able to achieve its required standards, although we had some minor accidents. On one sortie one of my main wheels would not come down and I diverted to the Air Station at Hal Far where I landed on the good wheel and managed a controlled ground loop without too much damage.

But it was not to last. Within three months, much to the dismay of the wives and the delight of the bachelors, we were ordered to join the Far East Fleet based in Singapore. Events in mainland China and particularly the shelling, with heavy loss of life including that of the Commanding Officer, of the frigate HMS *Amethyst* up the Yangtze River caused an outcry. Awkward questions were raised about why the Admiralty had seen fit to withdraw all carriers from the Far East, thus denuding the Fleet of air cover at a time and in an area which was still most unstable. Hence *Triumph* was dispatched to fill the void.

Before departing, Captain Hutton was relieved by Captain Torless who was a qualified Observer but had had little recent carrier experience. We sailed in early August and arrived in Hong Kong a month later, having enjoyed some flying en route. After operating off Hong Kong we returned to Singapore where the ship would carry out self-maintenance and the air group flew ashore to Sembawang where there had been a small naval air station in the past. It had been re-opened for our benefit.

This was a grass airfield with one runway where flexible metal tracking had been laid to provide a surface usable even during monsoon rain conditions. This was very much the Air Group's airfield as we had to provide all the support facilities ourselves. We were, however, splendidly assisted by local civilian staff who were responsible for household duties and provided drivers for the transport from jeeps to aviation fuel tankers and fire tenders.

Singapore Island had three RAF airfields at Tengah, Seletar and Changi and the fighter squadrons were actively engaged up country in support of the Army's on-going contingency operations against the communist insurgency. We worked closely with 60 Squadron who were equipped with an earlier mark of Spitfire and during one of our periods at Sembawang we deployed six aircraft to Kuala Lumpur to take over their duties and provide them with a break in their routine. For us it was an introduction to the difficult task of attacking targets in deep tropical forest and against some surprisingly well-directed fire from the ground.

Over-flying primary jungle the whole time required us to be trained in jungle survival and this was undertaken at the extremely efficient and thorough jungle survival school in Johore Bahru. We took this training very seriously; jungle was to us a much more hostile environment than the sea.

★　　★　　★

About a month later we returned on board and headed back to Hong Kong. We flew regularly and suffered a number of accidents during deck landings; the crash barriers had taken their toll and fires were not infrequent. It highlighted yet again the fragility of the these aircraft, particularly the Seafire. However, it is fair to say the Seafire was not responsible for any of our fatal accidents.

We were still suffering from deprivation of the Navy's right to procure and operate its own aircraft after the formation of the RAF in 1919. While the Inskip ruling of 1936 permitted the FAA to operate aircraft from carriers at sea it would never have survived the war without the provision of rugged, deck-worthy aircraft from the USN. Although the Swordfish played an amazing role, most famously in the sinking of the *Bismarck* and at Taranto [where the Japanese first appreciated the effect of an attack on a fleet in harbour] as well as on converted tankers and mini carriers, the Navy's own fighters stood little chance in the air war except against the Italians.

The Grumman Avenger, Wild Cat and Hell Cat and the Chance Vought Corsair were the wartime success stories, but after the war all US aircraft had to be returned or destroyed. Not until the Sea Fury did we have a British fighter aircraft with an adequate undercarriage for carrier operations. Fortunately it was on its way.

We practiced catapult launches (very slow and cumbersome procedures) and rocket-assisted take-offs. On one occasion soon after these trials the wings of the Senior Pilot's [Dizzy Steer] aircraft started to fold as he gathered speed down the flight deck. Catching sight of this in the corner of his eye he made an instant decision to abort and by brilliant handling brought his aircraft to a stop right on the forward edge of the flight deck. It was an incredible piece of luck that this failure did not take place during one of the catapult or rocket-assisted launches, as the aircraft certainly and the pilot probably would have been lost and the reason for the failure never revealed.

After Singapore and Hong Kong early in 1950 *Triumph* sailed North to Japan where we operated off Kure [near Hiroshima] and where the ship was later able to go alongside. This was in the designated British Commonwealth Occupation Force area, the occupying forces by this time being all Australian. These included a fighter Squadron (No.7) equipped with Lockheed Mustangs and commanded by Wing Commander Bay Adams based at Iwakuni air station to which we disembarked and from which we carried out a number of joint exercises.

This was very much General MacArthur land and the control of the US forces was masterful, as Japan came to terms with defeat, the atom bomb and the collapse of its dreams of the Greater South-East Asia Prosperity Zone.

We were lucky enough to have time to travel and see something of Tokyo, Osaka and Kyoto. I also found one of my fellow cadets, who I had not seen since we joined up eight years before, living with a Japanese family in Kure while on his final year of language training. He was dressed Japanese style and ate and lived totally in their culture. It gave me a fascinating insight into this astounding country. We saw even more when we sailed with other units of the fleet to exercise off the northern island, Hokkaido, with US Air Force units based there.

By this time there had been changes of Commanding Officer in both Squadrons, Lieutenant Commander Ian MacLachlan taking over 800 and Lieutenant Commander Ben Lyons 827. Pat Jackson moved up to take over as Air Group Commander from Stan Orr. This was also when I became Air Group Administration Officer which was akin to being the adjutant and responsible for all Air Group paper work, routines and movements, the latter being the not infrequent move from ship to shore and vice versa.

Proceeding south after our time off Hokkaido, the ship passed through the Korea Strait on the night of 2 July when we were greeted by the news that North Korea had invaded the South. The immediate relevance to us came quickly when the ship turned north to rendezvous with the USS *Boxer*, a USN carrier like the USS *Valley Forge* with which we had recently exercised, and a combined force of aircraft was launched from both ships to attack Pyongyang, the North Korean capital, the next morning.

The United Nations quickly took action to place all forces resisting the invasion under their banner and our aircraft were painted with bold black and white stripes on the wings to aid recognition of friend from foe as used at the time of the Normandy landings. This was not, however, always successful. On one sortie, when investigating over-flying traffic, which turned out to be Boeing Super Fortresses from Okinawa on a bombing mission, my wing man (Sub-Lieutenant White) was shot down by the top turret gunner while giving him a 'good-morning' wave. Fortunately he was able to escape from his burning cockpit and, although blinded, made a safe water entry and was soon picked up by the SAR helicopter from the USS *Boxer*. He regained his sight some weeks later as he recovered from his burns in a US military hospital.

The air group flew a large number of sorties in support of the army ashore and our two soldiers who formed the Carrier Borne Air Liaison Team (CBALs) were the main link in the briefing and debriefing chain. A major and a captain, they played the vital role for which they were trained and indeed relished this opportunity.

The ship remained on station until the end of the month when she returned to Kure for a week and aircrew were given privilege leave for about four days on the quite magical island of Miajima in the Inland Sea.

By this time the Admiralty's plans for additional support bore their first fruits with the arrival of the repair carrier HMS *Unicorn* bringing some much-needed replacement aircraft and aircraft repair facilities. With an operational flight deck she could also receive serviceable aircraft in need of routine maintenance and, in extremis, act as a spare landing deck.

Triumph returned to station on 8 August. We frequently flew as top cover for the Firefly bombing attacks and carried air-to-ground rockets with which we sank a number of junks and inshore patrol boats, attacked aircraft hangars and fuel tanks as well as spotting for gunfire support by the cruisers and destroyers. I also flew a number of photo reconnaissance sorties along the North Korean coast.

On 4 September we provided maximum support for the amphibious assault on the island of Inchon. This was a ferocious battle and showed the USMC had lost none of its skill at this form of warfare. Working with the American pilots we heard more voice transmissions than we were used to as they would give verbal reports direct to their ship after carrying out a shore attack. One of the islands commanding the approach to Inchon was called Walme-do and this received a tremendous hammering from USN dive bombers. The attack commander reported over the air, 'We hit the island so hard I thought it was going to roll over and sink'.

The Air Group lost a number of aircraft, but the pilots were all re-covered and our wonderful old amphibian, the Walrus, came into its own when flying well beyond the range of the US Navy helicopters to rescue a downed US pilot close inshore. Most tragically our CO, Ian MacLaughlan, was killed and the Senior Pilot, Lieutenant Thomas Handley, assumed command.

Apart from the set piece operations such as at Inchon and the sensational first encounters with MiG 15 jets in air to air combat, and the shooting down of one of them by Lieutenant Hoagy Carmichael which occurred later, the daily attack and support sorties could become monotonous and the results of attacks not always apparent. Opposition from ground fire accounted for most of the losses sustained.

Triumph was in due course replaced by HMS *Theseus* and the navy was thereafter to maintain a carrier on station throughout the following years of the Korean War. This has been well documented by Commander John Lansdown who served as Air Engineer Officer in one of the carriers in his book *With the Carriers in Korea*. There is no doubt the FAA reached a peak of operational performance during this period, achieving sortie rates hitherto considered totally unrealistic and the part played by the aircraft maintenance crews was outstanding. This was very much the Navy's air war as far as the UK was concerned.

The embarked squadrons alone provided the UK's offensive air contribution in the Korean war, dedicated to support of the United Nation's forces throughout the full three years. Sadly it was very seldom that the opportunity to give direct support to our own troops, like the gallant Glosters, arose. There can have been few Fleet Air Arm pilots at the time who did not take part, including volunteers from the reserves, and they bore the brunt of the losses; among them were twenty-seven pilots killed in action.

Our friends from the Australian No 7 Squadron at Iwakuni had been re-equipped with Meteor jets and moved north to give support from land bases in Korea. They were in the thick of the action from the start and sustained their share of losses, one of which, quite early on, was Bay Adams, the C.O. In October *Triumph* began her passage home, while six of us, who were needed urgently for new appointments, were sent home by BOAC, at this time flying four-engined Argonauts on relatively short legs. We took all of four days to make the journey from Hong Kong with overnight stops in Singapore and Colombo.

AIRBORNE EARLY WARNING

Service Trials Unit

On return from the Far East I was appointed to 703 Squadron, the Service Trials Unit (STU) responsible for the clearance of all aircraft and weapon systems for use by operational squadrons as well as the testing of all flight deck equipment(mainly catapults and arrester gear) of all new or re-fitted carriers prior to the embarkation of their own squadrons.

Before I could take up my appointment I needed to complete a conversion course to qualify on the Sea Hornet (a scaled-down version of the de Havilland Mosquito with enhanced performance; fitted with a hook, it was the Navy's current night fighter) and another to convert to jets.

The conversion course for the Hornet took place at the Naval Air Station at Brawdy in Wales. Here the Navy took its first step towards privatizing non-operational flying tasks by contracting with a company, Airwork, to provide all the flying instructors and maintenance personnel, most of them ex-RAF or FAA. This example of the use of contractors, whenever this could be more cost-effective, was to be widely expanded by the Navy and copied by the other Services over the years to come. The legendary Mosquito, fitted with dual controls, was used for instruction.

From Wales I went to the Naval Air Station at Culdrose in Cornwall for the jet conversion course in 702 Squadron, commanded by a great New Zealander, Lieutenant Commander Peter Perrett. Dual-control Gloucester Meteors were used for this purpose, followed by the single-seat de Havilland Vampire – an exhilarating experience without incident barring a complete loss of power to the wheel brakes when coming in to land in a Meteor.

I was instructed by Donald Gibson, the Commander (Air), to make a wheels-up landing on the runway. Allowing the aircraft to touch down gently on the two engine nacelles kept the aircraft steady and otherwise fully intact. Repairs to the nacelles were quickly completed and the aircraft was flying again the next day.

When I joined 703 Squadron based at Ford near Arundel in Sussex, commanded by Lieutenant Commander Bartlett, the Squadron was much preoccupied with testing the newly invented steam catapult

which had been installed in HMS *Perseus,* secured at a berth alongside the Naval Air Station at Sydenham near Belfast. This allowed
aircraft to be catapulted from the ship at various weights and end-
speeds, flown round, landed on the airfield and then taxied back
directly under the ship's crane and hoisted on board again. More
clockwork mice!

It was in 703 that I made my first deck landing in a jet, a hooked
Vampire. Both the Vampire and the Meteor in the squadron had
been fitted with A-frame hooks [attached to the fuselage rather than
the tail] to enable carrier trials to take place. My landing in HMS
Vengeance was uneventful but the Vampire was not equipped for
catapult launch and I was required to make a 'free' take off.
Compared with the piston-engined aircraft the jets were extremely
slow to accelerate and the wind over the deck required for take-off
was imprecise.

It was agreed that the ship would provide all the speed it could – it
was a windless day – and my aircraft would be positioned as far aft as
possible. As I passed the island structure it did not seem possible to
get airborne and the aircraft practically fell off the end of the flight
deck. The sixty feet to the sea gave me just enough space to ease into
a climb but not before I had given the impression of a hovercraft to
those watching as jet exhaust created a cloud of spray to make the
aircraft almost invisible.

My time in 703 was cut short by a call from the Admiralty to see
the Director of the Naval Air Warfare Division, Captain Richard
Smeeton. He explained that I would shortly be off to the USA to be
trained in Airborne Early Warning (AEW) and ultimately to
command the first squadron in the RN. I was to take a team consisting
of a second pilot, Peter Hiles, two observers, John Winstanley and
George Gatis, all lieutenants, who would be the first airborne intercept officers, and two Chief Petty Officer aircrewmen, Charlie Homer
and Stanley Collier, who would be their assistants.

Airborne Early Warning had been born of necessity during the war
in the Pacific to see beyond the radar horizon of the ships and hence
detect low-flying aircraft approaching the fleet. The requirement was
for a very large megawatt power radar and a dome of at least eight feet
diameter. It was an outstanding achievement to meet this requirement
before the war ended: fitted under the belly of a Grumman Avenger
it was deployed in early 1945 in the US Pacific Fleet.

★ ★ ★

After the war, among its many assistance projects, the United States Department of Defense inaugurated the Mutual Defense Assistance Programme (MDAP) under which some countries could be supplied with equipment they might not otherwise obtain. The RN had identified AEW as an extremely important capability and the supply of thirty aircraft had been agreed. By this time the Douglas Skyraider had replaced the Avenger as the platform aircraft and the first ones were due for delivery in November 1951.

After crossing the Atlantic in the *Queen Mary* in May we reported for duty with the Naval Staff in Washington. Here we were briefed in detail about administrative routines required by the US Navy, given a substantial advance of pay and advised to open an account with the Riggs Bank used by the Embassy. This being a Saturday, Peter Hiles and I sought some social activity and were invited to join a lively wedding reception in the Mayflower Hotel on Massachusetts Avenue. Despite air-conditioning it was very hot and jackets were soon shed. At the end of the evening I discovered I had also shed my wallet.

This was a major drama as funds were vital, not least for the provision of wheels which were a social essential. Happily I was able to raise my distant cousin in Los Angeles, explain my predicament and breathe a sigh of relief as he undertook to wire me immediate replacement dollars. What a star.

Early the next week we reported for duty with the Fleet Airborne Electronic Training Unit Atlantic (FAETULANT) at the US Naval Air Station, Norfolk, Virginia. Joining us in Norfolk was the final and key member of our team, Lieutenant Lindsay Bryson, a brilliant electrical engineer to whom the whole AEW programme was deeply indebted over the years. Bryson's distinguished career included serving as Controller of the Navy as a four-star Admiral, the first Electronics specialist ever to have held this appointment.

Bryson's hundred-horse-power brain quickly absorbed the intricacies of this hugely powerful radar and its down-link to ship or shore and soon demonstrated a mastery of the equipment which far outshone all the US Navy instructors.

On completion of our training in Norfolk we were posted to Composite Squadron 12 (VC12) based at the Naval Air Station at Quonset Point in Rhode Island. VC12 was the parent squadron for all AEW flights assigned to Atlantic Fleet aircraft carriers.

The Skyraider was the last piston-engined carrier aircraft to be designed by the distinguished Ed Heinemann at Douglas Aircraft: a rugged dive bomber with a huge load-carrying capacity, plenty of endurance and considerable agility as well as steadiness in a steep dive.

At Quonset Point Peter Hiles and I first flew the basic Skyraider in its attack variant, designated AD-3. This was to be a preliminary familiarization prior to flying the AEW version, designated the AD-4W. Here I was also introduced to the US Navy's budget system whereby every item of equipment and all operating expenditure (such as fuel and spares) had a notional cost. Called the Naval Industrial Fund (NIF), in the squadron these letters stood for Nothing Is Free. It kept everyone cost-conscious and was a discipline I would have welcomed in the RN.

The AD-3 was a delight to handle and without under-wing stores had the agility to give any fighter aircraft a run for its money. Peter Hiles and I occasionally indulged in some formation aerobatics and enticed one enthusiastic USN pilot, Dick Turner, to join us in this illicit pursuit. Illicit in the sense that VC12 was a strictly fly straight fly level squadron. I was happy to meet Dick again some fifteen years later when he was serving as a captain in the Pentagon.

Moving on to the AEW version was still to enjoy all the basic characteristics of the original, despite the huge radome and the massive electronic equipment packed into the fuselage, together with the two operating bays for the observer/controllers. Overload tanks were available to give extra endurance to the four and a half hours fuel carried internally: hence comfort, for all the crew, was important. Electric-powered canopy and seat position as well as auto-pilots were new experiences for us as were the 'hard hat' helmets with boom or throat microphones.

Rhode Island was close enough to New York for social weekends in the big city and to the Canadian border to visit friends at Prescott on the Saint Lawrence River. One of their house guests was to become my wife three years later.

AEW in the Royal Navy

On return to the UK and before the aircraft were delivered I spent a certain amount of time familiarizing myself with administrative support for the MDAP programme which was centered on the US Navy headquarters in London and driven by one Commander Mitchell. He refused to recognize that a mere lieutenant had been designated to command the RN squadron (in the USN it is invariably a full commander) and, no matter how I protested to him I was always 'Commander'. I gave up trying to convince him otherwise and he was comfortable with that until the first aircraft arrived.

These were delivered by sea to the River Clyde in November where they were unloaded and towed to the RNAS at Abbotsinch (now Glasgow Airport) for preparation and test flying before joining the squadron at Culdrose. A small hand-over ceremony took place between the US Admiral from their Headquarters in London and Vice Admiral Walter Couchman, the Flag Officer Air (Home). It was the first time I had appeared in uniform and when Commander Mitchell came over to shake my hand he exclaimed, 'Shit Commander, you're only a fucking Lootenant,' with a big smile.

The squadron, No 778, had been formed to introduce AEW to the RN and to train the first operational crews. We were pioneering AEW which would grow to be one of the defining military capabilities of the future. Precisely similar equipment was fitted to RAF four-engined Lancaster aircraft for North Sea surveillance some years later.

While the US continued to improve and expand this capability, efforts by UK industry centred on a programme to modify the Nimrod aircraft. This turned into an embarrassing technical and hugely expensive disaster and a belated decision was made to purchase the AWACS system fitted to the Boeing 707 in 1986.

My Squadron staff consisted initially of the two full crews who had been with me in the USA. Peter Hiles assisted me with the test flying after aircraft had been prepared for flight following transport from the USA, and with the conversion of new pilots as they joined. The senior observer and aircrewman dealt with the training of the back-seat operators who were to be, in effect, fully fledged 'Air Direction' officers, empowered to take fighter aircraft under direct control for the interception of aircraft detected by the Early Warning radar.

The Squadron began flying its ADWs at Culdrose before the end of 1951 and early in the new year had a great opportunity to display the enormous power of the radar to the whole country. During a heavy storm off the south-west of Cornwall a merchant ship had been swamped and nearly lost. Her crew had been taken off, but the Captain was determined to stay on board. This was the merchant ship *Flying Enterprise* and on her was Captain Carlsen.

There was heavy media cover as the ship was gradually driven further and further away into the Western Approaches and all contact was lost despite the RAF flying numerous long-range patrols. Finally we were asked to help. I set off early on the morning of 5 January 1952 with John Winstanley on the radar and the renowned BBC air correspondent, Charles Gardner, in the other seat, much to the disappointment of Stan Collier, my regular crewman. We had no more than a general idea of the ship's position, but we had fitted long-range tanks which increased our endurance to over eight hours.

Climbing through heavy cloud to over 10,000 feet we had radar cover out to 125 miles and settled down to a long search. We estimated the ship to be between 250 and 300 miles out and after an hour she should have been within range. There were a number of radar echoes which John began to track and finally narrowed the possibilities to three. He had to pick out the one which was stationary. He made his selection and we descended through cloud to break at about 500 feet with the unmistakable sight of a hull nearly fully submerged and only the deck house above the water. We made a low pass and a figure appeared waving excitedly. Charles Gardner was busy taking pictures and recording the event for broadcasting.

We returned to Culdrose after nearly five hours in the air, most of it in cloud and nearly all over a very wild sea and force eight gale, and all on a single engine. It was one for Wheeler's line book! We passed the position of the ship to the RAF and a Lancaster of Coastal Command was dispatched with some safety equipment which was dropped to Carlsen. Overall, not exactly the task of an Early Warning Aircraft but at least an eye-catching example of the versatility of its radar.

Early in 1952 I took an aircraft to Farnborough for tests to establish deck-landing parameters for the arrester wires and catapults and then to HMS *Eagle* for live deck-landing trials. These were all entirely normal. At Farnborough I met another bachelor living in the mess, Lieutenant Commander Tom Innes, currently involved with Avro's chief test pilot, Roly Falk, in testing the Avro Delta development aircraft. The programme required them to take the aircraft through the sound barrier, approaching in steps of 0.1 Mach each flight, a form of Russian roulette which Tom admitted was touching his threshold of fear.

Training continued throughout the first six months of 1952, during which time four crews, who were to comprise the first AEW operational Flight, were qualified. To recognize the transition from a purely training role to operational status the Squadron was given an 800 designation and 778 Squadron became 849 Squadron on 1 July 1952.

In September the Squadron embarked a flight, which included those of us who had been in the USA, in HMS *Eagle* for the autumn deployment on a major NATO Strike Fleet exercise in northern waters. Operating by day and night and in weather which grounded all the other aircraft in the carrier group, the flight demonstrated the huge extension to the reconnaissance area covered by the potential 200-mile-radius radar as well as the detection of low-flying aircraft. Conditions were such that when some major surface units failed to make a rendezvous we were called upon to locate them.

Also embarked was the first squadron to be equipped with Supermarine Attacker jets, No 800, commanded by Lieutenant Commander George Baldwin. One day George landed on behind me, his hook failed and his aircraft entered the specially designed barrier, which, while almost stopping the aircraft, tore off its wings and the fuselage continued to slither up the deck, coming to rest alongside my aircraft. I was still in the cockpit, looking down on George who gave me a cheery wave. He was wearing a leather flying helmet and my immediate thought was, if any aircrew deserved hard hats like ours it was them.

Building up the operational flights towards the target of one for each operational carrier and the introduction of the new aircraft as they arrived in Scotland was a task well met during the remainder of 1952 and the first half of 1953. By the time of the Coronation Review of the Fleet in June the Squadron was present with sixteen aircraft in the Fleet Air Arm fly past.

I handed command of the Squadron to Lieutenant Commander Baring at the end of July 1953. He was tragically killed in an helicopter accident while still in command.

51

In 2002 I was invited back to Culdrose to celebrate the 50th anniversary of the formation of 849 AEW Squadron. Sadly Lindsay Bryson was not fit enough to join us, but Peter Hiles and Stan Collier were in good form.

WASHINGTON DC

Naval Staff Course

Following my spells of Squadron command I was appointed to the office of the Second Sea Lord, Chief of Naval Personnel and a member of the Admiralty Board. This was my first introduction to the way business was conducted in Whitehall in general, but, as I was to find out later, the pace was rather slower than on the Naval Staff.

I had by this time become engaged to the girl I had met in Canada during my first spell of duty in the USA. She was the daughter of a much respected doctor with a substantial practice in the town of Evanston on the shore of Lake Michigan, just north of Chicago, and we were married in a chapel on the campus of North Western University. It was something of a shock for her to arrive in England where food rationing was still in force some eight years after the end of the war, and accommodation was a small flat near Turnham Green.

Shortly after taking up my new appointment I was informed that I had been selected as Flag Lieutenant and personal pilot to the Admiral, British Joint Services Mission in Washington, Vice Admiral Sir Geoffrey Barnard. He would not be taking up his appointment for six months and had asked that I attend the Naval Staff Course at Greenwich during this period. So my brief stint on the staff of the Second Sea Lord came to an abrupt end.

The buildings of the Royal Naval College, Greenwich, which stands in a commanding position on the Thames, were designed as a hospital for disabled men of the Royal Navy by Christopher Wren. He was in effect commanded to do so by Queen Mary II at the end of the 17th century, despite the fact that he was already building St Paul's Cathedral, Hampton Court and a number of City churches. Enough surely to keep him fully occupied.

The hospital was closed and the buildings handed over to the Navy in 1873. The Navy fully appreciated this architectural jewel. It became a college for advanced training and students were fortunate indeed to enjoy not only the outstanding beauty of the college and its riverside setting but also its relatively easy access to London's many attractions.

The Naval Staff Course was one of the few remaining single-service staff courses attended by officers of commander and lieutenant-commander rank in the RN and Commonwealth navies. Courses at more senior level were invariably tri-service and very often inter-national, which created whole new opportunities for study while greatly complicating issues of access to classified information.

Those attending were given the chance to extend their education and also to be reminded of much that had been diluted by the pressures of day-to-day operations, This was for most of us refreshing and compelling. The directing staff were high fliers and the visiting lecturers outstanding. This free-ranging part of the course was matched by the application of staff training and analysis to the production of sound operational plans. The 'solutions' produced by students demanded the burning of much midnight oil to meet stringent time scales. I drew the line at 3 a.m. If the task could not be completed by then, I was not cut out to be a staff officer.

British Joint Services Mission (BJSM) Washington DC

Happily I managed to qualify, albeit having missed the last three weeks after an urgent call from Washington, and by the end of 1954 I was installed with the rest of the Royal Naval staff in offices provided for us by the United States Navy situated on Constitution Avenue in the heart of Washington, DC, known as the Old Navy Buildings. It was a particular privilege to share the building with a number of USN Bureaux and an easy familiarity was established which enhanced the already close ties between the two navies which had been operating together again for nearly four years in Korea.

The depth and breath of historic, cultural and social links between our two countries were as solid as a rock and the special relationship between the USN and the RN was one of the strongest. The shared naval traditions form a bond which goes back beyond the Declaration of Independence and even Mount Vernon is named after a Royal

Naval Admiral. At Trafalgar HMS *Victory* had Americans pressed into service among her ship's company.

A common language ensured a dialogue embracing naval theory and practice as well as strategy and tactics. The writings of the US Navy's Captain Mahan are accepted as having influenced Admiral Fisher in his restructuring of the Royal Navy before the Great War, while the US Admiral, Samuel Eliot Morison, a professor at Harvard, also had a chair at Oxford.

Royal Navy carriers played a significant part in the later stages of the war in the Pacific and the equipping of many Fleet Air Arm squadrons with the more capable US Navy aircraft created a strong bond between the airmen of both services. Many of the RN pilots had been trained in the USA during the Second World War, a programme which was re-introduced during the Korean war.

The armoured decks of the RN carriers withstood Kamikaze attacks better than their US counterparts and working closely together on air operations created mutual respect and helped the USN to adopt without hesitation the innovations in carrier equipment introduced by the Royal Navy after the war.

While the aviator nexus was particularly strong the submariners were not far behind, developing bonds which grew from the advent of the nuclear boats. In the wider context of command and control, radars and electronic sensors were often interoperable but usually on a strict UK/US only basis.

The 'air' office on the Admiral's staff was headed by Commander D.B. 'Dick' Law. Well known and admired in the USN, he had been the first pilot to land a jet aircraft at the new New York airport later to be named after John F. Kennedy. Law had been in North America leading a Fleet Air Arm aerobatic team giving displays all over Canada and the USA. He had a mixed bag of aircraft, made up of Sea Furies, Hornets and one Sea Vampire. It was in that aircraft that he landed on completion of their flying display at the inauguration of the airport.

The air engineer, Commander Nick Goodhart, a naval pilot who also held a number of world records as a glider pilot, and a civilian staff officer, Stewart Miller, who had been there for years, completed the team. I was welcomed into their group and remained one of Law's closest friends until his untimely death in 1998.

*   *   *

The Lockheed Expeditor aircraft which had been assigned to the Royal Navy staff during the war became time-expired and had been replaced by a de Havilland Heron, a larger four-engined version of the successful Dove. A home in America had been provided for the Expeditor by the USN and this had been a carefully guarded privilege which the Navy was not about to give up. The compromise was the Heron, provided jointly by the Navy and RAF for the use of all three services, supported by an RAF sergeant engineer and with a full-time flight lieutenant pilot. The Navy were, however, always to have first call.

The aircraft was stationed at Andrews Air Force base in Maryland about a forty-minute drive from Washington. Flying in controlled airspace and having to comply with complex flight regulations, without which no clearance to take-off could be obtained, was a whole new experience. It was not long before I was joining the stack of civilian aircraft waiting to land at Washington National airport where I had to pre-position the aircraft every time I picked up a VIP-coded passenger. My Admiral was coded seven, low on the scale but still entitled.

There were no direct flights to Washington from the UK and senior military and civilian visitors expected to be met in New York. On one occasion I spent more than three hours 'stacked' over New York in very unpleasant weather without ever being cleared down to pick up my passengers.

In addition to flying the Heron I was granted five hours a month flying USAF Lockheed Jetstars from Andrews and almost as many hours as I wanted flying Skyraiders from the Anacostia Naval Air Station just across the water from the National Airport. When a hurricane warning threatened the Washington area all aircraft had to be evacuated and, as scores of officers departed the Pentagon for the three airports, the roads quickly jammed, only to be cleared and jammed again by a second wave of cars, manned this time by the wives with overnight toothbrushes for their pilot husbands. I took the Heron to Canada.

I got to know the staff of the Rear Admiral who headed the Bureau of Aeronautics, responsible for the entire Naval Aviation budget, (nearly as big as the entire UK Defence budget) and was required to justify this in front of the Armed Forces Sub-committees in both Congress and the Senate. This clearly demonstrated that the USN was in charge of its own funding. I wished it was the same in the UK, but the Admiralty Board found the whole concept of appearing before a parliamentary committee quite abhorrent.

While nuclear submarine co-operation was increasing, it was developments in aircraft carrier operations in the RN, which were adopted by the USN and which were accepted as having been vital to the success of carrier operations in the jet age, which created the greatest impact. First came the concept of the 'angled deck', the brainchild of Captain Denis Cambell and Mr Eric Boddington, which allowed aircraft which missed the arrester wires to 'go round again' – several times depending on fuel state – instead of ending up in the crash barriers. Apart from the massive saving in cost of lost aircraft there came the ability to launch and land at the same time, saving vital minutes steaming into wind. A reduction in the number of arrester wires needing to be installed was an added bonus.

While the USN were quick to adopt the concept, they initially had trouble with the word 'angled'. Their first suggested alternative was 'canted', which we persuaded them really did give the wrong impression, and then on through 'tilted, 'slanted', 'off-set' and many others. It reached a point where the opinion of the Chief of Naval Operations, Admiral Robert Carney, was sought and his response was, 'I don't give a damn what you call it so long as it isn't "cock-eyed" – I reserve that exclusively to describe the opinion expressed by Monty about aircraft carriers'. (Field Marshal Montgomery had recently declared that he saw no future use for them.)

The second innovation was the use of a stabilized light source to guide a pilot onto the deck instead of the 'batsman' or 'paddle waver'. This was invented by Commander Goodhart, the member of staff I have mentioned above.

Then came the replacement of the hydraulic powered catapults by steam from the ship's main engines. Already aircraft weights and high launch speeds had stretched beyond the capability of hydraulic systems and there had been some tragic accidents.

Finally came the direct acting arrester gear, developed by the Royal Aircraft Establishment at Bedford, which provided for the increased weight and landing speeds of the new jet aircraft.

The US Defense Industry

The Admiral was given access to all USN research and development work and travelled widely to naval and civilian establishments all over the States. He was often accompanied by a specialist staff officer but he was always accompanied by me, sometimes as his pilot, often as his staff officer and frequently as both. We also made a visit to Hawaii as guests of the C-in-C Pacific, Admiral Felix Stump, flying in his personal aircraft, a commercial DC 6 crewed by his own staff.

Looking at the US defense industry and its close association with many University post-graduate projects – the first surface to air ship-launched missile was developed by Johns Hopkins University near Baltimore – I could not fail to be immensely impressed. However, their scientists bemoaned the fact that their research was always tied to projects; they were never given a clean sheet of paper and asked to think the wildest thoughts. 'As you do at Oxbridge,' they would say. But Oxbridge would ask, 'Why can't we have some funded projects like they do in the USA?'

We had visited a wide cross-section of industry and seen some of the ten or so projects all aimed at achieving vertical take-off. (At Ryan in San Diego we had to be there at dawn to see their 'tail sitter' perform as it could only operate in zero wind!) and Frank Piesecki was developing his big tandem-rotor helicopters, now still going strong as Boeing-Vertol Chinooks.

It was also a great experience to work with staff officers of the highest calibre who, apart from the air group, included Commanders John Coote, a submariner and yachtsman who left the Navy to join the Beaverbrook newspaper chain, and the extrovert Val Bailey, who was to be a distinguished commodore in command at Plymouth, and Commanders Ian Easton, Bunny Holford and Rodney Sturdee, all of whom became admirals. The Chief of Staff was Commodore Peter Gretton, one of the great U-boat hunters of the Atlantic battle.

Admiral Lord Mountbatten

Admiral Barnard's social programme in Washington was run by a delightful American lady who knew everyone the Admiral needed to know in Washington and was known by them and all the staff as 'Maggie'. I was only marginally involved, but I was responsible for the

Admiral's driver, a splendid and very courteous black man called Hiawatha Lee. He, poor man, had to suffer the agonies of driving an Austin Princess seven-seat limousine known to all as the hearse. A funereal pace was its favourite speed and any exertion above this normally incurred a severe penalty, like overheating or brake failure.

During the visit of the First Sea Lord, Lord Mountbatten, and Lady Mountbatten it was necessary, against my better judgement, to send all the Mountbatten luggage by car from Washington to New York on conclusion of the naval part of his visit and the start of his private programme which was to be launched at a black tie dinner with the Pilgrims at which he was the guest of honour. The car, with Mr Lee at the controls and Mountbatten's valet riding shot-gun on the thirteen pieces of assorted trunks and suitcases, set off at 10 a.m. for the three-hour journey. I had allowed for it to take six hours and there was still a cushion of another two hours on top.

Lady Mountbatten had been speaking at an International Red Cross dinner in Richmond, Virginia, the previous evening. I had flown her there in the Heron and stayed overnight to fly her to New York the following morning. Lord Mountbatten had gone by train from Washington to the Naval shipyard at Philadephia and thence to New York where they were to stay at Mr Winthrop Aldrich's Fifth Avenue apartment. On arrival at La Guardia Airport at about 3 pm Lady Mountbatten was met by the British Consul General with his Rolls Royce and I was happy to leave her in his safe hands and flew back to Andrews. Little did I know what I had left behind.

Captain Peter Brayne-Nichols, Mountbatten's Naval Assistant, recounted later that when he and Mountbatten had arrived at 5th Avenue about 3.30 there was no sign of the car. The temperature began to rise. Lady Mountbatten arrived some half hour later and called for calm. Long before the mobile phone there was no way of knowing what had gone wrong. The temperature continued to rise. Brayne-Nichols, who happened to have his dinner jacket with him, suggested Mountbatten could borrow it. This was a mistake. It was seriously too small, with sleeves ending near the elbow. The temperature by this time was off the scale. Literally they were saved by the bell which rang after the hearse had limped in at six pm following a nightmare drive. The Princess was never again permitted to venture beyond the bounds of the District of Columbia!

★　　★　　★

It was a wonderful time to have been in the USA. General Eisenhower was President and Richard Nixon the Vice. The UK was building commercial jet airliners and selling them into the US market. Capital Airlines presented their first Vickers Viscount with Rolls Royce Dart turbines for christening by Mrs Nixon in a major media occasion and the traditional champagne ceremony. Nixon in his address praised the UK for this 'first' and expressed his regrets, as a Californian, that it had not been made in the USA. He capped this by grabbing the microphone after the ceremony and announcing, 'At least it is Californian champagne'. 'What a ham,' moaned the press.

We lived in Spring Valley in the north-west of the District and quite near the home of the defeated democratic nominee for President, Senator Estes Kefauver, always most approachable and cordial. There was an active social scene, mainly restricted to weekends, and plenty of opportunities for my wife to visit her parents. Our first child, Jonathan, was born in April 1956.

I had many occasions to fly my Admiral on visits to the RN officers serving on exchange appointments with the US Navy and Marine Corps as well as on the SACLANT Staff at Norfolk. One visit was made on our way back from a base in Florida. The weather had become progressively worse as we flew north and my hopes that it would not be as bad as forecast were soon dashed. We entered cloud over the Carolinas as night set in and were bounced around for the next two hours which unsettled my passengers who did not enjoy rough weather in this small aircraft.

I was conscious of the conditions but reports indicated it would get no worse. We had a precise time of arrival to make and it still looked achievable. As we approached Norfolk I was given a very complex route through the local air traffic lanes which I followed as far as the point of hand-over to Norfolk Naval Air Station. I reported I was four-engined, with no co-pilot and asked for a vectored radar approach to the runway. This was immediately agreed and weather at base reported as 500 feet cloud base and one mile visibility. No problem. We broke cloud at 200 feet in pouring rain.

We had been airborne for nearly six hours, the last three at night and in cloud. When I left the cockpit to rejoin my Admiral who had been greeted by Captain John Frewen, (later to be C-in-C of the Home Fleet) the senior RN officer at Norfolk, Frewen's only comment was, 'You were fifteen minutes late'. That said it all.

THE FALKLANDS

It was time for me to go back to sea and I was appointed to HMS *Protector* (Captain John Wilkinson) as Executive Officer in May 1956. The Ministry of Defence, in response to requests from the Foreign Office to maintain a guardship on station in the South Atlantic, had reconfigured one of two ships originally built as anti-submarine net layers. *Protector* had a distinguished war record, although torpedoed off Crete and put out of action until the end of the war.

The guardship was required to operate in Antarctic waters and to protect the interests of the United Kingdom and its related claims to sovereignty in certain parts of Antarctic territory. She should also operate in support of the Falklands Island Dependency Survey (FIDS) which had various bases on the peninsula, maintained throughout the year and supported by the Royal Research ship *John Biscoe*, an operation in which the Governor of the Falklands was closely involved. At the same time Hunting Aerosurveys were mapping the entire area by aerial photography with their maps 'locked' by cairns consisting of black fifty-gallon oil drums positioned by helicopter in locations precisely defined.

1955 was designated the International Geophysical Year in which the UK, Australia and New Zealand were all involved. The UK was represented by the Royal Society, whose expedition advance party, commanded by Surgeon Lieutenant Commander David Dalgliesh, had sailed south in the research ship *Tottan* to establish a base at Halley Bay at the south-east end of the Weddell Sea.

At the same time Sir Vivian Fuchs was launching his British Transantarctic Expedition with Sir Edmund Hillary and their advance party was also heading south in an icebreaker, the *Theron*, to establish their initial base in much the same area. However, they reported 'Drifting in heavy pack ice at about fifteen miles a day. Position not precise'. *Protector* was 1000 miles away on the west coast of Graham Land, but Captain Wilkinson said he would sail round into the Weddell Sea and to the ice edge so that her helicopters could assist *Theron* to find her way out.

When this was finally achieved, Captain Wilkinson sent a boat to bring a party to *Protector* for dinner. Vivian Fuchs tells the story in his book. 'One after the other we clambered up a swaying rope ladder to the deck above. When Ed Hillary's turn came, a sailor was heard to say, 'Hold tight Sir, think you can manage it?' followed by the coxswain's, 'He's all right. Climbed Everest didn't he?'.

We had no such excitements the following year.

The ship was equipped to operate two Sikorsky S51 helicopters and provided with an adequate hangar and a flight deck constructed over the net-deck at the stern. The highly infammable petrol for the helicopters was carried in two large cylindrical tanks fitted either side of the hangar, resting on sloping crutches and retained in position by heavy wire strops, the design concept being that in emergency the strops, which were fitted with a quick-release mechanism, would be slipped and gravity would do the rest.

As the aircrew were relatively junior, the appointment as Executive Officer had to be held by a practising airman who was also the Captain's adviser on all aviation matters. For me, it was necessary to qualify on helicopters and I carried out my conversion at RNAS Lee-on-Solent while the ship was in Portsmouth dockyard in preparation for her next deployment. Initial helicopter training was carried out in the small Hiller with its Franklin engine fitted behind the pilot at head height which was to have fatal consequences for one pilot on my course who landed too heavily during an engine-off practice landing.

I then graduated to the Sikosky S51 from the *Protector* flight. We were fortunate to have two helicopters from the original batch built in the USA and fitted with the proven and highly reliable Pratt and Whitney engines. I was to fly regularly during the deployment.

The unique conditions for navigation required a level of experience between the Captain and Navigating Officer which could only be gained on the job. It followed that after the first deployment in 1955 the Captain and Navigator should become 'out of step' and so Captain Wilkinson remained for a second year and a new navigator, Lieutenant John Evans, joined for his first year.

John Wilkinson was a splendid Commanding Officer, calm, prepared to be advised by his specialists and now confident about operations in ice. He was a very private man and seldom enjoyed company. He did not find it easy to communicate but could be drawn out on occasions. John Evans was outstanding and a huge support to his Captain.

Our seaman complement was drawn almost exclusively from the

members of the Portsmouth Field Gun Crew, who, with their Petty Officer trainer, had volunteered for the ship. They were a splendid group and well matched by the Royal Marine Detachment commanded by the intrepid Captain 'Jungle' Bazely. Being on detached service we also boasted a doctor, Surgeon Lieutenant John Kemp, and a Padre, Eric Milner, and of course a top-class engineer, Lieutenant Commander Hegaty, a gifted all-rounder and Russian linguist. Lieutenant John Brigham commanded the helicopter flight with Lieutenant Mike Rawlinson as his Observer, and with a second pilot and Observer.

New on this deployment was a team from the Hydrographer of the Navy commanded by Lieutenant John Wynne-Edwards, charged with a considerable survey assignment which would require them to remain in one area for much of the time. For this they were provided with a prefabricated building – designed and delivered in kit form by ex-aircraft manufacturer Boulton and Paul – and a thirty-six-foot fully equipped survey launch.

Passage South

We sailed in early September and our arrival in Rio de Janeiro was marred by there being no reply to the twenty-one-gun national salute and the seventeen-gun salute to the Brazilian Admiral fired by the ship. All was made clear by a perspiring Naval Attaché who greeted the ship at her berth. He had made a cock-up over GMT and local time, resulting in our hosts not expecting us for another four hours!

All was forgiven by the Brazilian Admiral and we settled into an enjoyable visit which should have lasted a full week, only to be inter-rupted by an urgent call for help from the FIDS. Two of their scientists and their six-dog team had become isolated on an ice flow due to the unexpectedly early break-up of a major ice field.

The challenging task of rounding up a major part of the ship's company, well deployed among the renowned flesh-pots of the Copacabana, was completed in good time and the ship bade a quick farewell to the Sugar Loaf mountain as we headed south at best speed: in *Protector*'s case, all of eighteen knots.

The passage to the ice gave us an unusually early introduction to steaming among first small 'bits', then 'bergy bits' and finally into leads between the major ice flows to the solid ice pack. We also met penguins in their native habitat for the first time and they were to provide us with endless entertainment for the rest of the deployment. They never let us down.

Helicopter reconnaissance was flown and the stranded dog team located much where we expected. The huskies were unimpressed by the helicopters and it needed all the persuasive power of their handlers to get them into the cabin – two at a time. On return to the ship the only trace of the rescue operation was the pungent smell of the huskies which totally overcame the normal aroma of hot engine and engine oil. Ultimately the huskies lost out in the bad smell stakes to the over-powering stench of whale blubber being processed.

No sooner had we completed this task than we had a cry for help from Hunting Aerosurveys. One of their Hiller helicopters, used to site the cairns vital to the photographs taken by their Catalina flying boats, had crashed when the pilot suffered a 'white-out' while positioning oil drums. Again we located the wreck and our air technical team were able to dismantle the machine into pieces small enough to be air-lifted out.

Port Stanley

Finally we made our way to Port Stanley in the Falkland Islands which was to be our base for the deployment. Here we made direct contact with the Governor, Mr Edwin Arrowsmith, and the FIDS HQ and had our first taste of shore leave. It was a stark contrast to Rio.

The Islands boasted a local Defence Force, not much above platoon size, and a football pitch of some use near the grass landing strip which was adequate for an irregular air service from the Argentine. We were able to explore the outer islands by helicopter and take part in the annual gosling slaughter. This unattractive pastime was essential to preserve sufficient grass to sustain the sheep population, the mainstay of the local economy. Geese were vermin and there was a bounty paid for every beak brought in. No one made a fortune.

Britain had first occupied the islands in 1833 by which time the earlier settlers had virtually wiped out the penguin, seal and sea lion population. They introduced sheep to replace the now extinct native wild life and the sheep in turn wiped out the tussock grass which had hosted the nesting sites for a wide variety of marine birds.

In the aftermath of the Falklands War British Government scientists looked seriously at the waters surrounding the islands and not just for oil. Vast fishing grounds were discovered and it soon dawned on the islanders that the sheep could share the grazing with the wild life. The penguins have found their way back and the eco-tourists now outnumber the local populace.

In 1956 it was a bleak existence. The islanders maintained contact with each other and with Port Stanley by a radio network, and a small float plane was available for emergency use. The Falkland Island Company was the only major commercial activity bringing in supplies from the mainland by way of a monthly round trip in its small freighter the SS *Darwin* to Buenos Aires and Montevideo and providing a market for the wool.

Mail came monthly by sea and occasionally by air. The islanders were inclined to send their children to school on the mainland and were dependent for major medical support from the same direction.

During our frequent visits to Port Stanley we had got to know the island and the islanders quite well. The helicopters helped. They were a unique group, fiercely British but with a realistic view about the fragility of their position and their dependence on the Argentine. Few of them expected their children to remain in the longer term.

On our first journey south to Graham Land the survey team were put ashore at Port Lockroy and assisted with the erection of their home base near a suitably sheltered anchorage for their survey boat. We then settled into a regular pattern of visits to the FIDS bases. We also visited all locations where the UK claimed jurisdiction and delivered HMG's official protests where bases had been established by other countries. We then usually invited their staff for drinks on board and played football against them on the ice.

Re-fuelling

Protector had no access to fuel in the Falklands and was dependant on supplies embarked on behalf of the Admiralty in the two whale factory ships owned by the Salvesen Company, the *Southern Venturer* and the *Southern Harvester*. Having carried the fuel south, these ships had the right to call on *Protector* to come and collect it when they required the tanks for storing their whale oil. In due course we had a call from

64

Southern Venturer to rendezvous with her in the South Bellingshausen sea.

The factory ship did not stop but continued at about four knots while *Protector* secured alongside, using a seventy-foot sperm whale as a fender. The oil transfer was painfully slow due to the very small pumps available and it took the best part of a day and a half to take on board 500 tons. As well as the oil we took onboard the smell; the smell of the blubber being processed pervaded every corner of the ship and took several weeks of the best Southern ocean air freshener to dispel.

The whale factory ships normally operated in company with six 'catchers' which harpooned the whales and towed them to the mother ship for processing. Two helicopters were carried to search for the whales and it was the provision of these helicopters which gave Bristow Helicopters their first commercial contract, Alan Bristow having only recently set up his company after leaving his job at Westlands. He himself flew on these expeditions in the early days.

At the shore-based factory at Grytviken in South Georgia the catchers performed the same role and, although the shore factory was able to make more complete use of the various products resulting from the rendering, the quality of the oil itself was said to be lower due to the much greater elapsed time from kill to processing. True or folklore, we never learned.

Mid-deployment came with a week in Montevideo where we caught up with mail from home and the ship's company enjoyed the hospitality of the local people whose memories of the battle of the River Plate were fresh in their minds.

Royal Visit

On return to the south we were joined by the Royal Yacht *Britannia* in Port Stanley with Prince Philip embarked. HM the Queen had decided to fly back from the Commonwealth Games in Sydney and HRH was taking the long way home. He wanted to go further south: he was keen to see penguins and the artist Edward Seago, who was included in his party, was keen to paint penguins. We went south – fast. However, we ran into a hazard in the shape of the Commanding Officer of the Royal Flight who is responsible for the safety of all members of the Royal Family wherever and whenever they take to the air.

His instructions were clear. First, when HRH was airborne in one helicopter another should remain in company as instant air sea rescue. So 100% serviceability of both helicopters was required. No problem. Second, there had to be a minimum cloud base of 1000 feet. Big problem, which became a big issue with HRH glowering at a 200-foot cloud base and proclaiming it to be 1000 feet while his private secretary, Michael Parker, beseeched him to keep calm.

Nevertheless we managed to fly him ashore several times and honour was satisfied all round. Edward Seago produced some wonderful paintings, most of which I understand now hang in Buckingham Palace.

Too close for comfort

An exciting moment arose late in the deployment when the ship was trapped between two major ice floes, the open water ahead having disappeared and the pack-ice closed astern. Helicopter reconnaissance offered nothing better than a report of clear water ahead some seventy yards beyond the pack.

The Captain accepted that, despite not being equipped with an ice-breaker's cut-away bows, we would have to force our way through. Going astern as far as possible, he rang on full ahead and charged the pack in the direction indicated by the helicopter. The impact was formidable as the ship shuddered to a stop. A crack in the ice had been achieved and a second run took *Protector* through.

The bow had sustained substantial damage, having been bent completely round and a major hole opened in the forepeak above the waterline. The Shipwright officer and his team were able to shore up the bow successfully to allow normal operations to be resumed with a two-knot penalty on speed. Not a handsome ship in the first place, *Protector* now had a real scar to show for her time in the ice.

A final visit to Punta Arenas, the southernmost town in Chile, provided a three-day break where again the ship's company received the most friendly welcome. Admiral Neuman, the area Flag Officer, was kind enough to make this a special occasion for me, taking my first steps on Chilean soil for twenty-seven years. Equally memorable for all of us was the spectacular passage through the famous Beagle Channel.

66

Homeward bound

Our route home would take us to South Georgia again, this time transporting a new Government Agent accompanied by his wife, to take up residence after a gap of several years. We embarked some thirteen large trunks and assorted crates carrying all the essentials for their three-year tour. There was no corner shop in Grytviken. I wondered what they would first realize they had forgotten.

I had decided that to help interest the ship's company on the long passage home we would embark some penguins and the Captain sensibly suggested that there had better be someone to take them over on arrival in Portsmouth. The London Zoo perhaps?

A signal to the Admiralty elicited a swift response from the Curator of Birds at the zoo, Mr Yealland, who would be pleased to receive them provided they were matched pairs of either Kings or Emperors and he included vital information on their diet, as wild penguins will not eat dead fish, and about survival through the tropics. A daily dose of Mepacrin was prescribed.

Having been assured by the doctor, John Kemp, that he could distinguish the sexes, the Admiralty issue swimming pool (100% canvas) was erected under the flight deck and filled with sea water. Connected by hose to the fire main, clean sea water could be guaranteed. A net from deck to deck-head was fitted around the pool area both to contain the penguins and to prevent unauthorized feeding, and wooden access ramps connecting the pool to the surrounding area completed the installation. Lieutenant David Smith, the ship's electrical specialist, had volunteered to act as keeper and was assisted by three sailors, with Leading Seaman Colswell in charge. All we needed now were the penguins.

After disembarking the Agent and his wife at Grytviken the ship moved to the area of the Bay of Isles and a colony of Kings. While the smaller penguins always scattered at the approach of a helicopter, the Kings and Emperors stood their ground. This made it easy for the doctor and his team to bundle six of them into the helicopter, and three matched pairs it was. Penguins are very social and faithful, so, as the doctor knew all along, there was no great skill required. There are no queer penguins.

Our only stop en route to Cape Town was at the tiny dependency, the island of Tristan da Cunha where a small population of less than 200 souls lived in almost total isolation. A rocky coastline made boat work impossible so all visits ashore were by helicopter. I confess the charm of the island escaped me but not our Padre who, on his return to the UK, volunteered to serve there and he did so for seven years. The local water did, however, yield a harvest of fresh fish for the pool and the penguins welcomed this change from their usual force-fed diet.

On arrival at the Simonstown naval base near Cape Town there was the normal interest in the ship but quite overwhelming press interest in our black and white passengers in and out of their pool. It was a splendid visit for the whole ship and I was able to renew contact with the Packer family, now with four boys.

After his naval service during the war Piet had qualified as a doctor and established himself as a noted ear specialist in South Africa. His great chum was a plastic surgeon who had just completed the re-connection of a vital organ which had been detached from a well-developed local inhabitant. I did not stay long enough to hear whether full functionality was restored.

Heading for home we set course first for Freetown for fuel and then Las Palmas in the Canary Islands for some recreation. In Freetown Wynne-Edwards arrived on board with a mongoose in his arms. Against all my better judgement, and my rules prohibiting live animals onboard, he pleaded that this was the only thing in the world his mother really wanted. I relented on condition the beast never left his cabin, never made a mess and his mother was at the dockside to claim possession. After all we would be home in ten days.

The penguins, with their white fronts conforming to the rig of the day, took their place on the upper deck to man ship as we entered Portsmouth harbour having confounded the odds and survived the tropics. One, however, was in not too good shape and expired only months after reaching the zoo.

As for the mongoose, when presented with the animal Mrs Wynne-Edwards let out a wild shriek, leapt onto a chair and refused to touch it. Fortunately for her son, Mr Yealland was on hand and added the mongoose to his collection of penguins.

The Captain asked me to add a section on the defence of the islands for inclusion in his Report of Proceedings. My opinion was that the islands were indefensible except at a cost which would not find room in any defence budget. I suggested a hand-over of sovereignty in twenty-five years to allow a full generation span for its acceptance by the islanders. I fully appreciated their instinctive dislike of the almost constant instability of the various regimes, military and civilian, in the Argentine, but their ever-growing dependence on the mainland would outweigh this. A fair price for their land should be offered to farmers wishing to relocate to the UK. This was 1957. The invasion came twenty-five years later.

4

MASTER AND COMMANDER

FLYING TRAINING COMMAND

After a fascinating year in the Antarctic it was time to return to front-line operations. I was fortunate to be appointed to the staff of Flag Officer Flying Training (FOFT), based at the Naval Air Station at Yeovilton in Somerset. FOFT was responsible for all training after the award of wings, and in the case of helicopter pilots for the basic and advanced flying training up to wings standard as well. I was to be responsible for all front-line squadrons.

Before joining the staff it was essential to do some refresher flying and I was put through this at Lossiemouth by joining an air warfare course flying Seahawks. This was interrupted by the sudden death of my father from indigestion; otherwise rather better diagnosed these days as acute angina for which heart surgery is almost always successful. He was sixty-two.

Rear Admiral Charles 'Crash' Evans was the Flag Officer, a wartime ace fighter pilot and a flamboyant character who was setting aggressive standards. From Yeovilton (home of the Night Fighter squadrons) his command extended to Cornwall (RNAS Culdrose home of Anti-Submarine Warfare) to Wales (RNAS Brawdy) and Scotland (RNAS Lossiemouth, home of the fighter and attack squadrons) and to RNAS Ford near Arundel in Sussex.

A new helicopter station at Portland was being created to provide a home base for small ships' helicopter flights and to provide support for ships undergoing work-up under the Flag Officer Sea Training. The development of this base was one of my responsibilities.

The Fleet Air Arm was in very good shape. The four-year slog of the Korean War had swept away any thoughts of an undemanding peace-time routine and transformed the performance of the carriers and their squadrons. Although the Korean War was fought before the FAA was re-equipped with jets, the transition was taking place and when the Suez débâcle occurred only a few years later all fighter squadrons were operating either Seahawks or Sea Venoms.

Lossiemouth under Captain Torrens-Spence was an invigorating place with an unflagging reputation for flying hard and playing hard, as was Yeovilton where the Commanding Officer was Captain Dick Law with whom I had served in Washington.

To make sure standards were set and maintained the fixed wing squadrons were required to carry out Front Line Armament Practices (FLAPs) which had to be undertaken away from home base. Rather than being a chore, FLAPs were immensely popular and raised performances all round.

This was also the time when swept-wing supersonic aircraft were entering service and the first FAA squadron, No.803, to receive the Vickers Supermarine Scimitar – descendant of the one-time world-speed record holder the Swift – had formed at Ford under the command of Commander Tom Innes. At Ford and not Lossiemouth because this gave the easiest access to the supporting Aircraft Establishments at Farnborough, Bedford and Boscombe Down, as some assistance was bound to be required from them during the work-up of this all-new aircraft and weapon system.

The comparatively huge Scimitar, nearly four times larger than the Seahawk, twin-engined and capable of delivering an atomic bomb, was considered to merit an officer of Commander's rank and experience in command of the first squadron.

Tragically, Tom was killed in a car accident on a dangerous road at Bury Hill near the air station towards the end of the work up and was relieved by Commander Des Russell who had been Training Commander at Lossiemouth, another brilliant and experienced pilot.

At the same time the Sea Vixen was on its way to replace the Sea Venom. This was another big increase in size but also in capability; equipped as it was with a long-range radar and second generation air-to-air missiles, it was a formidable all-weather and night fighter. Meanwhile the Buccaneer was coming along to provide a real low-level strike capability. Added to all this, the two-seat Hunter trainer was to provide dual instruction but specifically for instrument training and testing. These were heady days.

While most of the staff, and particularly my section, flew regularly between air stations and on training exercises, there was an extra dimension provided by carriers on passage up or down the English Channel. Whenever this occurred the Admiral requested use of the deck for an hour or so in order for his staff officers to keep in carrier-landing practice.

Night Flying

Night flying at Yeovilton took place four nights a week and, while this was not much enjoyed by the local populace, they were extremely tolerant. Despite the heavy flying programme, normal mess life continued in the Wardroom and one memorable night we were joined half way through by an American in a Day-glo flying suit whose appearance was explained by his unplanned arrival after a thirty-four-hour non-stop flight in a single-engined Mooney from Texas.

He should have made his landfall in France but had been blown off course, was completely lost and running out of fuel when he picked up the voice of a Wren controller at Yeovilton on the emergency frequency. Radar contact was quickly established and he was homed safely to land.

The Executive Officer of the Air Station and President of the Dinner formally welcomed him to what he hoped would be a suitable evening meal. After an unrelieved diet of Hershey bars he expressed himself well pleased – to be alive!

Farnborough

I was also responsible for the Fleet Air Arm participation in the Farnborough Air Show. As the Navy did not maintain a permanent display team, the most suitable front-line squadron which was dis-embarked at the time would be nominated to work up a display. One year this was a Seahawk squadron commanded by Pete Perrett.

Smoke had been used to enhance displays for some years but Perrett's men came up with a scheme to add blue and red colour by the addition of ICI dyes which remained stable at the very high temperatures which were experienced at the tail of the jet pipe. Always keen to be first in the field, this seemed like a great opportunity to show a lead and as trials progressed satisfactorily I gave the go-ahead.

The Squadron duly performed to great acclaim at Farnborough with a diamond formation of nine aircraft which took off and landed in formation having displayed their tri-colour smoke to marked effect. On the fourth day the pilot flying in the 'box' at the bottom of the diamond, Lieutenant Roger Dimmock, [later, as a Rear Admiral, to serve as FONAC] experienced a fire. He immediately slipped out of the formation, turned to open country and ejected while Perrett completed the display. An urgent investigation took place with the coloured smoke as the prime suspect, so it was back to white smoke for the rest of the week.

Change of Command

After about a year Charles Evans left to take up his appointment as Flag Officer Aircraft Carriers and was replaced by Rear Admiral Denis Cambell who had recently been promoted after a very successful tour in command of HMS *Ark Royal*.

More of an academic, he was as stimulating intellectually as his predecessor had been in drive and sheer energy. As the inventor of the angled deck his was a name to conjure with in naval aviation circles on both sides of the Atlantic. He spoke modestly of this achievement and had obviously been hugely entertained by the initial doubts of all the highly qualified test pilots who appeared unable to get their minds round the simple relative velocity triangle involved in landing at an angle to the ship's heading.

Towards the end of my second year I received news of my next appointment, as Commander (Air) of HMS *Victorious*. I therefore took the opportunity to go back to Lossiemouth and put in some hours in the Scimitar. Lossiemouth had recently been equipped with the aircraft and conversion of young pilots straight out training was well under way.

As a family we had been living in rented accommodation first in West Coker and then South Petherton. On my appointment to *Victorious*, a Portsmouth-based ship, we decided to make a move and were lucky to obtain a married quarter in Southsea.

COMMANDER (AIR)

HMS *Victorious* was one of six fleet carriers of about 30,000 tons displacement, with six boilers driving three shafts and giving a 30-knot top speed. Designed in the thirties, they entered service in 1940 and had a busy war. *Victorious,* while serving with the US Pacific fleet, survived two Kamikaze direct hits and remained operational.

In 1950 work began on a modernization programme to bring the ship up to the required state for operating the faster and heavier jets which were due to enter service. She ended up at 35,000 tons, with a flight deck angled at nearly nine degrees. She was also the first, and only one of three, to be fitted with the new 984 3-D radar and Comprehensive Display System (CDS) (the others being *Hermes* and *Eagle*) which revolutionized aircraft control.

After a long refit the first days of sea trials are a testing time and *Victorious* had been fitted with a complete new suite of radars and electronic equipment which had to be tuned before embarking her squadrons. When the time came, tragedy struck. The Scimitar squadron was first to land on and, as is customary, the Commanding Officer leads. Commander Russell duly hooked a wire only for the arrester system to fail and the aircraft to fall over the edge of the deck into the sea.

Such was the press interest in this 'new' ship, and the embarkation of the Scimitars in particular, that the BBC outside broadcast team with Richard Dimbleby were present. The television-viewing public witnessed not only the loss of the aircraft but also the loss of the pilot who did not escape from his cockpit.

That the pilot failed to escape and hence was not picked up by the attendant helicopter was a matter of deep concern and all procedures affecting safety equipment were reviewed. One of the recommendations was that in future the aircrewman in the rescue helicopter should be a qualified diver, able to assist the escape of a possibly injured or trapped aircrew under water. This was quickly implemented and saved many lives, both service and civilian, over the years.

I joined the ship on 21 May 1959, landing a Sea Venom, borrowed from 893 Squadron, on board in the channel. I was greeted on the flight deck by Commander Dickie Richardson, from whom I would take over and who had stood by the ship during the last year of her refit.

The ship was on passage back to Portsmouth and had been in commission for less than a year after her modernization. Captain Charles Coke was in command. Early in the war he had developed the concept of directing fighters to their targets by radar, creating this vital wartime specialization. We had first met when he was the Naval Attaché in Washington and I was in the USA with AEW.

Charles Coke was a charming, immensely talented officer and something of an artist and epicure. As a 'private' ship with no admiral embarked, the Captain lived in the Flag Quarters in harbour and it was widely accepted that he kept the best table in the fleet. But it could also be said that this would not have been difficult!

With an admiral embarked, and this time it was Charles Evans as the Flag Officer Aircraft Carriers, Captain Coke became the Flag Captain and dined at the Admiral's table. The story is told that when confronted with his first main course and a steward presented a sauce boat, Charles Coke courteously enquired,

'Pray tell me, what sauce is this?'

'It's not a sauce sir, it's gravy,' a somewhat startled steward responded.

'Well in that case I don't think I'll have any thank you.'

Very much in command but with a deceptively laid-back manner, he was highly respected and probably the only captain of a major aircraft carrier who failed to become an admiral. He later confided in me that to have commanded the first ship to bring this latest development of his original concept of 'Fighter Direction' into the fleet satisfied all his personal ambition and higher rank had little appeal. I am sure the deafness of his wife also played a major part in his decision to retire.

The Heads of Departments were a strong team. Martin Ollivant, the Executive Officer, was outstanding as were the heads of the two Technical Departments. Engineering embraced everything from all 'hotel services', running water, heating and air conditioning, to the main engines and all flight deck machinery from catapults to arrester gear.

The Electrical Department provided services becoming ever more demanding, as, quite apart from the heavy end of power supplies, the hyper-sensitive control systems needed very precise levels of power for radars and weapons. Where flying operations are involved all systems must be available all the time.

The Supply Officer or 'pusser' was Commander Jock Petrie Hay, a tremendous asset to the ship and at the forefront of improving catering in the fleet. *Victorious* was the only ship to have lobster on the ship's company menu on a regular basis and a cold buffet and salad bar presided over by proud young chefs. Who cared if only a handful of men chose the lobster? The fact that it was on the menu showed what sort of ship this was. With other ships in Gibraltar it was said a large number of cap tallies indicated there were many visitors enjoying how a galley should be run.

In view of the level of responsibility carried by all those involved in flying operations I felt it completely wrong for the 'tot' (the measure of rum allowed to all crew members over the age of twenty) to be issued at the traditional midday time.

This is a cherished routine for the entire ship, but Commander Ollivant was quick to appreciate my reasons and made the necessary arrangements for all those concerned to have their ration only on completion of their duties for that day.

Lieutenant Commander Geoff Higgs, who had been the Senior Pilot of 803 Squadron from formation, was now in command and the squadron was showing no signs of stress from the harrowing start to the commission. Under his sound leadership the Scimitar was soon being accepted like all the other aircraft and it became apparent that no special treatment was required.

The 849B AEW Flight was commanded by Lieutenant Commander Brian Stock (my old schoolfriend). The C.O. of the Helicopter Squadron 825 was Lieutenant Commander John Ashton and Lieutenant Commander Eric Manuel commanded the Venom Squadron 893.

Deployment to USA

After exercises off Norway the ship was soon to depart for the USA. Operating aircraft while crossing the Atlantic meant that no diversion airfields were in range and the Scimitars took this in their stride.

The main object of our deployment was to take part with the USN in an air defence exercise 'Riptide' and demonstrate the capability of

76

our new control equipment. During the exercise, in which two USN carriers took part, the *Essex* and the *Wasp*, we cross-operated aircraft between the ships and handled three different USN jets in *Victorious*.

On completion came a visit to Norfolk Naval Base in Virginia where there was great interest in the 984 radar and CDS which had outperformed the equipment in the US ships. For the first time a radar display showed not simply a 'blip' but letter and number symbols which indicated if the target was unknown or, if known, the type of aircraft, its height and heading and, if appropriate, remaining fuel and ammunition.

Fighter controllers at their displays spoke directly to the pilots while the senior Direction Officer, Commander Air or Captain, instead of having to interrupt a controller when seeking information, was able to visit his own display and discuss tactics through a headphone.

After Norfolk came a short visit to Boston, followed by a week in New York where we were happy to welcome on board Ed Heinemann and his wife Zel, plus other top people from Douglas. It was unique to be able to show the designer some of his creations in an operational setting on a foreign aircraft carrier. They kindly gave us a return match on the town and I was very pleased to host the Heinemanns at home many years later when they visited London.

The Royal Naval Film Corporation

On return to Portsmouth the ship was made available to the Royal Naval Film Corporation (RNFC) to host a dinner for leading members of the film industry. The RNFC was just one of Lord Mountbatten's many initiatives which arose shortly after his wedding to Edwina Ashley, grandaughter and ward of the famous royal financier Sir Ernest Cassel, when the glamorous couple were visiting the USA and much fêted, particularly in Hollywood.

Lord Mountbatten quickly turned this popularity to the advantage of the Royal Navy by persuading the major moguls of the industry to allow ships to show films at sea without payment of fees or royalties. Thus the RNFC was formed to manage this bounty and ships all over the world had access to the latest releases while paying no more than the actual production cost of the additional copies.

It was a splendid evening with Lord Mountbatten in a much relaxed mood and happy to enjoy the speeches, particularly that of 20th Century Fox's Spiras Shouros in very fractured English.

Change of Command

Soon after sailing from Portsmouth *Victorious* made a courtesy visit to Hamburg, the first time a carrier had made the journey up the Elbe to this most famous of the three Hanseatic ports. It was an important visit in Navy to Navy terms, but was also hugely popular as Hamburg is a very sailor-friendly port.

Charles Evans also marked the end of his time as FOCAS here and he was able to celebrate ashore in his own inimitable style.

During dinner at the residence of the Canadian Ambassador I met a young German couple who told me of their interests in Mediterranean islands, having created a residential area in Sicily at Taormina and now in Ibiza. I had been to Taormina at the end of the war but Ibiza and the Balearic islands were new to me. They had two young sons who were thrilled to visit the ship and we parted with their wish that I should visit them in Ibiza. I thought little more about it at the time.

Captain Coke was relieved in August by Captain Richard Janvrin, an Observer who had taken part in the historic raid on the Italian fleet in Taranto. He was another splendid Captain and an experienced Whitehall warrior.

The squadrons were disembarked when he joined, so I borrowed a Hawker Hunter from Yeovilton and flew him to Lossiemouth which was now the home base for the Scimitar squadron. I took the opportunity to go supersonic for Captain Janvrin's first time over the Moray Firth before we landed.

Victorious took part in a number of exercises as part of the NATO Strike Fleet off north Norway and simulated nuclear strikes on shore targets were often carried out under strike direction of an AEW Skyraider. On one occasion an AEW aircraft was launched to give strike direction to Scimitars tasked to carry out a low-level simulated attack on land targets some 200 miles north of the ship.

The strike proceeded successfully, but contact with the directing aircraft was lost after it had reported being an estimated 180 miles distant but outside radar cover. Equipped with long-range tanks, the Skyraider had an endurance in excess of seven hours, but concern mounted as radio and radar cover was not regained.

Searches were duly launched and wide areas swept by all squadrons during the next two days. On the third day a signal was received from the Admiralty passing on a report from our Naval Attaché in Moscow that an aircraft had ditched alongside some Russian trawlers. The position given matched the expected latitude, but the longitude was several degrees west of where the aircraft should have been operating and where all our searches had been concentrated. The immediate reaction was to suspect the Russian report, but it proved to be quite correct.

The pilot, Lieutenant Barry Hartwell, and his crew were first picked up by a trawler and then transferred to a depot ship from which they were ultimately returned to HMS *Urchin*, a ship of the Fishery Protection Squadron which had been diverted by the Admiralty to make a rendezvous. The subsequent investigation into the cause of the loss of the aircraft was frustrated by many hundred fathoms of salt water.

The Mediterranean

Some months later in the Mediterranean Lieutenant Hartwell gave an almost repeat performance. Having landed two sailors at a NATO airfield in Sardinia to go on compassionate leave and collected the mail for the ship, he experienced a total engine failure just after take-off for the return flight. He had no time to make an emergency call before ditching in the lake immediately ahead.

After swimming ashore he managed to commandeer a donkey on which he returned to the airfield where his predicament had been totally unobserved. His debriefing back on board was clouded by the deep decline into which the entire ship's company had descended on hearing the fate of their mail. He probably wished he had not come back.

During one of our NATO exercises we were visited by the NATO C-in-C South, based in Naples, the renowned naval aviator Admiral 'Cat' Brown. On completion he requested to be flown ashore to Naples which was just within the relatively small operating radius of a Sea Venom. The Commanding Officer agreed to fly without his navigator and take the Admiral.

After the night catapult launch the Admiral scanned the instruments and seeing the fuel gauge said, 'I assume that's your reserve tank'. On being informed that it represented all they had, he fell silent for the rest of the flight. Praying perhaps.

Flying Trials

Geoff Higgs carried out the first night-landing trials of the Scimitar. These took place in Lyme Bay and, as an extra precaution in the event of an overshoot after failure to pick up a wire, a destroyer was stationed ahead with cross-tree lights burning to provide an horizon. There was little natural wind and the ship was making a healthy thirty knots towards the coast while a number of touch and go landings were made.

I worked closely with the Captain and the navigator, Lieutenant Commander Rodney Bowden, and sought permission for one final landing when our course was taking us straight towards the beach. The destroyer ahead signalled an anguished,'I can hear the dogs barking'.

Captain Janvrin held his nerve, Higgs landed safely and the dogs went back to their kennels. We had proved the Scimitar could become night-operable, but it was not for the faint-hearted.

Early in the new year the ship was made available for the first deck-landing trials of the Buccaneer (Blackburn Advanced Naval Aircraft – Black Banana as it became known) and further Scimitar trials to clear the aircraft to carry '4 stores', i.e. two large underwing stores each side, the stores being 1000lb bombs and long-range fuel tanks.

The Scimitar trials were carried out by David Morgan, a Vickers test pilot who had also served in the wartime FAA. The Buccaneer trials were shared by 'Block' Whitehead (ex-Lieutenant Commander) the Blackburn chief test pilot, and Commander Pridham Price, then commanding C Squadron at Boscombe Down. The rest of the trial team was led by Denis Higton, the C Squadron civilian programmer and all-round enthusiast.

To begin with our visitors wanted the whole ship to themselves which they considered normal practice, but I persuaded them that I had to keep our squadrons in practice and that a limited programme would not impact on their trials. In the event all the visitors enjoyed the increased tempo which the combined operations engendered; they completed their tasks in record time and could even enjoy watching some night flying.

At the end of 1959 893 Squadron had been replaced by the Sea Vixens of 892 Squadron commanded by Lieutenant Commander 'Shorty'

Hamilton. Lieutenant Commander Alan 'Spiv' Leahy took over command of 803, and the Skyraiders of 849, replaced by AEW Gannets, commanded by Lieutenant Commander A.D. Levy, completed the transformation. Only the Helicopter Squadron 825 remained, with its Westland Whirlwinds.

After the flying trials and spring exercises the ship entered Portsmouth Dockyard for docking and a three-month maintenance period. A combined recommissioning and 21st anniversary of the ship's launching was held on 14 September 1960 prior to sailing for work up in the Mediterranean. Based on Malta, this culminated in a major NATO exercise 'Royal Flush' which included *Hermes* and *Ark Royal* and three USN carriers, *Saratoga, Independence* and *Intrepid.*

A visit to Naples at the end of November was followed by more exercises off North Africa near Tobruk and then passage to Gibraltar when a force eight gale was encountered and the ship hove to to prevent damage to aircraft parked forward. There was severe damage to boats and catwalks and the rudder chose this time to jam five degrees to starboard which enlivened activity on the bridge to an even higher pitch. By juggling with revolutions the Captain was able to maintain a slow but steady course into wind and gave thanks that this had not happened the previous night when doing twenty-seven knots three miles off Cape Bon.

Gradually way was made to the shelter of the island of Minorca. Here it was possible to anchor off Mahon, Nelson's oft-chosen harbour, where the ship's divers managed to clear the fouled rudder using cutting gear which was flown from Gibraltar in one of HMS *Albion's* Skyraiders.

The ship returned to Portsmouth for Christmas and there was another change of command, Captain Janvrin being relieved by Captain Jock Gray who had no background in aviation but was, in the short time I served with him, enthusiastic and realistic about the task ahead.

My time was swiftly coming to an end and I was warned that my next appointment would be to head the Work-Up Team for the Indian Navy's carrier INS *Vikrant.* I saw the chance to get a step ahead in this new challenge if I could arrange for some of the Indian Seahawk pilots to be deck-qualified in *Victorious* before I departed.

I was aware that the Squadron, No 310 and known as the Flying

81

Tigers of Bengal, were working up at Brawdy where the Commander Air was an ex-C.O. of a Venom squadron in *Victorious*, George Black. Having received approval from all the Commanding Officers and both FOFT and FOCAS, Black led a trio of Indian pilots, the C.O., Senior Pilot and one other, on board. They each completed four landings and four catapult launches and returned to Brawdy with tails well up. It was to pay huge dividends later.

This was also the time when 803 Squadron received its first pilot straight out of the training pipeline. He was to be the first to make a virgin deck landing in the Scimitar. The pilot was Lieutenant Joe Billingham who showed no trace of nerves and landed as if this was his hundredth rather than his first deck landing. The robust way that 803 Squadron had introduced the aircraft played a major part in its acceptance as just another naval aircraft.

The Sea Vixen squadron were equally robust. Their aircraft were just as big and less crisp in response to heading changes in the last stages of the approach: quite a challenge, particularly at night. On one sortie the pilot, Lieutenant Marshall, found the fuel in the drop tank under the starboard wing would not transfer, and the jettison mechanism for the whole tank also failed. Marshall was cleared to approach after all other aircraft had been landed only to have the starboard undercarriage leg collapse as the aircraft entered the wires. As the tank scraped along the deck it split open and the heat generated was enough to reach the high ignition point of the turbine fuel. There was a spectacular fire which completely destroyed the aircraft, but both Marshall and his observer, Sub Lieutenant Maddox, escaped unhurt.

The ship was soon deployed for the Far East. We were routed round the Cape and a full 'Shop Window' was carried out for senior South African officers and key civilians who had been embarked for the day prior to entering harbour at Cape Town.

An otherwise very happy visit, and a chance for me to meet up with old friends, was marred by distress at seeing how our national policy of not supplying the South African Government with weapons which could be used to suppress the civilian population was so narrowly interpreted as to prevent even the supply of submarines. This vacuum was quickly filled by the French who took the opportunity to respond positively to each and every request.

After exercising with the South African Navy, *Victorious* took passage to Aden where I disembarked, having been relieved by Commander A.B.B. 'Nobby' Clarke, an old friend and one of Dick Law's original display team.

My two years had been immensely rewarding. The ship had been at the cutting edge of the new developments in aircraft and command systems, the only RN carrier to have a fully angled deck and thus able to demonstrate the flexibility this provided, and the first to carry nuclear weapons and have a nuclear strike capability.

My family had a short spell in Southsea during the summer of 1960, but as our second child was due my wife took off for the United States and remained there until the end of my time as Commander Air. A daughter, Alison, was born in February 1961. We intended to buy a house in reach of London and this seemed the right time. We settled on one which was being constructed in West Byfleet, Surrey.

INDIAN SUMMER

The Indian Navy decided to follow in the steps of the Australian, Canadian and Netherland navies and chose an aircraft carrier of the Majestic class, six of which had been ordered for the Royal Navy. This ship had been launched on the Clyde in 1945, named *Hercules*, but never completed. Purchased by the Indian Government some ten years later she was towed to the Harland and Wolff yard in Belfast for modernization and completion.

As head of the RN Work-Up Team charged with introducing the Indian Navy to aircraft carrier operations I first went on board on 4 March 1961 when the ship was alongside awaiting the arrival of the Indian High Commissioner to the UK, Mrs Vijayalakshmi Pandit, for the formal commissioning and naming ceremony.

The hangar had been decked with flags, there was a platform for the VIPs and behind that an Indian flag draped over a plaque which would commemorate the occasion. This was to be unveiled by Mrs Pandit, re-naming the ship INS *Vikrant*, meaning Herculean.

The Commanding Officer, Captain Peter Mahindroo, said he

much looked forward to us working together and I took an immediate liking to him. The Head of the Electrical Department, Commander Krishnan Dev, was appointed as my guide and proudly showed me the arrangement for unveiling the plaque, a button which would activate the motor to pull the cord and draw the flag aside. I asked if he was completely sure there would be no electrical failure at the critical moment and he took me behind the scenes to display where one of his staff would stand, hidden from view, and pull the cord by hand should there be any problem.

The ceremony was conducted impeccably and the ship formally accepted on behalf of the Government of India from the Civil Lord of the Admiralty, Ian (Lord) Orr-Ewing.

The other members of the Work-Up Team were Lieutenant Commander Charles Rushbridger, an Observer and experienced Operations Officer, and Lieutenant Commander Wally Dann, an equally experienced Air Direction officer. In the months before the Squadrons embarked we got to know the ship and its equipment and to ensure the air department and flight deck crew were properly trained.

When the time came for aircraft to land on, the ship was in every respect ready to 'receive aircraft'. The first to land on was the Commanding Officer of the fighter squadron, No 300, Lieutenant Commander Balbir Law, who showed all the panache to be expected after his initiation in *Victorious*, and caught the target wire. He was followed by the other three pilots in his flight and then the Senior Pilot, Lieutenant Commander Archarya, and Lieutenant Ram Tahaliani followed with their flights.

The ship then sailed for the Mediterranean to embark the Anti-Submarine squadron No. 310 off Toulon some four days later. The arrival of the French Breguet Alizé aircraft powered with Rolls Royce Dart turbo-propeller engines was something of an anticlimax after the sleek Seahawks.

This Squadron was commanded by an Observer, Lieutenant Commander M.K.Roy, who flew with his Senior Pilot, Lieutenant Andy Anderson. Two Alouette helicopters manned by French civilian crews provided planeguard facilities for daytime operations.

*   *   *

84

The ship then proceeded to Malta where the work-up began in earnest within range of the naval air station at Hal Far, a diversion airfield being an essential safety ingredient for any newly commissioned ship and her squadrons. Happily the ship and all her officers (I learnt later that to have been selected for the first commission in *Vikrant* was an indication of high standing) quickly got into their stride and the good weather helped us to make excellent progress.

To begin with I needed to be everywhere at once: in Flyco (Flying Control – next to the compass platform) and in the arrester gear rooms for land on and in Flyco and the bridge and at the catapult howdah for launching!

However, the navigator, Lieutenant Commander Oscar Dawson, was successful in keeping the ship in her assigned practice area and the Captain was a tower of strength who soon had the ship dead into wind for launch at the precise time stated on the flying programme with the correct wind over the deck.

The Operations Room ran smoothly under the unflappable Rushbridger and Wally Dann ensured that those airborne were under positive control when required. Here he was very ably supported by Lieutenant Duggal, the ship's most senior Direction Officer, who quickly established his authority and ability and hence soon won the confidence of all the aircrew.

Soon after embarking Balbir Law turned over command of the Seahawk Squadron to his Senior Pilot and filled the vacant post of Lieutenant Commander Flying. This key appointment required a mature and experienced pilot capable of running the entire flying programme on behalf of Commander Air. Law had to learn on the job and from me, and at the same time build up his own deck-landing experience.

I was determined that he should become night-qualified by the end of the work-up and this required that he complete at least forty day deck landings and catapult launches. So, as the last of sortie of the day, he made four launches and landings while building up his numbers. Law was an outstanding officer and pilot in whom I had every confidence, otherwise it would have been impossible to schedule him for flying after every tiring day. He duly took night qualification in his stride and when he was promoted and became Commander (Air) the Indian Navy had its first fully qualified officer in that appointment.

When Archarya took over command of 300 Squadron, Ram Tahaliani became the Senior Pilot. As part of the package offered by the French Government in return for the selection of the Alizé as the Anti Submarine aircraft, the Indian squadron was granted any number of facilities free of charge, including the right to nominate a pilot to undergo training as a test pilot. Tahaliani was the man. This was in stark contrast to the UK which imposed charges for everything, 'including paper clips', as the young pilots put it. An uncomfortable contrast, but I was only too familiar with this aspect of UK policy.

An IN officer, Commander Y.N.Singh, was appointed as the Commander (Air) and perhaps he had the hardest task during the work-up. Although qualified as a pilot he had limited operational experience and of course was unfamiliar with everything that was happening, while nevertheless being nominally responsible. The Work-up Team set the targets for achievement, knew what could and could not reasonably be expected and when to put the pressure on and when to ease off.

Half way through the work-up the ship visited the French naval base at Toulon for some self-maintenance and shore leave. This covered ten days and with nothing on my agenda I took an overnight train to Barcelona and a flight to Ibiza where my friends from Hamburg were building some summer homes. I was easily persuaded to take a long lease on a small property at a peppercorn rent. It was to result in many happy years for our family and their friends.

On resuming the work-up it was time to prepare for night flying with all approaches to the deck in daylight being made under radar control of a small team under the senior air controller, a Lieutenant Commander, who turned out to be totally incompetent. If contact was lost on the final approach no instructions were given and pilots would have been left in serious danger. Drastic action was needed to restore confidence.

I had to advise the Captain that the officer should be relieved of his responsibilities forthwith if we were to complete the work-up. The Captain gave me immediate support and Lieutenant Duggal was called on to fill the vacant post. Morale was quickly restored.

*   *   *

86

The head of naval aviation on the Indian Naval staff in Delhi was Commodore David Kirke on loan from the RN. A tough and uncompromising character and long-time FAA pilot, he was an excellent final arbiter to whom I could turn when and if things really got beyond local solution.

I did seek his approval when the Indian Destroyer *Rajput* arrived from Bombay to act as planeguard for night flying and instead collapsed into the dockyard with a string of engine room problems. As the aircrew were in peak form and the weather and moon conditions favourable, a combination which would be unlikely again during our work-up, I had sought an alternative in the Search and Rescue fast motor boats operated by the RAF.

The Officer Commanding the RAF gave his permission, his boat crews were full of enthusiasm and Captain Mahindroo agreed with me that this offered the only possible alternative. David Kirke concurred. Fortunately the sea remained calm, the squadrons provided aircrew to the rescue boats for any technical advice should it be needed and the night qualification was completed for all pilots without any diversions ashore. A great achievement by any standards.

There remained only the Operational Readiness Inspection (ORI). The Team wrote up the scenario and produced all the operation orders and the associated 'incidents' to which the various departments had to respond. A testing time in any ship. *Vikrant* rose to the occasion throughout, a splendid example being set by the Captain, and a fitting end to an excellent work-up.

Vikrant went on to serve for thirty-six years, mostly as the Fleet Flagship, setting standards to which the rest of the fleet aspired. At least six of the first commission officers rose to command her over the years; some became Naval Advisers to the High Commissioner in London, some attended the Imperial Defence College, several became admirals and two of them, Oscar Dawson and Ram Tahaliani, rose to the very top, becoming Chief of the Naval Staff.

I was fortunate to meet many of them again over the years. One of the Seahawk pilots, who left the Navy to start a career in business and broadcasting, Shamu Verma, and his wife became frequent visitors to London and Balbir Law, who decided to leave the Navy as a captain, married and lived in Suffolk, have both remained in touch.

I was to see many more of the others in India during my post-naval years.

The Work-Up Team were proud to have played a part in giving INS *Vikrant* a real 'flying' start and setting standards which were to be accepted and maintained brilliantly. I was told our ORI scenario was published in hardback!

5

DRIVING SHIPS
AND DESKS

CONTROLLER OF THE NAVY

Naval Assistant to the Third Sea Lord and Controller of the Navy

During the seven years I had been away from Whitehall much had changed. The Suez operation had taken place while I was at sea in the Antarctic, Macmillan had replaced Eden as Prime Minister and Duncan Sandys had completed his highly controversial two years as Minister of Defence. Mountbatten became Chief of the centralized Defence Staff and Admiral Sir Charles Lambe, after a brief spell as First Sea Lord, had died in office and been replaced by Admiral Sir Caspar John who had himself just completed three exhausting years as Vice Chief, two of them under Mountbatten.

Duncan Sandys had been appointed Secretary of State for Defence with much more power than his predecessors had enjoyed as the Prime Minister sought to make huge savings on defence expenditure by grasping the opportunity offered by the advent of nuclear weapons and advanced missile systems, and by collaboration with the United States to reduce weapon development costs. Harold Macmillan was convinced this could only be achieved by centralization in Whitehall and reducing the power of the individual Service Chiefs.

He needed a man not afraid to wield a knife and fully able to resist any attempts to preserve single service prejudices. Sandys had just such a reputation and his appointment was greeted with foreboding by all three Services and particularly by the Navy which Sandys had already pronounced to be 'a luxury the country can no longer afford'.

By the time the White Paper was published it had been much toned down by the strenuous and well-founded arguments put forward by Mountbatten and the three Service Chiefs. Mountbatten, although a supporter of more centralization in Defence, could never agree with Sandys's view that nuclear weapons would ever actually be used. He saw them only as a vital deterrent against a Third World War but of no other significance.

The idea that missiles would spell the end of the manned aircraft was openly refuted by the Chief of the Air Staff and the premise that the V-bombers would be replaced by the Blue Streak ballistic missile now being developed was patently unsound on grounds of vulnerability and slow reaction time. Taken with the enormous cost and political sensitivity, further development of the missile was abandoned by the more open-minded industrialist Harold Watkinson who replaced Duncan Sandys in 1959.

Mountbatten and Sir Solly Zuckerman, Chief Scientific Adviser to the Ministry of Defence and Mountbatten's old colleague from his time as Chief of Combined Operations during the war, sought an alternative solution to meet the requirement for the UK to maintain an independent nuclear strike capability. This was narrowed down to a choice between procuring the Skybolt air-launched missile being developed for the United States Air Force and making the necessary modifications for it to be carried by the V-bombers, or the US Navy's Polaris submarine-launched ballistic missile.

The Navy, who saw the new carrier programme as its top operational priority and was not prepared to take on the cost of providing the nation's nuclear deterrent which could easily make financing the new carriers impossible, had no difficulty in supporting Skybolt for the RAF and so the Chiefs were able to give this project unanimous support. An agreement was signed for the procurement of Skybolt from the United States in June 1960.

However, within eighteen months, despite the desperate efforts of the RAF to keep Skybolt alive, which included persuading the MoD to pay half the development costs, the US Department of Defense cancelled the project. Taking vulnerability into account, submarines were clearly superior to aircraft as launch platforms; they could remain constantly on alert and undetected and provide guaranteed second strike capability.

Meanwhile the more centralized accounting being introduced in the MoD did much to allay the Navy's fears about the cost of Polaris, which would now be funded centrally as a national strategic system.

Vice Admiral Sir Michael Le Fanu

This was the situation in Whitehall when I joined the staff of the Controller as his Naval Assistant in September 1962. The effect of this bruising period was still much in evidence and it had not ended. The Controller was preparing to accompany Macmillan to a meeting with President Kennedy in the Bahamas with Polaris very much on the agenda.

I had first met Admiral Le Fanu at a lunch in the spring, given for him by the Flag Officer Air (Home), Vice Admiral Sir Desmond Dreyer, at his headquarters at Lee-on-Solent. At the same lunch was the current Naval Assistant, Captain Louis Le Bailly, a very distinguished engineer who was to become one of the most successful Chiefs of Naval Intelligence, and it was he who told me in confidence that he would be moving on in six months and I was to succeed him.

Admiral Le Fanu had taken over as Controller in October 1961 at the age of forty-eight. He had previously served as Director General Weapons reporting to his predecessor and before that he had been Flag Officer Second in Command of the Far East Fleet, based in Singapore but very much the sea-going Admiral. This did not stop him having a cordial relationship, on and off the golf course, with the Prime Minister, Lee Kuan Yew. Me, Lee Fan Yew, you Lee Kuan Yew.

The Admiralty deplores unemployment among senior officers and in the few spare weeks he had before taking up this appointment he was charged with the task of devising an organization capable of undertaking the construction and operation of Polaris missile submarines, should this ever be required. What foresight!

Richard Baker wrote a perceptive biography of this unique officer under the title *Dry Ginger*, which reflected both his colouring and the fact that the daily rum ration was abolished while he was First Sea Lord. LeF, as he was known, had married a girl, Prue, who, crippled by polio, 'could never have children'. So they had three. Prue drove an adapted car, crawled when there was no wheel-chair and clawed her way upstairs on her stomach when there was no one to help. When

91

I was there with LeF or someone else we made a 'seat' with crossed hands, and carried her. Nothing daunted her.

As predicted, LeF went right to the top. When First Sea Lord he was selected as Chief of the Defence Staff only to be struck down by leukaemia as he took up the appointment. My two years as his Naval Assistant were the most fascinating of any I spent in Whitehall.

Nuclear Propulsion

While many other developments were in some sort of trouble, progress with the submarine nuclear propulsion programme had gone well. Although soon after the war the marine engineers were concentrating on the hydrogen peroxide steam turbine design acquired from Germany and installed in HM Submarine *Explorer*, (a somewhat hazardous project which found the submarine unfairly but inevitably referred to as the 'Exploder') the Admiralty also saw fit to appoint both naval engineer officers and members of the RN Scientific Service to the Atomic Energy Research Establishment (AERE) at Harwell.

Atomic energy was always seen as a potential power source for warship propulsion, appearing to offer huge benefits in vastly reducing the requirement to refuel at sea and in the case of submarines to remain submerged at all times, thus acting as a true submersible.

However, ten years were to pass before work began in earnest. This was in 1955, when the USS *Nautilus* first went to sea under nuclear power and the RN began development of the first British nuclear submarine, the *Dreadnought*. The small team at AERE was expanded and the Yarrow Admiralty Research Department (a small Admiralty-staffed-and-funded organization based at the Yarrow Shipbuilders yard on the Clyde and part of the Controller's Department) and Vickers Engineers Ltd became involved.

As the RN was some years behind the USN in development, US practice was sensibly followed and work on a prototype began at Dounreay near Thurso. The design was based on a Pressurised Water Reactor (PWR) and the aim was for the prototype to 'go critical' in 1962. It quickly became apparent that, moving as they were into completely new engineering and chemical fields, this was going to be an extremely expensive and time-consuming project, co-ordinated by the Naval section at AERE.

This effortlessly became one of those projects where the engineers could say that science was on their side, but they could give no estimate of either when or at what cost. Meanwhile the USN was operational at sea and Admiral Mountbatten was not a man to play 'catch up' for long. More practical assistance was required.

The man responsible for the US Navy's nuclear programme was Rear Admiral Hyman Rickover and, when he visited the UK in 1956, Admiral Mountbatten made sure they would meet. Mountbatten made an immediate impression and the meeting was judged such a success that another visit took place the following year when a deal was struck.

The Rickover/ Mountbatten relationship has been well documented, but two comments bear repeating. One was that Rickover asked Mountbatten whether he wished British pride to be satisfied or to get a nuclear-powered submarine to sea as fast as possible. Mountbatten answered firmly that speed was of the essence; clearly the response Rickover wanted. The other was a quote in the Naval Institute Proceedings some years later that at their first meeting 'the introvert iconoclast from the Ukraine fell under the spell and aura of the grandson [*actually great-grandson*] of Queen Victoria'.

US regulations did not allow the transfer of nuclear reactors or their fuel to foreign countries and difficulties were experienced in putting a deal together. Discussions at top level between the Atomic Energy Authorities of both countries on pooling information led to considering the possibility of purchase by the UK of a complete submarine or at least a complete PWR reactor.

Action on these lines would have required enactment of new US legislation and this encountered opposition, not least from Rickover. However, he was prepared to support an amendment to the act allowing the UK to make a commercial deal with the US manufacturer. Not Government to Government but Government to company.

The necessary amendment was approved in 1958 which resulted in a UK Government signing an agreement with a US company, Westinghouse. No other country attempted to follow. Not only was plant acquired from Westinghouse but engineers from Rolls Royce and Vickers were trained by the US companies and RN officers trained at sea, starting with Commander Peter Samborne who was to be the first captain of *Dreadnought*, having absorbed the methods and standards instilled in the USN by Rickover.

The Royal Navy had been presented with a priceless gift – a complete plant with full supporting documentation enabling the RN to become a Nuclear Navy at a fraction of the cost and many years in advance of having 'gone it alone'. As a result HM Submarine *Dreadnought* was launched by Her Majesty the Queen on 21 October 1960 – Trafalgar Day.

Meanwhile the Dounreay reactor prototype became the test bed for new ideas concerning possible alternative materials for the primary circuits and other concepts as well as acting as the essential training facility for submarine crews.

Admiral Rickover

Personalities featured largely with Rickover and we were fortunate that, besides Mountbatten and Admiral Le Fanu, the senior member of the Royal Corps of Naval Constructors assigned to the nuclear programme was one Roland Baker. A cheerful extrovert in contrast to the ascetic Rickover, they developed a mutual respect which lasted long enough for the RN to produce the *Dreadnought*. However, this was as far as Rickover was prepared to go and he steadfastly refused to exchange any information on future developments despite the cordial relations which had been established.

Fortunately the Navy were able to avoid the excesses to which the USN was exposed by the stranglehold which Rickover established on the education and training of all USN personnel over a period of nearly thirty years and which resulted in the loss of many potentially great leaders. It was not uncommon for officers of commander rank to tender their resignation on the grounds that 'the nuclear submarine service is on a disastrous course due to the ageing, anachronistic leadership of Admiral Rickover leading to an alarming attrition rate in the submarine service'.

Not until the appointment of the young John Lehman as Secretary of the Navy by Ronald Reagan was the nettle grasped and the retirement of Rickover ordered. In a quite extraordinary meeting between the President and Rickover in the presence of Lehman and Secretary of Defense Caspar Weinberger in 1982 it was finally achieved. In his memoirs Lehman gives a detailed account of Rickover's intemperate and at times almost violent reaction to his removal from office when President Reagan invited him to the White House for a farewell meeting. He went so far as to tell the President to 'cut the crap' when a future advisory role was suggested.

Polaris

Despite the emphasis on things nuclear I had been selected as the Controller's new Naval Assistant because the importance attached to the new aircraft carrier programme merited an experienced airman to be part of his personal staff and, probably more obviously, I was available. As things turned out, we battled hard to keep the new carrier in the programme, but the decision to adopt Polaris and the need to set up a management capable of driving the resulting procurement through to time and cost soon dominated our lives.

At the Bahamas meeting Polaris had become the central theme and while the Prime Minister was determined to retain an independent nuclear capability he now had no viable alternative and the President's men were of a different mind. They wanted to see the UK capability subsumed in a European/NATO force.

However, President Kennedy took a wider view; he wanted the UK to continue to honour the agreement to station US nuclear submarines in Scotland and nuclear-capable US Air Force squadrons in England. If the UK was to shoulder these risks for the USA then he was prepared to honour the original undertaking given by President Eisenhower.

Eventually a compromise was found whereby the UK agreed to assign the Polaris submarines, as well as any other nuclear-capable forces, to SACEUR and to accept the missiles without prejudice to the subsequent formation of a multinational force. The UK also maintained the overriding right to use the missiles should Her Majesty's Government believe that 'supreme national interests' were at stake.

Early on, the Controller was able to persuade his Admiralty Board colleagues that only by precisely following the management structure pioneered by the USN would it be possible for the UK to achieve the tough financial and timescale parameters which had been set. But, above all, the programme was to be managed by Project Evaluation Review Technique (PERT), or 'network scheduling'. This was entirely new to the UK, both to the defence procurement agencies and to industry, who were stuck in the time-warp of a bar-chart mentality. It was to change the face of procurement for ever.

There were some heavyweight industrial players in the shape of Vickers, in its capacity both as Shipbuilder and Engineer (at that time separate companies), Foster Wheeler who would be responsible for the power plant, and Rolls Royce and Associates, a new company formed to manufacture the nuclear core. All of them were already involved in the Dreadnought project. Lockheed would, of course, supply their Polaris missile.

In essence what had to be done was to stretch the Dreadnought design to incorporate the sixteen-missile armament and all its control equipment. It was a huge task. These would be enormous craft, displacing over 8000 tons, with a submerged speed of thirty knots. Similar boats were being built in the USA by companies with massive resources and able to draw on a seemingly endless supply of graduate engineers. The pool of talent in the UK was much more modest and so far with experience limited to this one project.

A Special Project Office with a direct line to the Admiralty Board via the Controller was set up with Rear Admiral Rufus MacKenzie as the first Chief Polaris Executive (CPE) His assistant (to be known as APE) was Captain Ray McKaig, another excellent choice who was a distinguished deputy and subsequently became a four-star admiral before his untimely death.

Working alongside the CPE there had to be a single representative of the companies involved with the same power to make decisions and keep the project on track. Leonard Renshaw, the then CEO of Vickers Shipbuilders, was the man.

One of the first tasks of the Executive was to introduce the industrial partners to PERT and critical path networking. This involved the appropriate managers from all three companies attending classes run by a team in CPE, very much a key activity in the early days. Then came the creation of the critical path network itself which clearly showed the interdependence of each component of the build and the corresponding critical dates for delivery and fitting.

Thus the E and R (Evaluation and Review) of the PERT kept progress under constant surveillance and overcame the previous management failing of never identifying slippage, in either cost or time, early enough simply because the critical effect on the whole programme of delay in the supply of some relatively small component was not apparent.

Needless to say critical path networking was quickly adopted for all major projects including dockyard refits whose progress to time and to budget had defied all previous management methods.

The Polaris programme initially called for the construction of five submarines equipped with sixteen missiles each. This was considered the minimum necessary to maintain two boats constantly on station and present a credible second strike (and hence deterrent) capability as defined by the nuclear theology of the time. This demanded the ability to 'take out' a stated number of 'major' cities. The number of hulls was reduced to four in late 1964 when Healey was under pressure to make more and more savings on defence expenditure and the entire Polaris project was under attack once again.

The programme was initiated in 1962 with an in-service date of 1969. That the first boat deployed to time and to budget was the only proof needed that, properly managed, meaning adequately resourced to manage, no project should prove too complex to be successfully completed. The high cost of low overheads remains the greatest enemy.

Funding and Procurement

Denis Healey, the charmer who referred to aircraft carriers as floating slums in his book *The Time of my Life*, describes the Ministry of Defence as unlike any other Whitehall Department. With half a million men in uniform and much the same number of civil servants scattered across the world and probably another million working on defence contracts, he considered no other minister had management problems on his scale. What he did not go on to say was that what really distinguishes the Ministry of Defence from other Whitehall Departments is the presence of military personnel in many key positions, bringing first-hand experience of what is needed and what it feels like to actually work at the 'sharp end'.

Whatever their influence, however, the military did not control the finances which remained firmly in the hands of the civil servants who maintained their own discreet links direct with the Treasury. This was when civil servants could still actually join the Admiralty, or the Treasury or the War Office, as a career where they could develop loyalties which became strongly defined and identified with their choice of service. All this was to be abolished over time as centralization became the new mantra in 1963 and gradually killed off the final vestiges of 'tribalism'.

One of the earliest manifestations of centralization was the formation of a central 'Programmes and Budget' division responsible for bringing in house the task previously undertaken by a small and dedicated team in the Treasury. In fact the man who had headed this team in the Treasury, Anthony Bell, was transferred to the Ministry of Defence to take on this task: a classic gamekeeper turned poacher situation. Gradually, of course, the Treasury rebuilt its own team and the work was duplicated, more people were employed and no better solutions achieved. One for the price of two.

I shared an office with the Controller's Secretary, Charles Denman, who had also served the Admiral in this capacity during his two previous appointments. Together with an assistant Secretary, Lieutenant Commander Mike Hudson (of whom more later), and a civilian Personal Assistant, we formed what was known as the 'private office'.

Three of the four Directorates which reported to the Controller were situated in Bath whence they were dispatched at the outbreak of war in 1939 and were now well entrenched in two major establishments on two hills overlooking the city. The fourth Directorate, responsible for all matters to do with aviation, remained in London.

Of the four Directors General, the Director General Ships, Sir Alfred Sims, was considered *primus inter pares*. He was also head of the Royal Corps of Naval Constructors and very sensitive on the subject. The primary position of the ship constructor which had lasted for five centuries was now being challenged by the new technologies which were propelling the equipment fitted in the ships into the forefront and making demands for funds which far outpaced those required for the hull itself.

While gas was beginning to replace steam in the ship's turbines with the attendant flexibility, weight reduction and ease of operation, speed remained much the same as it had been for fifty years, but new missile systems would extend effective weapon ranges tenfold.

The warship builders themselves were also feeling this wind of change and the Controller was convinced that there would never be sufficient work in future to sustain the number of companies now involved. There were thirteen; among them John Brown, Fairfields, Scott and

Yarrow on the Clyde, Harland and Wolff in Belfast, Cammell Laird and Vickers on the west coast, Hunter and Hawthorn Leslie on the east and Vosper Thornycroft and Samuel White in the south.

All of them were capable of building warships of frigate or destroyer size, some specializing in submarines and less than half of them capable of building ships of cruiser size and above. In addition the Royal Naval Dockyards retained the capability to build frigates, based on the premise that if major refits had to be undertaken, then the skills to build a complete ship were required and must be nurtured. One of the yards, Chatham, had the ability to build submarines.

The commercial shipbuilders maintained an active Warship Builders Association which lobbied, up until then successfully, for work to be shared proportionately among them all, but it was clear to LeF that this state of affairs could not be allowed to continue and I quickly became involved.

The solution had to lie in the introduction of competition and in turn this would require the Ship Department to be capable of issuing definitive tenders. The mere suggestion of this raised strong objections from the Ship Department and Sir Alfred leapt on the first fast train to London to confront the Controller. At the same time the Naval Staff objected to the fact that, once a design had been 'frozen' at the time of the tender, they would no longer enjoy the opportunity to change the specification.

These objections were, however, as nothing compared to the outcry from the warship builders. 'This will be the end of the industry,' they wailed. 'Consider the employment issues.'

We considered all the issues. Yes, the Naval Staff would have to stick to the specifications as agreed in the tenders. Yes, the Ship Department would have to carry out more detailed design work. And yes, shipbuilders, you will have to compete with one another, and yes, some of you will not survive.

We were able to make an unanswerable case for competitive tender to the Naval Staff in financial terms. We were presently being held to ransom. Shipbuilders were allowed to charge on a cost-plus basis and happily accept every change introduced by the Naval Staff during building while they watched the profits escalate.

This did not stop the Ship Department joining a carefully orchestrated attempt to prove the impossibility of our proposal, but we held firm and they knew our proposal was fundamentally sound. The decision was made to proceed and the shipbuilders were informed. They threatened a boycott. We went ahead.

The deadline date for submission of responses to the first tender approached without a single offer. The time was set for midnight and Admiral Le Fanu, Charles Denman and I waited in the office as the hour approached. We had no idea which way it would go. There were no rumours. The shipbuilders had been silent. We took no bets.

At five minutes to midnight a messenger arrived with a large envelope. One of the major companies had broken ranks. Within the next ten minutes the other offers came in. The stranglehold had been broken. The method of ship procurement had changed for ever. It was to take another twenty-five years for a similar discipline to be imposed on aircraft procurement, but it took only five years for the number of shipbuilders to drop to six and subsequently three.

The Private Office

The role of the 'private office' was not only to provide all the essential back up for the Controller but to act as a conduit for information which would not normally have reached him through formal channels. While the secretary was, in effect, the Personal Staff Officer, ensuring the safe and timely completion of all Admiralty Board business in the widest sense, the Controller having an important part to play in all Board issues not just those affecting his own department, the Naval Assistant was his eyes and ears.

There were certain issues which came to Board level sponsored by one or other of the members and on which there was no consensus. The new aircraft carrier was one. While supported broadly by all the members as a single-service matter, when it became an inter-service battle for approval and deeply opposed by the other two services, resolve tended to weaken.

The Controller felt that the proposals and submissions which reached him from his Directors General were all, as he put it, 'clinically clean, drip-dried and polythene wrapped'. He needed to know if there had been some input at an earlier stage which might have been overlooked, even suppressed, on the way up; in fact what lay behind the deathless prose served up in the stream of papers crossing his desk every day. It was thus essential for the Naval Assistant to have an active network of contacts both in the Directorates and the Staff Divisions.

To be clear on how firmly he should support every issue raised LeF confided in Charles Denman and me not only to seek our opinions but more to obtain a feeling for what the view might be generally at below Board level. If the issue was one on which we all felt very strongly, was it a resigning issue? 'Do I pick up my cards?' as LeF put it. Obviously a last resort.

Matching Resources to Projects

It was the Naval Staff who initiated the new, and rightly designated, 'Staff' requirements. These were generated by officers recently at sea in command or second-in-command level, men who, in the ten years or so needed for requirements to become hardware in the Fleet, should see the fruits of their endeavours. These were the staff officers whose task it was, working with the Royal Naval Scientific Service and industry, to steer an initial project though its feasibility studies to a fully funded requirement, be it a new ship class, aircraft or weapon system.

In the final stages the project had to pass scrutiny by the Fleet Requirements Committee, jointly chaired by the Controller and the Vice Chief of Naval Staff, where the dreams of the Naval Staff met the realities of financial and often industrial constraints. The Naval Adviser played a crucial part in keeping information channels open, preventing entrenched positions being adopted and in general acting as a facilitator.

In the end, however, it was cost, balanced against the ability of the contractor to meet the technical specification, which determined the outcome. The 'best' was often presented as the requirement and became the enemy of the 'good' which might actually become the most cost-effective solution. Industry naturally joined with the Naval Staff in wishing to push the boundaries as far as possible, and sometimes beyond their capabilities.

The more I worked with the Directorates, who all pleaded that the new competitive tender method was imposing impossible burdens on their existing staff, the more I was convinced that existing manpower was not being used effectively. I felt this was particularly so in the Ship Department where I discovered that more manpower was being deployed on design work for the modernization of six existing frigates than on the design of a completely new frigate class for which the budget was greater by a factor of ten.

Admittedly these were rounded figures but they highlighted the problem and gave me the opportunity to discuss this with the Director General who revealed that he was quite unaware of how or on what basis his manpower was in fact allocated. I suggested that an understanding of this factor alone would be helpful and he readily agreed.

My own view was that the management of the entire Ship Department should be overhauled and that could only be done effectively by outside consultants. Management Consultancy was in its infancy at this time, with the US McKinsey & Co on the scene early, as well as an English company Urwick Orr & Co, who I sounded out unofficially.

I was fully aware that nothing could be achieved without the full co-operation of the Department concerned and equally that Sir Alfred would never accept a root and branch review, so I had to adopt an oblique approach to Urwick Orr who normally contracted on an all or nothing basis. Would they, I asked, be interested in becoming involved with the Ministry of Defence? This they certainly were.

Having established that, I explained the Ship Department situation and that if they were prepared to start with the limited brief of manpower allocation there would be no telling how far this could lead. They took the point. All consultancy contracts sow the seeds of follow-on work.

Armed with Urwick Orr's agreement in principle and an outline budget, I took my plan to the Controller. Both he and Charles Denman immediately saw the possibilities but also the problems as this proposal broke completely new ground and in a highly sensitive civilian-staffed Directorate. I was instructed to sell my idea to the Secretary of the Navy, Sir Michael Carey, the top naval civil servant and the last to hold the famous title immortalized by Samuel Pepys.

My subsequent meeting with Sir Michael greatly exceeded my expectations. He embraced the suggestion wholeheartedly and was particularly delighted with the concept of introducing management consultants to improve efficiency and productivity to a largely civilian-staffed Directorate. He went on to say how much he looked forward to announcing this initiative to the Public Accounts Committee at his next appearance. He asked for an estimate of costs and declared himself able to accommodate the figures I had obtained from Urwick Orr in his budget. There would now be no going back; it was already his idea! I had the go-ahead.

The study was duly completed and, as predicted, resulted in a full-blooded review of the whole department. But this was after my time. A new Controller, Admiral Sir Horace Law, was in post and Sir Alfred was able to resist implementation of the full recommendations. However, as time went on, most of them came to be introduced as 'in house' changes: improvements and hence not 'imposed'.

Today Management Consultants flourish in all Departments of State with costs apparently not a matter for concern. While I would be happy to take credit for having fired the first shot in gaining accept-ance in the Civil Service for the use of Consultants I am appalled at the way this has spiralled. The pendulum has swung too far. Consultants are now too often used, as they are in business, to ensure the acceptance of change or new policies which management either lacks the will or the determination to do for itself. When politicians find the decision process too difficult they appoint a Royal Commission, others appoint consultants.

Out and About

While the Polaris programme became very dominant and recruiting and setting up the Polaris Executive took a large part of our time, the Controller kept up a formidable programme of visits to major contrac-tors as well as ships and naval establishments. This exposed me to the senior management of a great number of companies, large and small, who all had stories to tell, contracts to win and concerns about the future. It was a time when I switched my senses to 'receive' only. Listening proved very valuable.

Visits to ships were his favourite activity. LeF loved to be at the sharp end and re-charge his batteries with contacts in every part of the ship and all sections of their ship's companies. A new class of ship or new piece of equipment recently installed were a particular pleasure.

The Controller made only one major overseas tour during my tenure. This was to visit his opposite numbers in Pakistan, India and Australia where there was much common ground. India was starting a building programme of frigates and the Australian Navy was about to order its first submarines, hopefully from the UK.

⋆　　⋆　　⋆

We had an excellent visit to Karachi where I stayed with the Naval Adviser, Captain George Kitchen, and his wife and had the pleasure of breakfasting in their roof garden. His wife said how much they enjoyed it, despite the occasional unannounced arrival of a small body part dropped by a circling vulture which had been scavenging in the local Parsee cemetery!

From Karachi we flew to Bombay and then on to Delhi where some of my old *Vikrant* shipmates were serving and made sure we had a great reunion. I stayed with the Naval Adviser to the High Commissioner, an old friend and fellow pilot Jock Cunningham, and his wife Mary, a one-time transport pilot herself.

The city was intolerably hot, but M.K. Roy (one of the ex-*Vikrant* squadron commanders) would borrow a couple of horses from one of the cavalry regiments stationed in the city and take me for a dawn ride in the perfect early morning temperature before dismounting at the Gymkhana Club for breakfast. A great way to start the days which, as in Karachi, were devoted to staff talks directed at the problems of procurement.

In Australia we spent some time in the Perth area. The Australian navy was at that time considering the development of a major naval facility on the west coast. Here I found my old friends, the Packers from Cape Town, now thoroughly entrenched with Piet, well known as the man who could make people hear in Western Australia.

Thence to Sydney and the naval yards, followed by South Australia for the Woomera missile range where much UK missile testing took place and then a weekend break when I was able to take the Admiral to the home of a cousin of my mother, Claire MacKinnon, who I have mentioned earlier. This was a sheep station near Ballarat, some 70 miles from Melbourne, where we did all our viewing on horseback; the sheep ran one to three acres and the Admiral showed a fine turn of speed in the saddle. Gates were another matter.

After that it was Canberra for talks with John Gort, the Navy Minister, regarding their submarine order. Tough negotiations with a tough politician who would go on to be Prime Minister. Happily the contract was eventually won, their submarines being built on the Clyde and one of them in Chatham dockyard.

This had been an extraordinary two years for me professionally but again much less happily on the family front. My time at the Ministry demanded very long hours and I was seldom home in Byfleet before nine in the evening. My wife considered this more as just an extension of separation when at sea and all she had to look forward to was yet another sea-going appointment. She was right.

By the middle of 1964 it was time to think about my next job and I only wanted one thing, command of an escort of any kind operating with the Fleet either at home or in the East. It was to be the Type 12 Frigate HMS *Lowestoft* and I would join in the autumn.

HMS *LOWESTOFT*

I was delighted to be taking over a running ship. Often an appointment is to a ship either building or in refit and a large part of time in command is devoted to battles with builder or refit yard to get the ship out on schedule and in fighting trim; valuable experience but it's not sea time.

Lowestoft was a Type 12 Anti-submarine Frigate of some 2,400 tons belonging to the 6th Escort Group and fitted with the latest long-range sonar, multiple ahead-throwing mortars and twin 4.7 inch guns. Capable of 30 knots from two steam turbines, this 'Whitby' class was to be the last without a helicopter weapon system.

Commissioned in 1962 *Lowestoft* had seen two captains in her first two years. Joining in September 1964 I had the advantage of three months hard running with the fleet largely taken up with anti-submarine exercises in the Western Approaches, nearly all in heavy weather conditions. I was leading a Task Unit of five ships against four submarines attempting to transit without interception. A testing last deployment for the ship, due to re-commission in the new year, ending up in Portsmouth where she had drawn the short straw and was designated duty ship for the Christmas period.

While available for duty at eight hours' notice half the crew could go ashore on a daily basis. The main contingency, however, appeared to be the need to retrieve the Prime Minister from his Scilly Island retreat if other methods had failed.

Early in January we sailed for Chatham to re-commission with a new crew on 12 February 1965. The Chaplain of the Fleet, the Venerable Archdeacon R.W.Richardson, conducted the Order of Service. We were old shipmates.

The Admiralty was drafting whole ships' companies to join a ship at the same time; the 'all of one company' concept. Join together, work-up together and operate together in a two-year cycle. A fine aim but over time it proved impossible in manpower terms and as in *Lowestoft's* case, she was on her third Commanding Officer before the end of her first commission. However, I was to enjoy very nearly two full years at sea with much the same crew.

I was fortunate to have as First Lieutenant, Lieutenant Commander Hamish McCloud, who as an aspiring submariner had failed his 'perisher' – the stringent examination for command – and returned to the surface. He proved to be a thoroughly sound officer who I recommended for promotion and was pleased to see him subsequently as Executive Officer of *Ark Royal.*

The other officers, with the exception of the Engineer Officer and the Gunnery specialist, Mike Ward, a recently qualified Australian on exchange with the RN whose daughter subsequently became a god-child, were fairly average. Indeed I was expected to 'bring on' a number of young and not so young officers who were having difficulty and on the whole they managed quite well.

On sailing we headed straight for a full work-up at Portland. The Portland Naval Base together with the Helicopter Station was the home of the Flag Officer Sea Training (FOST) whose staff and facilities provided the best work-up programme the Navy has ever produced. In seven intense weeks ships were able to hone their own skills and tune their weapons to full operational standards. The staff officers and chief petty officers, led from the front by the Commander Sea Training, commuted by helicopter from ship to ship at sea in the exercise areas, trouble-shooting, directing, correcting and in general working to produce the best possible performance from every ship.

Submarines, helicopters, target aircraft and refuelling tankers were all available and so successful was the training that many NATO nations sent their ships to be put through the course of which one week was spent alongside for self-maintenance and to exercise the ships' companies in 'support of the civil power'. Every ship had to be capable of providing a platoon-strength body of men with rifles and machine guns and these were tested realistically in set-piece exercises using civilians from the local area. There was also time for some sport and I turned out for a ship's rugby XV for the last time!

106

*   *   *

The daily routine at sea was for all ships to leave harbour at 0800 under the command of a different ship every day. The nominated Commanding Officer was not informed until about 0100 and he was required to order and direct the formation in which ships should depart and continue to manoeuvre in close company until instructed to disperse them to individual exercise areas by a senior staff officer. Daily exercises were usually completed in time for ships to be anchored in their designated positions by midnight.

The pressure on the entire ships' companies was intense, particularly on the Captain, who rightly was under close inspection the entire time. He also had to become completely confident, fighting his ship from the Operations Room, sitting at his own radar console, wearing a split headset with one ear for his ship and the other direct to the other captains involved in the action. Every ship that completed the course was proud of the distinction.

After Portland came a number of Fleet exercises with a break in mid-summer to act as escort to HM Yacht *Britannia* during Her Majesty's Royal Visit to Germany. Having arrived by air the Queen departed by sea, embarking in Hamburg where her highly successful tour ended with a grand dinner on board *Britannia* attended by the President, Heinrich Lubke, the Chancellor, Ludwig Erhard, and most of the other dignitaries who had made this such a memorable visit.

Lowestoft, in company with HMS *Blackpool*, spent three days in the naval base at Cuxhaven before moving up the River Elbe to Hamburg and securing close to *Britannia*. On Her Majesty's arrival in Hamburg, the Mayor of this famous Free and Hanseatic city broke tradition by descending the steps of the Rathaus to greet her. The Queen directed that the compliment should be returned by breaking the tradition that all escorting warships should follow in the wake of *Britannia*.

Thus, on completion of the dinner and the departure of the guests, the two German escorts, the destroyers *Hamburg* and *Bremen*, preceded *Britannia* down the Elbe with *Lowestoft* and *Blackpool* astern. The event was covered by BBC outside broadcast with Richard Dimbleby in *Lowestoft*, the ship floodlit and what appeared to be every private boat on the Elbe darting between the ships. Avoiding action was impossible and the hooting and shouting accompanied by random fireworks gave the whole night a carnival air. I could only pray we ran

107

no one down and was greatly relieved when we had cleared the city on our way down towards Cuxhaven and the open sea.

After more exercises came a week at Largs off the Ayrshire coast as 'guardship' for the Clyde regatta when we enjoyed wonderful sailing as well as an opportunity to entertain some of the Clyde shipbuilders. It was a great pleasure to see Eric Yarrow again.

Then came transit exercises with submarines on the way south for a final visit before deployment to the Mediterranean. This time to London, wearing the flag of the Commander-in-Chief, Admiral Sir Charles Madden, who was making a farewell call on the City.

For a Captain a visit to London presents a fair challenge requiring a tight 180-degree turn just below Tower Bridge as it begins to rise and the need to time a sternboard through, as the bridge becomes fully open; all in the best interests of returning the traffic over the bridge back to normal as quickly as possible. After that, securing alongside HMS *Belfast* presents no problem.

On departure I had arranged a families day, embarking them all from the *Belfast* and taking them back under Tower Bridge and down river to Greenwich where they disembarked. A modest event but very few ships have the opportunity of a visit to London and the day was greatly enjoyed by a substantial number of families, including mine.

Mediterranean and Far East

After passing Gibraltar we exercised en route to Malta where, on entering the Grand Harbour, Valletta, we heard that we were soon to join the Far East fleet in company with the carrier HMS *Eagle* (Captain John Roxburgh). *Lowestoft* was to act as 'planeguard' when *Eagle* was flying aircraft and *Eagle* would act as our refuelling tanker.

Before this, we had time to take part in two important NATO exercises in the Eastern Mediterranean, both of them in thoroughly unpleasant weather, and were happy to join *Eagle* for passage through the Suez Canal. *Eagle* carried out flying exercises at regular intervals on our way to Mombasa where we made a brief stop before *Lowestoft* was ordered to detach and proceed independently to join the rest of the 6th Escort Group in the Far East.

★   ★   ★

The remainder of the year was spent operating between Singapore, where the ship was for Christmas, and Hong Kong. It was the first time we had been in company with any of the other ships in my division (*Lowestoft* was half-leader) or the Group leader, Captain John Templeton-Cothill (inevitably 'Tumbledown Cottage') in HMS *Rhyl*.

John Templeton-Cothill was out of an unusual mould. Brought up in France, he spent much of the war as a liaison officer with the Free French Forces. Sensitive and artistic, his taste stretched the capabilities of the dockyard when he asked for special trompe l'oeil effects in painting his cabin and for them to procure special fabrics for his curtains and covers.

To avoid the installation of an unsightly air-conditioning unit in his cabin he settled for drawing cold air from an adjacent compartment which involved having an opening cut through behind the kneehole of his desk. He paid the penalty in the chilling effects on his most vulnerable nether regions.

I had not been to the area since 1951 and much had changed. Both Singapore and Hong Kong were now 'boom' towns, having fully recovered from the years of Japanese occupation. Hospitality ashore was lively, rather more so in Hong Kong than Singapore. After *Rhyl* and *Lowestoft* had operated in company for a few weeks both ships' companies were rather disappointed to be ordered to return to Mombasa as the situation in Rhodesia was becoming critical.

On arrival we expected to have at least a week in harbour for self-maintenance and recreation. After a couple of days viewing big game in the Tsavo Park under the guidance of the Resident Naval Officer East Africa, Lieutenant Commander Roberts, an old shipmate from HMS *Victorious,* and another day deep sea fishing off Kilifi, John and I headed for a weekend with friends in Nairobi.

Rhyl had accepted to be 'ready' ship at eight hours' notice to sail despite a minor boiler defect. However, when the call came the *Rhyl* boiler was still in pieces and it was *Lowestoft* that put to sea after I had caught the 0500 a.m. newspaper and milk flight back to Mombasa. We had managed to get all our men back on board with the exception of the navigating officer to whom I had unwisely given an extra twelve hours' leave in order to visit his sister up country.

109

*　　*　　*

Lowestoft was ordered to start the Beira Patrol which was to be maintained for several years. Instructed to turn south only after losing sight
of land, we were to blockade the port of Beira through which the
Smith regime was deemed to be importing oil. There being no
instructions on the level of force to be used, the Admiralty must have
assumed that an order to stop would be obeyed. I harboured no such
illusions. With McCloud and the Gunnery officer we devised a
creeping gun attack on the stern to be used if a ship failed to stop after
a shot across the bows. This would be aimed to protect the integrity
of the tanks.

I was happy not to have been faced with implementing this plan. In
the event, some years later when a tanker did refuse to stop, no action
was taken, a humiliating climb-down well illustrating the lack of political will to follow threats with appropriate action.

After several months *Lowestoft* was relieved of these duties and
returned to Mombasa where my own relief awaited me. I had
completed just under two years in command and was lucky that since
the re-commissioning eighteen months earlier most of the ship's
company had stayed together. They worked hard and played hard.
They took every change in programme with a smile. 'Not so much a
programme, more a way of life' was the splendid approach. The few
that I had to send to detention returned with an 'it's great to be back'
attitude. I was going to miss them – all 243 of them.

We had been deployed for just on a year without home leave and
there arose the usual crop of domestic problems invariably dealt with
most efficiently by the Chatham base staff. This was spearheaded by
a small group of Chief Wrens who, all with their own cars, were able
visit the home concerned and report on the veracity and gravity of
the situation. In two cases sailors were flown home. There was only
one effort to work a flanker by a young stoker whose neighbour at
home had reported his wife's attempt to commit suicide by putting
her head in the oven. The Chief Wren duly reported, 'The kitchen is
all electric'.

For my family it had not been a happy experience. My wife was
quite unable to come to terms with separation and continued to
harbour hopes that I would resign and move to the United States. Our
son was now boarding at preparatory school and this was a traumatic

110

experience for her, although the Headmaster confirmed to me that, on his own, Jonathan was happily involved in work and play. I looked forward to a spell at home to see whether things could be sorted out.

THE MINISTRY OF DEFENCE
NAVAL STAFF DIRECTOR

In September 1966 I returned to Whitehall as Director of Naval Air Warfare (DNAW), the Naval Staff Division with responsibility for all matters concerning naval aviation. This embraced everything from the development of new equipment, including aircraft and weapon systems and their support afloat, to flying training and operations through the appropriate Flag Officers. DNAW was also responsible, on behalf of the Admiralty Board, for issuing releases for the introduction and operational use of aircraft and airborne weapon systems at sea, and for solving subsequent problems which inevitably arose.

I joined at the end of a period of intense inter-Service battles over new equipment. The possibilities of joint procurement of similar aircraft for both the Navy and RAF had reached a climax with the proposed development of the small Hawker Harrier vertical take-off ground attack aircraft into the P1154, a Mach 2 fighter required by both the RAF and the Navy. While the RAF was always keen to support every new concept, the Navy had doubts about the capability of the P1154 from day one. Its design speed depended on developing after-burning in the plenum chambers of the engines, a completely new challenge where swivelling nozzles were involved.

The Chairman of Hawkers, Sir Arnold Hall, had admitted to me over dinner one evening that while they thought science was within reach they could not estimate the cost or time it would take to achieve. This led to the comment by one of the Navy's most senior test pilots, Captain Eric Brown, in testimony to the assessment committee that, 'If the Navy chose the P1154 the only way their pilots would ever exceed Mach 2 would be to buy a ticket on Concorde'.

This was also soon after the time when the order for the new carrier CVA-01 had been cancelled and the Minister for the Navy (no longer called the First Lord of the Admiralty) Christopher Mayhew and the First Sea Lord, Admiral Sir David Luce, had both resigned.

It was generally perceived that the Navy had not fought its case effectively and to some extent this was true. Whether more experienced Whitehall in-fighters would have done better is questionable. My predecessor, Captain George Baldwin, was no Whitehall virgin and his deputy, Captain Ray Lygo, was an accomplished corridor fighter not afraid to spill blood. They both fought tenaciously but failed to garner the support at top level which should have been present from the start. Resignations after the event are empty gestures.

Denis Healey had been Secretary of State for two years and admitted that he worked harder there than anywhere else in his life. He was much in love with 'think tanks', drawing on the studies of the Hudson Institute and the Rand Corporation and setting up a Project Evaluation Group (PEG) within his own office staffed by five 'bright' officers and civil servants.

Despite the efforts of the Foreign Secretary, George Brown, who enjoyed playing a power game with the assets provided by the armed forces and moved aircraft carriers around by name, the government decided to abandon its overseas commitments, cease to have a role in 'policing the world' and withdraw from all overseas bases. Hence there would be no grounds for retaining carrier-based air power. To those in the Commonwealth who took particular exception to this unilateral action Healey offered the prospect of long-range RAF deployment which resulted in some hilarious attempts to 'move' locations of islands to fit this new scenario while asking carrier-based aircraft to take photographs of potential sites!

In his autobiography Denis Healey, a great wishful thinker, says that, after many studies, he had concluded that, 'In most places which concerned us, we could support land operations more cheaply and effectively with land-based aircraft'. He had already pronounced his views on aircraft carriers so we had few illusions about his attitude.

There were some who perceived that, while the Navy had 'lost' its carriers, the RAF had somehow 'won'. In fact they had lost too. They failed to get approval for their new attack aircraft, the TSR2, and were made to take the Buccaneer and Phantom, both developed and acquired by the Navy, instead.

However, Healey did agree that the existing fixed-wing carriers HM

Ships *Eagle, Ark Royal* and *Hermes*, plus the helicopter carriers HM Ships *Albion* and *Bulwark*, could run on until the mid-seventies. There was nevertheless a battle to complete the refit of *Ark Royal,* as there were, it was claimed, substantial costs still to be saved. The Home Secretary, however, reminded the Cabinet that cancellation of the work in Plymouth dockyard would cost more in unemployment benefits to the area than to continue the refit.

The RAF had received a crushing blow in the cancellation of the TSR2 programme, which, with the new aircraft carrier, was seen to be an 'East of Suez' requirement, now forsaken. Conceived in 1957 as the long-term replacement for the Canberra bomber, the prototype first flew in late 1964. With the capability to deliver nuclear weapons, it was a cornerstone of the future RAF.

Collaborative Programmes.

As part of the attack on development costs which were rising at about 10 times the rate of inflation, Healey determined that all future major programmes should be part of a joint requirement with another European partner. With his opposite number in France, M. Debré, and Pierre Messmer, who was responsible both for the French Air Force as well as the French aviation industry, whose combined skill in selling French military equipment and particularly aircraft overseas had deeply impressed him, he established two major collaborative programmes.

The first was to provide the TSR2 replacement, a two-seat attack aircraft using a variable geometry (swing) wing, (to be known as the AFVG) and the development of an entirely new single-seat fighter/ground support aircraft, the Jaguar.

The second joint venture involved helicopters in three programmes shared between Aérospatiale and Westland. These were for a battlefield troop carrier on which the French would have design leadership, the second for a small-ship anti-submarine helicopter to replace the Wasp in the Royal Navy and as a new concept for the French Navy, and as a tactical battlefield helicopter for land forces of both nations on which Westland had leadership. The third was for a light training helicopter on which the French again had been given the lead. Hardly a fair share between nations, but Healey had already sold the pass.

*   *   *

Not all these programmes ended in tears, but none of them fulfilled the naïve expectations which had been inflated by Healey. In the case of the helicopters, all three entered the British armed forces in the numbers originally agreed in the international contracts and upon which production workshare between countries was based. On the other hand the French, while taking up their full quota of 'their' two helicopters, acquired less than half the number of Lynx stipulated in the inter-government Memorandum of Understanding.

Healey did follow the French example and set up a Defence Sales Organization headed initially by Raymond Brown, who with Ernie Harrison had founded Racal (ultimately Vodaphone) and supplied the Navy with brilliant communications equipment for many years. Ray Brown was hugely successful in this appointment and set a very high standard for his successors. Healey, on the other hand, had signally failed to understand that French procurement philosophy for their services is based on overseas sales prospects rather than military staff requirements. This speeds up the selection process no end.

The two French-designed helicopters specifically met easily identi-fied commercial requirements for off-shore transport and general training and sold strongly into those markets. The French had clearly outwitted the ponderous British in finessing the best options.

The Lynx was designed to withstand demanding battlefield criteria and operations from ships in sea conditions which would keep most navies in harbour. However, the French recognized the need for a commercial helicopter in this category and produced the Dauphin which, unencumbered by military specifications, also became highly successful in world markets.

These agreements set the precedent that future programmes would not be approved without a collaborative partner. Henceforth programmes seldom benefited the UK as much as they did our part-ners who were able to drive bargains which they knew we could not refuse, given that without them we could do nothing.

While the Ministry of Defence locked procurement into the vice of collaboration our partners enjoyed the fruits of the development for half price and shared in production work while remaining completely free to compete against us in the world market. Thus the French never joined British Aerospace in selling the Jaguar abroad but competed actively against it with their Mirage family of aircraft and in the case of the Lynx they never honoured their commitment to buy the battle-field version.

Nevertheless, in the best tradition of political short-termism, Healey claimed in his book that, 'we made a great success of the Jaguar project and a package of helicopters'. The long-term damage to the UK's technology base was immense but it came in stages, with each stage being accepted as 'inevitable'. Much as in the 'salami slicing' of the Defence Budget, it avoided any suggestion of a 'big bang' which would have created widespread alarm.

Meanwhile the USA went ahead with an aircraft, the F-111, and Healey toyed with the idea of purchasing some to fill the perceived gap before the introduction of the AFVG. The F-111 was originally promoted by MacNamara (Secretary of Defense) as a joint USAF/USN programme but ran into extreme hostility from the USN whose track record for producing brilliant aircraft in this size range far outstripped that of the USAF, the US navy's McDonnell F4 having become a major component of the USAF – to the tune of over 14,000 aircraft – despite having folding wings and a naval pedigree!

The USN did not consider the F-111 met the stringent require-ments demanded by carrier operations. They saw it as an aircraft being pushed into production not on its merits but by the pressure of Texas representatives in the Senate and Congress as production would be in their State. MacNamara, when boss of the Ford Motor company, having produced the only complete failure in its history with a model named the Edsel, no one should have been surprised when the US Navy dubbed the F-111 the 'Texas Edsel'.

Vice Admiral Tom Connelly, the Deputy Chief of Naval Operations for Air, masterminded the Navy's case and won. It cost him his promotion but the Navy called their subsequent new fighter, the Grumman F14, the 'Tomcat'.

Development of the Harrier, in which the US Marine Corps were showing great interest, continued, although the RAF were not happy with having to return to a single-engined aircraft. Healey, when chairing one of the procurement meetings where I represented the naval staff, rounded on Air Vice Marshal Reginald Empson, dismissing his argument for a second engine with the words, 'The trouble with you Reggie is that you are like a wife, always demanding a fur coat'.

Pressure on the budget proved relentless and soon a choice had to be made between withdrawal from the AFVG or the Harrier programme. The RAF chose to give up the former, accepting that they would never get a twin-engined Harrier, but one engine was better than none.

The Buccaneer remained the only UK aircraft to have a high-speed low-level performance; made possible by milling the wing from one solid billet of metal, it was also the first attack aircraft to be fitted with a 'head-up' display (HUD) in which the US Navy showed much interest. They requested that one of their test pilots should evaluate the sight and I was able to make special arrangements for this to take place from Lossiemouth, using the local practice bombing ranges.

In addition the Buccaneer was the first aircraft to have a flight recorder fitted which constantly monitored the flight profile as well as engine and flying control parameters. Thus pilot accuracy as well as technical performance could be analysed after landing.

However, the Buccaneer (with Gyron-Junior engines) was having a problem at sea and several aircraft had been lost due to uncontrollable 'pitch-up' on leaving the end of the catapult. I instructed C Squadron at Boscombe Down to send their most experienced test pilot to join *Eagle* in the Far East. Lieutenant Commander David Eagles (later to become one of the two ex-Naval test pilots to carry out all the test flying for British Aerospace on the Tornado) was the man and he typically met the problem head on by being catapulted off himself.

He experienced exactly the same problem and he too had to eject. After much more testing at Boscombe Down a technique, involving pre-set flying control positions and a 'hands-off' launch, allowed operations to start again but full confidence was not restored until Spey-engined aircraft reached the squadrons.

Back in Whitehall more immediate cuts in the defence budget were ordered and the axe fell on ten Buccaneers from the Navy's programme. I pointed out that while the notional saving was one million pounds per aircraft this would be reduced to four million overall after taking into consideration nugatory costs. The Treasury responded by saying they would allow the full ten million to count towards savings in the current year and push the cancellation costs into the next year. And industry thought it was alone in creative accounting!

116

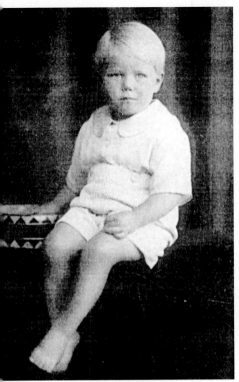

1 & 2. The author in 1926 and in 1976.

3. St Paul's School 1st XI, 1942. The author is second from the right in the front row.

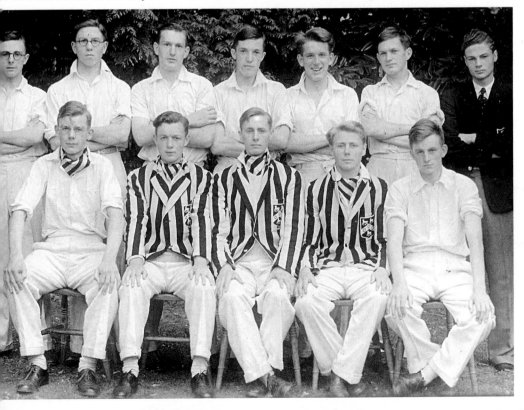

4. Surrender day in Malta, 29 September, 1943. Aboard HMS *Nelson* in Grand
   Harbour, Valetta. General Eisenhower greeted by Vice Admiral Sir Algernon Willis,
   Flag Officer Force H. Behind them are General Alexander and Air Marshal Tedder.

5. Marshal Badoglio, Head of State, arrives to sign the document of Italian surrender.
   With him are General Eisenhower, General Alexander and Admiral Cunningham.
   Behind are General Gort, Air Marshal Tedder and General McFarlane.

6. HMS *Nelson* in camouflage paint.

7. USS *Savannah* hit by a glider bomb close on *Nelson*'s beam, off Salerno, 1943.

8. HMS *Glasgow* hit by shore batteries off Cherbourg, 26 June, 1944.

9. HMS *Keppel*, 1944.

10. HMS *Protector* off the Antarctic coast, 1956.

11. The author on board HMS *Triumph*, 800 Squadron. Behind him is his Seafire 47.

12. HMS *Triumph*. Aircraft ranged for take off, Korean coast, 8 August 1950.

13. The author *(right)* with Lt John Winstanley, his observer, after they had found the *Flying Enterprise*, 849 Squadron, 5 January 1952.

14. A Skyraider of 849 Squadron operating from USS *Valley Forge*.

15. *Victorious* in New York in 1959 – "between two Queens"!

16. *Victorious* enters Oslo harbour in 1960 after a NATO exercise.

17-19. Accidents can happen; Sea Vixen landing on *Victorious*.

20. Scimitar launch.

21. Visitors' Day on *Victorious* in Cape Town.

22. INS *Vikrant*. The author with Captain Mahindroo, Commander Singh and the air crew, who have just completed the 1000th accident-free deck landing, 1961.

23. Admiral Sir Michael Le Fanu with Lord (George) Nelson *(sixth from left)*, Chairman of English Electric. The author is on the far right. 1963.

24. HMS *Lowestoft*, 1964-66.

25. Presentation of New Colour to the Western Fleet aboard HMS *Eagle*. *From the left:* Admiral Sir John Bush, the Commander-in-Chief, Princess Anne, Prince Charles, Lord Mountbatten, the Queen and the author. In the background is the Royal Yacht *Britannia*, July 1969.

26. Refuelling and re-storing at sea. *Eagle* with her for'ard lift down.

27. A view of the two hangars in *Eagle* with visiting Harriers in the upper hangar.

28. *Eagle* putting the message over.

29. The first launch of a Phantom from *Eagle*, 1970. This photograph, taken by the author, shows the engines in afterburner and the catapult bridle falling away.

30. "The best way to say goodbye to visiting guests"!

31. Russian spy ship keeping in station. *Eagle* in the background.

32. Farewell Dinner for Admiral of the Fleet Sir Caspar John, GCB, at RNAS Lossiemouth on 1 September 1972, with present and previous Commanding Officers. The author is second from the right.

33. The author with Admiral Kidd and General Haig, the three major NATO Commanders.

SACEUR   SACLANT   CINCHAN

34. Taking over as C-in-C from Admiral Lewin, 1975.

35. Kirstie having just launched 'her' ship HMS *Glasgow*, 1976.

36. Daughter Mhairi presents a bouquet to the Duchess of York with Kirstie looking on, 1986.

The Phantom Programme

Despite all this the Navy's planned procurement of the McDonnell F4 Phantom was allowed to proceed. Healey was quick to appreciate that the Navy's choice was not only based on an outstanding aircraft with a performance in excess of anything in the UK, even more importantly it had been chosen by the Navy for its unique Westinghouse radar.

This radar was many years in advance of its peers and being made available to the UK only, in fact to the Royal Navy only. It did not take Healey long to order the RAF to follow the Navy's lead and they eventually acquired the aircraft in much greater numbers.

Healey had also made it a condition that 50% of the aircraft supplied should be fitted with parts manufactured in the UK. It had always been the intention to fit Rolls Royce engines, in this case the Spey with re-heat, and this went part of the way to meeting the requirement, but airframe components would also have to be included. This would inevitably push up the cost for these relatively small quantities but Mister Mac, (Jim McDonnell), said he would open up the whole US production line to UK manufacturers to give them the volume needed to become competitive. UK manufacturers failed to take up the challenge and the UK version ended up costing 50% more than the standard US product.

However, the US product would have severely restricted operations from the shorter RN catapults in terms of weapon load and endurance. Re-engined with Rolls Royce Speys, performance was restored, but this required substantial redesign to accommodate the greater air intake demanded for bypass engines and an extendable nose wheel to enable a precise angle of attack to be set for catapult launch. Achievement of re-heat itself was not without a problem for Rolls, as no re-heat had been fitted to a high bypass engine before. Rolls Royce were in uncharted water. The time specified for igniting the re-heat fuel was critical when required for an over-shoot on deck landing. Milliseconds count.

This became an issue when Rolls admitted that, while the re-heat worked successfully, it could not meet the critical time set by the Navy. At this point the RAF nearly broke ranks, saying they would be content with the USN version and praising its higher maximum speed. I was invited by Adrian Lombard, the Director of Engineering at Rolls Royce, to attend a meeting called by Air Vice Marshal Mavor,

117

Assistant Chief of the Air Staff (ACAS) Operations, to address this issue. As the Navy now had a large number of pilots serving in US Navy Phantom squadrons we had much more experience of the aircraft than the RAF, and Lombard wanted my input.

I was convinced that Healey would never approve a purchase unless Rolls Royce engines were fitted so I had to be clear if and how we could handle operationally this failure to achieve our specification. The Navy's problem was the re-heat time on deck overshoot; the RAF's was top speed. I therefore convened a meeting of experienced night flyers. They had already accepted that landing at night, or on one engine at any time, would require going into after-burner on touch down and without waiting for the feel of having missed the arrester wire. If we had to live with something less than our specified re-heat time, this landing technique would have to be extended to every landing.

As to overall performance and the RAF's concern about top speed, the feed-back from our pilots on exchange with the USN in squadrons with Vietnam experience was that acceleration was the prime require-ment and this was not a problem with the Spey.

The meeting with Rolls Royce went to plan. I was able to present the Navy's position with confidence and at the end Mavor admitted rather ruefully that even if the RAF had stuck to their guns Healey would have spiked them.

Chapman Pincher nevertheless had a field day with a two-inch banner headline in the *Daily Express* declaring that Rolls Royce had failed and the Phantom programme was in disarray. No doubt one of his many sources in the RAF had tipped him off. I telephoned to remonstrate. 'What,' I asked him 'would you have said if we had opted for the Pratt and Whitney J79 engines?' 'Then I would have been able to make just as much noise because you hadn't bought Rolls Royce. We have to sell newspapers.' An honest man.

Industry and Production

Throughout this period there was pressure by the government on Hawker de Havilland and BAC (British Aircraft Corporation) to merge, as a successful future for both of them could not be foreseen. The two companies spent much time and effort in trying to agree valu-ations on which proportional holdings in any merger could be based, but failed. In due course the inevitable nationalization resulted. Westland escaped this treatment as it had already absorbed all the other UK helicopter manufacturers as well as the fixed-wing elements of Saunders Roe and Fairey.

DNAW was also much involved in the air-to-air and air-to-surface missile acquisition programme. There was inevitably a competition between a US weapon, already in production or service, and a UK/European alternative, usually still on the drawing board. Even when a decision was eventually made after navigating the tortuous channels of the procurement process, a quite separate decision had to be made on the number of missiles to be ordered.

A missile production line must have a defined life if costs are to be kept down. Order a 'batch' and the price is X. Keep the line open on a 'trickle' basis and the price per missile becomes 4X or more. So, how many do you want? How many wars do you anticipate? How long will it be before the missile is replaced by something better? How much money can you allocate? As the late Derek Rayner, the distinguished CEO and Chairman of Marks and Spencer and later a Life Peer, at that time on secondment to the Procurement Executive, was quick to appreciate, all these decisions have to be made without the benefit of test marketing. 'Quite unlike introducing a new line in knickers in one part of the country before deciding to go nationwide' as he put it.

On the helicopter front we were still having serviceability problems and in the case of the Lynx, which the Navy would have chosen to be powered by a well proven engine, Rolls Royce saw the opportunity to design a new, more efficient small gas turbine to compete with the Americans. The government were persuaded by the argument and granted the usual launch-funding for development.

Much to its dismay the Navy was now forced into accepting a completely new engine for which it would be the only foreseeable customer, thus forfeiting the advantage of economy of scale and having other users with whom to share in-service development costs.

Our worst fears were to be realized. The new engine, named the Gem, was just that: a brilliant, extremely advanced and complex design more suited to operation at constant speed and altitude than the rough and tumble of the battlefield, ingesting sand, dust and leaves and, at sea, the ravages of salt water. So bad was its serviceability that the letters GEM soon stood for Great Engineering Mistake. As one engineer officer put it to me, 'When we asked for a tractor they sent us a Maserati. When they saw it in the field they said they understood the problem and took it away. When they returned they brought back a Maserati on tracks!'

The Gem gradually improved but was never installed in any other vehicle. The relatively small sales limited the interest of Rolls Royce, although they kept their best efforts for exports, the Lynx being sold to seven NATO navies. The British Army and Navy have persevered with it and it is a tribute to their skill and determination that it served so well in the Falkland war.

The Future Fleet

Overlaying everything else at this time was my membership of the Future Fleet Working Party (FFWP). Set up by the new First Sea Lord, Admiral Sir Varyl Begg, felt by many to be a paragon of inter-service objectivity, it was chaired by the Assistant Chief of the Naval Staff for Policy, Rear Admiral John Adams, supported by the Assistant Chief for Operational Requirements, Rear Admiral Anthony Griffin. The Directors of the Naval Staff Divisions were all members.

The Terms of Reference required the FFWP to determine the future size and shape of the Navy, no less. There were no conditions imposed other than that the future fleet would not have aircraft carriers nor would there be worldwide commitments.

As the work progressed something which had been absolutely clear to many of us dawned on all the others. The carrier was not only a vastly capable platform for deployment of aircraft, anti-submarine helicopters and long-range anti-aircraft missiles, but it also hosted the huge command and control radar and communications without which no naval task group could operate and which are as vital in times of tension as they are when in action. Where and how would these be re-provided in a fleet of which the nuclear submarine might be the capital ship?

Inexorably, combining all these capabilities in one surface ship instead of attempting to split them between many emerged as the only credible, operational and cost-effective solution. So, if it was to be a big ship, why not give it a flat deck so that helicopter operations could be facilitated and a marine Commando embarked? Even perhaps embark RAF Harriers? Three in one, a Command ship, a major Anti-Submarine ship and an Amphibious assault ship. But it can't be called a 'Carrier'. O.K; how about a 'Through-Deck cruiser'?

John Adams reported progress regularly to the First Sea Lord who cautioned him about designing a carrier by any other name. He would not be fooled. When John attempted to steer us away from this concept we immediately challenged him as to whether our Terms of Reference allowed us complete freedom, as we had assumed from the start, or were we now to be 'directed'? John soon backed down and the report was duly presented to Admiral Begg. A new fleet with multi-capable through-deck cruisers at its heart.

Predictably, Admiral Begg disowned the entire report, but in due course the ships were built to carry out the tasks assigned and played a key role in the Falklands.

People

During my time as DNAW I was very well supported by two excellent deputies and a number of thoroughly overworked desk officers who each had to cover a wide variety of tasks and projects. The pressure was well illustrated when the RAF joined our Phantom programme and set up a parallel staff which outnumbered my team by more than three to one. Captain Roy 'Gus' Halliday was one of the deputies; he was later to become a very successful Head of Naval Intelligence. The other, 'Tubby' Frazer, with a wealth of wartime experience as an Observer, died of an heart attack while in the office. He would have been the last to claim it was due to overwork.

As DNAW I kept in very close touch with the Naval Air Command and made regular visits to various units. While the Flag Officer, now Vice Admiral Sir Richard Smeeton, was situated at Lee-on-Solent, the Flag Officer Flying Training was at Yeovilton and there was a constant exchange of information and ideas at all levels of staff. It was at Yeovilton that Admiral Smeeton decided to site the Fleet Air Arm Museum which was conceived by him and opened by the Duke of Edinburgh in 1966.

One of the lighter moments came when a close friend invited me to dinner with his local MP. This was Robert Maxwell, who enjoyed gambling, and so dinner took place in the Ladbroke Club. Maxwell was an entertaining guest and interested in the defence procurement battles. After dinner we took to the tables with our few £1 chips while Maxwell started with £500 which he lost in the first few turns of the wheel.

The management recognized a big player and they stepped up a gear as Maxwell moved into thousands and started winning – big time. As his pile grew he assured me he would soon be able to buy me some Harriers if not a new carrier. It was all very jolly and at the end he picked up a five-figure cheque and departed in his Rolls Royce. Not bad for a Labour MP!

My two years as DNAW were drawing to a close and I was told my next appointment would be command of the carrier HMS *Eagle*. Almost at the same time I heard that my mother had died. She was seventy-eight, had survived her husband by eleven years and been suffering from cancer for several months. She was one of life's great 'givers' and genuinely never expected any return. She maintained all her good works in her local village and managed to be a wonderful grandmother right to the end. She had survived her mother by a bare six years.

On the family side, boarding school ceased to be a nightmare but this had been just one more demanding appointment with uncertain and inevitably long hours and, for my wife, no light at the end of the tunnel. I commuted daily from our house in West Byfleet and, as usual, I sent the family to her parents for the summer holidays. In 1967 my wife decided not to come back. I flew over to see if there could be any way forward but this proved to be impossible. Our separation began and ended in divorce a year later.

I moved out of the house and into a flat in London where I found my old friend Peter Shand Kydd also in the process of divorce. He had become involved with Frances Althorp, who was in the same situation, while I had met a young lady from Scotland, Kirstie Landale, whose family had strong ties with Hong Kong. As a foursome we saw a lot of each other over the next two years and all re-married within a month in 1969.

Peter kept a yacht in Mallorca on which we spent occasional holidays and once sailed to Ibiza. While my venture there had completely failed to attract my wife, who decided it was much too primitive during her only visit, we all found it enchanting. Frances was to bring her family, with the exception of eldest daughter Sarah, to the house for summer holidays with us several years running. By this time we had a small boat and all the young learnt to water ski. Kirstie was an expert teacher and while Jane managed well, Diana was the star and Charles just too young to get far.

HMS *EAGLE*

Admiral Le Fanu had commanded *Eagle* years earlier and admitted it had been the most challenging and demanding appointment of his career, not excluding his current job as First Sea Lord. I did not expect it to be anything less for me but I could not have looked forward to anything more keenly. I could never understand why some of my peers chose the command of shore establishments, however prestigious, instead of taking a top sea command.

Except for a few short intervals there have been ships named *Eagle* in the Royal Navy for nearly 400 years. These included the sixth *Eagle* which took part in the capture of Gibraltar but was wrecked off the Scillies in 1707; the tenth was Admiral Lord Howe's flagship during the American War of Independence and the immediate pre-decessor, the fourteenth, which was laid down in 1913 as a battleship but launched in 1918 as one of the first aircraft carriers.

The present ship, built by Harland and Wolff at Belfast, was laid down in 1942 and launched by the Queen (then Princess Elizabeth) in 1946. She finally entered service in 1952. *Eagle* and *Ark Royal* were not only the biggest to be built but also the only two carriers to have two aircraft hangars, one above the other.

HMS *Eagle* was fifty-three thousand tons of warship capable of a speed of thirty knots on the power of eight giant boilers feeding four steam turbines in turn driving four massive propellers. No naval officer could fail to enjoy the excitement and pleasure of a more statuesque and demanding 'Grey Mistress'.

The ship had completed an extensive refit in 1964 and emerged with an angled deck, a completely updated electronic suite headed by the full 3D Radar and Comprehensive Display System. This was the same as the one I had become accustomed to in *Victorious* and which was to be denied to *Ark Royal*. Cost and the short remaining operational life of the carriers was the reason given, but *Ark Royal*, although fully able to operate the Phantom night fighter, was to remain handicapped by a totally outdated command and control system. HMS *Eagle* was in Plymouth naval dockyard when I took over command from Captain Ernle Pope in October 1968, I was the fourth captain since the refit.

Eagle's aircraft complement was made up of an attack squadron, No. 800, of Blackburn Buccaneers commanded by Lieutenant Commanders S. Mather, and later Joe Billingham. This was the Mark II version fitted with Rolls Royce Spey engines. The all-weather fighter squadron of de Havilland Sea Vixens, No. 899, was commanded by Lieutenant Commanders Geoff Hunt, and later Michael Layard. The Anti-Submarine squadron, No 826, of Westland Wessex Mark 3 helicopters, commanded by Lieutenant Commander Kemp, and D flight of airborne early warning squadron, No 849, of Fairey Gannets commanded by Lieutenant Commander Tim Goetz, completed the air group.

The Executive Officer and Second-in-Command, Commander Alec Weir, was outstanding, as was the head of the Air department (Wings), Commander Ted Anson, a very experienced carrier pilot who had commanded a Buccaneer squadron as well as a frigate. I was fortunate to have them both.

Apart from my secretary, Lieutenant Commander George Greaves, who was a tower of strength and managed to ensure my office ran impeccably, the one officer with whom I spent more time than any other at sea was the Navigator, Lieutenant Commander Barry Wilson. His was a hugely responsible job as my right-hand man at sea.

I have explained the importance of all the other heads of departments in *Victorious* and I had an equally good team here. The medical staff was headed by the Principal Medical Officer, Surgeon Commander Bob Adamson, supported by two juniors and a dental surgeon. Among the three doctors, there must be a specialist surgeon and an anaesthetist as the carriers are fitted with fully equipped operating theatres.

All big ships carry chaplains and very big ships have three. One is always Church of England, one a Roman Catholic and the other drawn from the 'free' church community. *Eagle*'s third man was Church of Scotland, David Harries, a splendid extrovert and card-carrying member of Equity who came to the ship after some apparently too extrovert activities elsewhere. Marginally reformed, he was a tremendous asset.

The Navy has a great advantage in that it does not attach a rank to its chaplains. They can move among the sailors without any barriers and they were an immense help in family welfare matters well beyond their pure pastoral work. With over three thousand men they had plenty.

In *Eagle* their secular activities extended to responsibility for arranging all bus tours in foreign ports which could amount to no more than a few local excursions or involve a massive transport operation moving large numbers of libertymen to and from Boston and New York or Naples and Rome. In the latter case the operation was placed in the hands of John King, the RC padre, and they quickly became known as Rosary Tours.

The sailors delighted in seeing the padres taking an active part in the earthly activities of the ship and the padres themselves appreciated these opportunities to reinforce their pastoral work. It was also a pleasure to see two padres combining their Sunday services, alternately taking the lead and markedly increasing the overall numbers attending.

Work-up and Operations

Sailing from Plymouth after a rather special re-commissioning service attended by a number of the great and the good but none more welcome than my old boss, Admiral Sir Michael Le Fanu, then First Sea Lord, the ship embarked her squadrons and headed west and then north through the Irish Sea.

With a substantial number of new sailors and officers embarked, the ship went directly into a major work-up period, much of it carried out in the Moray Firth some thirty to a hundred miles from the Naval Air Station at Lossiemouth, which gave us staunch support throughout.

The comprehensive display system (CDS) worked well and had matured considerably since my time in *Victorious*, but it was still based on the massive Ferranti Poseidon computers (almost as big as a small house) which were largely analogue. Two Chief Petty Officer technicians had been with the system since its installation and knew how to look after it. The Admiralty, with unusual perception, stretched the rules so that these two key men could remain in post.

Today the computer power required would be installed in two or three cabinets and demand only a fraction of the air-cooling and electric supplies.

The only break in an intensive six-week period, which ended with an Operational Readiness Inspection by the Flag Officer, was a long weekend at anchor off Lossiemouth. This allowed one day of shore leave for each half of the ship and started well with all the ship's boats running a hectic ferry service to the small harbour.

However, as the day wore on the winds increased well above the forecast and the sea conditions at the entrance to the harbour became unsafe. So one half of the sailors spent the night ashore and the next day was taken up lifting them all back by helicopter, the Captain at Lossiemouth, the redoubtable Winkle Brown, flying one of them. The other half of the ship's company never got ashore. This could have generated much ill feeling but was taken in good spirit by those disappointed and this was to set an excellent example for the future.

Fleet operations followed when the ship was supported by a screen of anti-submarine and anti-aircraft destroyers or frigates. Ships are normally in relatively close formation, in assigned stations and always ready to turn as required for flying operations which usually call for high-speed manoeuvres, more often than not complicated by the presence of a Soviet spy ship.

There have been well-publicized instances where the carrier has collided with an escort, cutting the smaller ship in half and incurring the loss of many lives. Happily the RN was never involved, but Captain Lygo, in HMS *Ark Royal*, was to have a near disaster with a suicidal Soviet destroyer which cut across his bows during night flying and nearly suffered a similar fate.

I made quite sure that individual captains understood the standard operating procedures and could be expected to anticipate how the carrier would behave. This was particularly important when my escort was provided, as it frequently was, by the Standing Naval Force Atlantic, a group made up of ships from the northern countries of the NATO Alliance, namely UK, US, Canada, Norway, Germany, Holland and Portugal. While this was a very professional force, individual ships joined and departed at varying times and one could never be sure when a captain last operated with a carrier, or, indeed if he ever had.

A two-week summer leave period in Portsmouth gave me the

opportunity to re-marry. My wife, Kirstie, was a member of the congregation of St Columba's Church of Scotland where the minister, Fraser McCluskey, who had parachuted in with the troops at Arnhem, agreed to marry us, but only if I was in uniform.

Eagle then proceeded across the Atlantic for exercises with the US Navy and some port visits where my wife was able to join me. The first of these was to the naval base at Norfolk, Virginia, where we berthed close to the USS *Kennedy* which made us look very puny. I was able to arrange for my two children, Jonathan and Alison, to join us in Norfolk for a few days and meet their stepmother. It was a happy occasion.

Following more joint exercises with the USN, we routed north for a visit to Boston. This was at the very start of the troubles in Northern Ireland and there was concern about a possibly hostile reception from this strongly Irish-American area.

In the event it was a splendid visit greatly helped by the publicity given to the large number of blood donors from the ship and to the quite fortuitous assistance given by two of our sailors to a besieged city policeman trapped by a gang on the notorious Boston Common.

... GEE! YOU MEAN YOUR NASTY OL' CAP'N MAROONED YOU IN NORFOLK - AND IS MAKING YOU WALK - ALL THE WAY TO BOSTON!?..

These acts of 'heroism' received wide media coverage and set the tone for a very popular week.

On return to home waters our operations were enlivened by a visit from John Farley, Hawker's chief test pilot, in one of the development Harriers. He made a number of landings and both vertical and rolling take-offs. To witness the occasion, Rear Admiral Fell, Flag Officer Carriers and Amphibious Ships [FOCAS], brought on board senior executives of de Havilland and McDonnell Douglas who had recently signed up to build the Harrier in the USA for the Marine Corps.

We also carried out at this time the deck-landing trials for the Phantom which made a large number of landings (with the single wire of the trial installation of the Direct Acting arrester gear) and catapult launches at varying weights and configurations. The aircraft belonged to C Squadron at Boscombe Down and was flown by the naval test pilots, Lieutenants Hefford and Burn.

Royal Fleet Review

We were next plunged into planning for the forthcoming Fleet Review by Her Majesty the Queen at which time she would present new Colours to the Western Fleet, an event which happens perhaps once every half century. It next took place in 2003. *Eagle* would be the flagship of the Commander-in-Chief, Admiral Sir John Bush, and there would be over twenty-five surface ships from cruisers to minesweepers, two nuclear and six other submarines and at least four large Fleet Auxiliaries in attendance. The review was to take place on 28 and 29 July with all ships anchored in Torbay prior to sailing for the steam past in Lyme Bay. Her Majesty would be embarked in the Royal Yacht *Britannia*. *

Included in the programme was a dinner to be given in honour of Her Majesty by the Fleet and hosted by the Commander-in-Chief in the wardroom of *Eagle*. Her Majesty would be accompanied by the Duke of Edinburgh, Prince Charles and Princess Anne, and Lord Mountbatten. The Queen had let it be known that after dinner she would be pleased to attend a traditional ship's company concert party.

* See p.250.

When I was first informed of this by Admiral Bush he said it would be a good idea for contributions to the concert party to be made by other ships taking part in the review. Well aware of how 'blue' most ship's company concerts become, I expressed my alarm at this proposal and fortunately was immediately supported by his Chief of Staff, Vice Admiral Peter Ashmore, who had, as an equerry to the Prince of Wales when he made a world tour in HMS *Hood* in the mid-thirties, experienced this problem at first hand.

I was thus able to persuade Admiral Bush that *Eagle* had to be responsible for all aspects of the concert, including all individual acts. I was confident that we had the talent, one padre being a member of Equity and one of the doctors an ex-Cambridge Footlights performer, but I had to find a way round the main problem which arises when sailors play the part of a girl. To get over this I suggested we should call on the real thing and ask for Wrens from his Northwood staff to be seconded to us.

And so it was. Apart from the traditional Elephant Ballet performed by the hairiest stokers dressed in tutus, we were able avoid the excesses without detracting from the fun of *Where Eagles Dare*.

The fleet programme called for all ships to assemble in Weymouth Bay and carry out exercises in preparation for the steam-past. The Commander-in-Chief delegated authority to me as Flag Captain to manoeuvre ships as required, giving the appropriate orders in his name. He and his staff were fully confident with this procedure as his staff were not 'sea-going' in an operational capacity.

All exercises were completed satisfactorily, although enlivened by patchy fog and a generous number of yachts behaving unpredictably and calling for rapid avoiding action. On completion all ships anchored in Torbay in their assigned stations.

Kirstie and I had been invited to the summer ball at the Britannia Royal Naval College at Dartmouth that evening and, as customary, I sought the Admiral's permission to go ashore. 'Certainly not,' said he. 'There is no one between me and the Fleet except you'. He had a point.

The weather the next morning was deteriorating but the rain held off. The ceremony was completed without any bad moments and the cloud base allowed a fly past by the Fleet Air Arm to take place as planned.The evening arrangements also started smoothly. Her

Majesty was obviously delighted to be on board the ship she had launched and was in splendid form during drinks before the dinner while the three hundred officers were taking their places at the tables in the Wardroom.

Over a thousand sailors from other ships were embarked for the concert and about an hundred officers for the dinner. I found myself sitting next to the Minister for the Navy, David (Lord) Owen, who had been to sea in *Eagle* some weeks earlier. There were no speeches and all went well with the exception of the passing of the port when the Chief Steward lost the plot. As only to be expected Her Majesty coped perfectly.

On completion of the concert party which began with David Harries doing a 'This is Your Life' on Lord Mountbatten, which had the royal party roaring with laughter, it was time to move visitors and guests back to their respective ships, starting with Her Majesty. The weather now let us down. The wind was still rising and the sea rough. The Royal Barge from *Britannia* had difficulty coming alongside and considerable agility was required in getting the royal party on board. Then followed the three visiting admirals who all managed to make the leap into their barges except for the Hydrographer of the Navy who found the barge canopy where the cockpit should have been and ended up spreadeagled on top. However, with some loss of dignity but nothing more, that exercise was completed. But so was the running of any more boats between the ship and the landing stages in Torquay.

We were thus left with a thousand visitors on board and probably fifteen hundred ashore. The good people of Torquay took care of the stranded sailors and we found bunks for the visitors. Special arrangements had to be made for the Wrens. The Royal Marine sentries behaved impeccably!

I was quite concerned for the safety of some of the ships in the anchorage overnight and one nuclear submarine had to proceed to sea. Otherwise the programme was restored. The fleet steamed past HMY *Britannia* in style and then dispersed to follow their separate instructions. *Eagle* was due to return to Plymouth for summer leave, but I had taken steps to organize for there to be a families day at sea first.

Involving families in the activities of the ship had always been one of my priorities. Regular newsletters and allowing families on board in harbour all help, but days at sea are altogether different. Sadly, opportunities are few but this one was not to be missed and I intended we would make the most of it. Course was set to arrive off the outer break-water at Plymouth at 0730 and the Commander had arranged for families to be brought to the ship in dockyard tugs. A minimum age had been set at six years, but it soon became evident to the Master-at-Arms that this could not be enforced and a crèche was quickly set up and staffed by eager volunteers.

With everyone safely embarked, the ship sailed for the exercise areas where an ambitious day of operations had been planned so that wherever possible families could see their husbands and fathers at work and even work with them. Very strict rules were enforced regarding safety and access, but these were never to cause concern. The main feature of the day was to see the aircraft in action and, while providing safe viewing positions meant watching had to take place in relays, no one was disappointed.

The day was rounded off on the passage back to Plymouth by a repeat performance of the concert party given not only for the families but also for those of the ship's company who it had not been possible to include in the hangar for the Royal showing. It was truly a day to remember. Even the most senior Chief Petty Officers, some of them with over twenty-five years' service, could not remember anything remotely as exciting. The Commander was quite over-whelmed by the letters of appreciation received after the event.

In the autumn we deployed to the Mediterranean for three months, starting with a visit to Gibraltar, followed by a series of NATO exercises, a short stay in Malta and a five-day visit to Naples. The ship was open to Neapolitan visitors on one day and this resulted in huge queues forming by each gangway leading to the ship.

Ship visits are always very popular with the local inhabitants, but this was the only time I saw urchin entrepreneurs selling tickets to the unsuspecting souls queuing up!

The ship was back in Plymouth for Christmas leave before returning to the Mediterranean in the new year. Again there were several exercises and a break in Toulon where Kirstie was able to join me. John Templeton-Cothill owned a small château near Orange and suggested we borrowed it for the weekend. He had established close ties with the French Navy and said they would provide us with a car and driver for the journey. 'You must ask to have Christian as your driver; he sleeps with my cook.' And so he did.

Just after leaving Gibraltar for Plymouth on our way home a signal came in to say the navigator's wife had suffered a brain haemorrhage and their two children had been found alone in the house after forty-eight hours. Despite his protestations (I'm sure he felt I couldn't get the ship safely home without him) he was soon strapped into a Buccaneer and home within three hours. Happily his wife made a full recovery and he rejoined the ship a few weeks later.

On our return and after more exercises in the Western Approaches we were programmed for a four-day visit to Liverpool. In naval ports like Plymouth, Portsmouth and Chatham the whole ship's company may go ashore in plain clothes and invariably do so. Anywhere else uniform is worn, and so it was to be in Liverpool. However, the Master-at-Arms had approached the Commander on behalf of the senior ratings, the Chief and Petty Officers, to request that in this instance an exception should be made.

The Commander was in two minds and I was surprised by the request because I was sure Liverpool would want to give them a tremendous welcome and this would not be possible if they could not be identified. I was assured that feeling was strong among all the 'Chiefs' and, knowing what a splendid group they were, I gave permission.

In the event I was proved absolutely right. No one in uniform was allowed to pay for his own drinks in the pubs, travel on all public transport was free as was access to cinemas and dance halls where all the girls loved the sailors. Liverpool really took them to heart. After the first day not one of the Chiefs went ashore in plain clothes.

Throughout the last months of my command the ship responded as splendidly as ever, working under pressure and producing results. The Air Department was truly integrated with the rest of the ship, which was in turn very proud of its air group. In the two years we never suffered one flying accident.

This was an outstanding safety record which reflected the very high standards achieved by everyone on board, nowhere more than on the flight deck where the performance of the young men working day and night in winds of thirty to forty knots is almost as critical as the skill of the aircrew in landing their twenty-ton aircraft. The flight deck remains one of the very few places where officers not only lead their men but are seen to be leading their men, round the clock and no matter what the weather. Lieutenant Commander John Eagle, the Flight Deck Officer, set an excellent example.

Two others deserve special mention. One was the voice of Radio Eagle's reporter and Disc Jockey, a Leading Signalman, Tony Revett, with me on the bridge as his assigned station, who spent all his spare time in the studio. These were the days when there were no television screens on the mess decks. Sadly I had cause to deprive him of his Leading rank but this did not stop him interviewing me on Radio Medway when I was Commander-in-Chief and he had found his calling ashore.

The other was Lieutenant 'Tugg' Wilson, the ship's photographic and safety equipment officer with whom I had served in *Victorious*. Then, as now, he had a perceptive sense of humour and an uncanny ability to translate this into cartoon form. *Eagle* published a daily paper, the *Eagle Express*, when at sea and two Tugg cartoons appeared in every edition, one always on the front page. The paper was of course widely distributed in the ship and, when in company with others, copies were delivered by helicopter.

Inevitably the Captain featured frequently and Tugg asked me as soon as I joined whether I wanted to vet each cartoon before publication as was the case with my predecessor. I didn't need to and he never got it wrong. Tugg left the Navy to try his hand in the national press and found his niche in the off-shore oil industry where the task of making the roughnecks on the rigs safety-conscious needed all the humour possible to attract and hold their attention. He continues to contribute to a large number of naval publications.

Towards the end of this time *Ark Royal* emerged from her long refit, but we were never able to operate together. However, the healthy rivalry between *Ark Royal* and *Eagle* continued until the end. *Eagle* had the reputation for being the smarter of the two but the name *Ark Royal* and the Queen Mother (who launched her) helped to keep her in the news and give the impression of higher operational activity. On one occasion the Commander-in-Chief of the time mentioned this to the Queen and was put firmly in his place by the lady who launched *Eagle*.

Finally a few words about ship-handling at its most critical when entering and leaving Plymouth dockyard. The passage from or to the outer breakwater took a little over an hour, the determining factor being the temperature of the steam turbines which rose when manoeuvring at slow speed. A dockyard pilot was always embarked but the responsibility remained with the Captain. It was quite usual for the navigating officer to con the ship using carefully plotted wheel-over positions and speeds and I was happy for Barry Wilson to do this. He was promoted from the ship and I was delighted to see him rise to Vice Admiral.

However, I always monitored progress, using bridge wing compass readings to ensure the ship was well within safety lines, and was prepared to take immediate action if required. This happened to me only once when leaving Plymouth for my last time and with a new navigating officer on his first run. I had carefully briefed him, but he was caught by a stronger than usual tide due to recent heavy rains which demanded an earlier than planned turn at the elbow and I had to take over.

Happily my final return to Plymouth passed off, not effortlessly, but smoothly and without incident. And perhaps some touch of emotion as this would be my last in command of one of Her Majesty's Ships.

6

FLAG OFFICER

ALL THE BIG SHIPS

On leaving HMS *Eagle* I was appointed as a Rear Admiral to become Flag Officer Carriers and Amphibious Ships (FOCAS), taking over from Rear Admiral Mike Fell. The command included the fixed-wing carriers *Eagle*, *Ark Royal* and *Hermes*, the helicopter carriers *Albion* and *Bulwark,* and the amphibious ships *Fearless* and *Intrepid.* FOCAS also had functional responsibility for the standards and practices in small ships flights. The Commodore Amphibious ships, Gus Halliday, who had been with me in DNAW, flew his pennant in various amphibious ships on specific operations, as an important assistant operational commander.

With FOCAS came the NATO appointment as Commander Carrier Strike Group Two (ComCarStrikeGroup 2), part of the Strike Fleet Atlantic, and we often worked together with other Strike Groups in live exercises which almost invariably took place in North Atlantic waters. The Strike Fleet, while being under the command of the Supreme Allied Commander Atlantic (SACLANT), was assigned targets both conventional and nuclear by the Supreme Allied Commander Europe (SACEUR) as part of the overall NATO strike plan. The Commander Strike Fleet was at that time Vice Admiral Jerry Miller, an extrovert aviator and brilliant pianist who played with the Strike Fleet orchestra when given half a chance!

Strike Fleet exercises took place twice a year and were the most important items on the calendar, testing and training to the limits of capability and sometimes beyond. As one Strike Fleet Commander reported, 'You have got to come up here and do it. You can play war games but not until you put it all together, until you go to the Norwegian coast and put the four elements of the Striking Fleet together – the carriers, the ASW, the amphibious and the Marines – and co-ordinate with other NATO Commanders, do you have the chance to make it work, and it does.'

Post-exercise discussions played an important part and in Oslo for these occasions it was not unusual for King Olaf (an honorary Admiral in the Royal Navy) to attend and then lunch on board the Flagship. He was an entertaining and courteous guest.

With my operational staff we also took part in command and control exercises at the US Naval War College in Rhode Island where the problems during periods of international tension could be worked through. All NATO strategic planning was based on deterrence and if a fighting war were to take place this would demonstrate a failure which may have been caused by lack of communication at almost any level: an over-reaction by a junior commander or an unjustified initial act sparking a similar response. Many of these were illustrated and dealt with by adjustments to rules of engagement and practised in these very realistic 'games' where senior members of the US State Department and Department of Defense played 'for' and 'away', also representing the Soviet reactions as well as those of the US. 'War Games' was a misnomer; they were really 'Deterrence Games'.

On one occasion Kirstie was invited by Admiral Miller to accompany me and took passage overnight from New York to Newport in his flagship the USS *Newport News,* a privilege not granted to USN admiral's wives.

My shore headquarters were on Portsdown Hill where the entire staff were housed. The administrative staff, headed by the indefatigable Captain Alan Leahy, were there all the time, and the operational staff only when not with me at sea, which was much of the time. The Staff Officer Aviation, Commander Jock Tofts, and Staff Officer Operations, Lieutenant Commander Tony Norman, were key players in a strong and experienced team. I inherited an excellent Secretary, Commander Brian Brown, a qualified pilot who was to become a four-star Admiral, and Flag Lieutenant, Patrick Bruce Gardyne, who was relieved by Lieutenant Peter Tuke in due course.

Operating with the US Navy

The carriers were seldom able to operate together except on NATO exercises and so, when one of them was alone in the Mediterranean, and there was also a USN carrier there under one of my fellow Carrier Group Commanders, I would place the ship under his operational command. Both ships profited from these joint exercises and indeed *Ark Royal* found herself working under Rear Admiral William Houser on a number of occasions.

This led to an amusing incident some years later when Houser was a Vice Admiral and serving in Washington as Deputy Chief of Naval Staff for Air. The year was 1974 and the second centenary of the foundation of the US Navy was being celebrated. The local newspaper in Mayport, Florida, a major naval port and one regularly visited by *Ark Royal*, carried a front page devoted to a banner headline CONGRATULATIONS TO THE US NAVY above a full-page photograph of *Ark Royal*.

A copy of the paper was placed on the Admiral's desk with the comment 'Goofed again – who needs this PR Department?' To which Bill Houser was able to respond, 'Don't worry, she was one of mine!'

Another good friend was Rear Admiral Ken Wallace who was commanding a Cruiser Squadron based on Mayport and was the host when I visited in *Ark Royal*. Ken was an outstanding officer who had been the first Captain of the cruiser USS *Longbeach*, the first surface ship to be nuclear-powered. After retiring, he became an expert consultant to the US Government on nuclear power and a key member of the investigation team following the accident at Three Mile Island. He and his wife Kitty remain close friends.

During this time we were fortunate that Port Everglades was prepared to allow *Ark Royal*, on completion of exercises, to visit on a regular basis. Port Everglades, just north of Miami, became a favourite location for the ship's company. Through the good offices of the Navy League, the local population took the ship to heart so much so that they requested her presence when the USA celebrated the two hundredth anniversary of Independence Day. This was duly arranged and *Ark Royal* and her Royal Marine Band formed a central part of the festivities.

It was also during this time that I was able to reach agreement for our carriers to take advantage of the extraordinary facilities for training offered by the practice areas of the USN in the Guantanamo Bay region off Cuba, unmatched anywhere else in the world. Here our carriers could take part in exercises where there was no restriction on electronic warfare, supersonic targets were available and live firings could be carried out against them. Phantom pilots flew every mission with live missiles (albeit fitted with non-explosive heads) and the tension during intercept exercises was easily detected in voice transmissions.

These air attacks were simulated by Douglas A3 twin-engined aircraft with underslung supersonic unmanned targets, which would be released at an appropriate distance while the launch aircraft turned away. The action took place at night and the approach made under cover of radar jamming. The fleet had to take electronic counter-measures, detect the approaching aircraft and assign fighters to intercept and shoot down the target.

For safety reasons all interceptions were monitored by a control ship and when a fighter reported his radar locked on, the control ship had to validate the target and the pilot could not release his missile unless he received the report 'you have a valid target' from control.

On one occasion an *Ark Royal* Phantom pilot, having gained a target and been correctly authorized to engage, released his missile which promptly homed in on the starboard engine of the launch aircraft and removed it completely and cleanly from the wing. The aircraft made a successful emergency landing back at base and at the subsequent post-exercise presentation the Admiral declared, 'We are not going to let this incident in any way detract from the realism with which we will continue to conduct these exercises'.

After one of these exercises permission was granted for *Ark Royal* to visit New York where a berth was normally provided at one of the piers used by the big Cunarders. By this time only the *Queen Elizabeth II* was in service and her more modern design resulted in less draft. To our dismay, when planning the visit, we discovered that the depth of water alongside was no longer sufficient for our two big carriers.

Our friends in the USN, however, rose to the occasion and, with the assistance of the US Coastguard, laid head and stern battleship buoys in the Hudson River abreast 80th street. So that the customary cocktail party for the great and the good could still be held, arrangements were made with the Moran Tug Company to shuttle guests to and from the Cunard pier. The Moran family had been founders of the New York Yacht Club and great supporters of all things naval.

The visit attracted considerable press interest and the opportunity was taken to send a Sea King helicopter ashore to bring the press on board while the ship was still some distance out. I joined them for the return journey to New York, the ship by this time approaching the narrows, and this allowed me to get ahead with my round of calls. The first was on the Admiral commanding the Third Naval District who was the host authority for the visit, and we were able to watch from his eighth floor offices in the new World Trade Centre, the splendid sight of *Ark Royal* steaming past. It was a sunny but bitterly cold day with a fresh breeze.

There followed my calls on the Mayor, John Lindsay, and the Governor of New York State, John Rockefeller. I had arranged for my barge to collect me from the Cunard pier for the return to the ship, but when I arrived it was nowhere to be seen and I was greeted by Jim Moran with the words 'She went thataway!' He then explained that the ship had clearly been unable to secure to the buoys and had returned down river to anchor in a berth off Staten Island. I gratefully accepted his offer of a tug to get back on board.

The Captain of *Ark Royal*, John Roberts, explained that, having secured to the forward buoy and in the process of securing aft, he noticed the bow was paying off alarmingly fast, being caught by the strong crosswind. The civilian river pilot who, by US law, must handle all ships (including military) made reassuring noises, but Roberts rightly assessed that the forward buoy was not holding and that his ship was about to be in danger of grounding. He ordered the aft picking-up rope to be slipped, turned the ship through 180 degrees on main engines and headed back down river.

In the Admiral's offices ashore they were quick to appreciate the situation and immediately assigned an anchor berth off Staten Island. The buoy was attached to the bow, hidden from sight of the bridge by the flare of the flight deck as the ship steamed towards her anchorage. It caused huge embarrassment to the Admiral and his staff, without us having to add anything to the agony.

In fact the Staten Island ferry, 'the best nickel value in the US', saved the visit for the ship's company. It was cheap, ran for twenty-four hours very frequently and the jetty was but a short boat run from the ship. Hospitality was generous, entertainment abundant and there were no signs of an Irish problem.

Embarrassment for the Consul General, whose staff had made all the arrangements for the reception which was to take place on board that evening, was more immediate. His staff had to inform 600 guests that the party was cancelled. In addition to frantic telephone calls, radio and television announcements were made, but still over two hundred people turned up at the pier. The next morning's papers carried front-page photographs of *Ark Royal* with the vast buoy close up under her bow. All the main UK papers copied.

This did not stop us entertaining many of the great and the good and the atrocious weather did not prevent the arrival of many visitors from Washington, including the British Ambassador, Lord Cromer, and supporting cast of Charles Powell (our paths were to cross again some 15 years later at No.10 Downing Street), and his vivacious wife Carla. It was also an opportunity to thank many New Yorkers for their hospitality to the sailors, but not on the scale we had originally planned.

HMS *Eagle*

The only window of opportunity to carry out an Operational Readiness Inspection of *Eagle* occurred when the ship was in the Far East. The weather was not kind, with near hurricane winds in the South China Sea, but the whole ship performed splendidly. Ian Robertson was a most able captain and there was nothing to show for the rather shaky start he suffered when *Eagle* touched bottom on her first entry to Plymouth under his command.

The ship was entering harbour after some severe gales and the Captain, the navigating officer and the dockyard pilot all allowed themselves to be deceived by the position of a marker buoy just off the Royal South Western Yacht Club. Buoys are certainly useful, but their position can be moved by severe gales and checks by land fixes are vital. Even with an experienced navigator, the captain must be able to maintain a separate safety plot in his head.

The ship had to be docked for repairs to the starboard outer shaft and the Captain had to face a Court Martial. He was found guilty of hazarding his ship and I, and my Commander-in-Chief, Admiral Sir William O'Brien, were satisfied with the penalty: a severe reprimand. There were calls from the Second Sea Lord for him to be dismissed his ship, but these were strongly resisted and the subsequent record of the ship proved this to have been right.

Ian Robertson had a widowed mother with whom he kept in regular touch and he felt she should hear first from him about his problem before reading it in the press. He told her he was to face a Court Martial and in answer to her question, why, he said, 'Well, it was all to do with this buoy'.

'Oh my God,' she exclaimed, 'not that!' The Americans are fortunate with their different pronunciation.

HMS *Ark Royal*

During a minor NATO exercise in the Mediterranean when I was in the shore headquarters, *Ark Royal,* (Captain Ray Lygo) with a small screen of frigates was operating to the west of Malta with the customary attendant Russian destroyer listening and watching. These 'spies' could usually be depended upon to keep safely out of the way and it was accepted that the NATO operating signals were no secret to them. However, on this occasion, during night operations with a Phantom in full after-burner ready to launch from the port catapult, the Russian cut right across the ship's bow.

A collision was unavoidable, but the captain's immediate actions avoided what could have been a complete loss of the Russian ship. By going full astern the impact on the destroyer was well aft on the port side, and it rolled steeply away before recovering. *Ark Royal* was by this time nearly stopped, as was the destroyer.

A boat lowered by *Ark Royal* with a Russian-speaking officer on board assisted in the rescue of a number of Russian sailors who had been thrown into the water by the impact. The Russian captain refused further assistance and steamed slowly away.

The usual diplomatic messages passed between London and Moscow and, while no apology was received, neither was there a complaint. As far as subsequent intelligence sources were able to tell the name of the Commanding Officer of the destroyer simply disappeared from their Navy List and we presumed he was gulag-bound. There were suggestions that a Board of Enquiry should be convened and even a Court Martial. I resisted strongly. The events were crystal clear and the action taken was absolutely correct. I was supported by the Commander-in-Chief and the matter ended there.

Amphibious Ships

The amphibious ships were as busy as the carriers and the Royal Marine Commandos seldom deployed at sea without being joined by a unit of the Royal Netherlands Marines, and invariably their Commandant-in-Chief, the Prince of the Netherlands, Prince Bernhard, took the opportunity to join them.

Another regular visitor was the Commander-in-Chief Allied Forces Northern Europe, General Sir Walter Walker, based outside Oslo. A Gurkha, he had a tremendous admiration for the Commando squadrons which had been working in close support of his troops in Burma. Walker remembered all the Naval squadron commanders personally and always asked about them whenever we met. He could never understand why they had not all been promoted.

The opportunity to join the amphibious ships on foreign visits seldom arose, but the Fleet Commander requested that HMS *Fearless*, Captain Simon Cassels, should lead a squadron of ships on a visit to Bordeaux and Flag level representation was appropriate. The visit was marking the 25th anniversary of the twinning of the city of Bristol with Bordeaux, the two having been at either end of the wine business for nearly 600 years. In fact one early use of the Navy had been in protecting the ships in transit between the two cities. The success of the visit owed much to the efforts of the Consul General, Keith Butler, an old friend from Naples, who was a tower of strength.

At this time M Jacques Chaban-Delmas was both Prime Minister of France and Mayor of Bordeaux and hosted a splendid lunch at the Mairie for senior ship's officers and the Mayor of Bristol and her senior aides. It was my duty to speak in reply to the toast to Her Majesty the Queen and I made sure I gave priority to my host's position as Mayor of Bordeaux. Captain Peter Branson, our Naval Attaché in Paris, was a great asset throughout.

A visit to Bordeaux cannot pass without mention of claret and it was a member of the family Achille Faux, owners of the famous Beychevelle vineyard in the Pauillac region, who was to be the guest of honour in his capacity as the member of the French parliament for the Gironde and a member of the Cabinet, at the dinner I gave in *Fearless*.

My Flag Lieutenant, Peter Tuke, had discovered at a late stage that Madame Achille Faux and her husband were not operating in tandem. He apparently had other interests in Paris where he spent most of his time and another lady had to be found in short order to balance the numbers. Peter was astute enough to persuade a charming young lady, the daughter of one of the major Bristol wine importers, to take the vacant chair. She was a great hit with the guest of honour who pursued her round the ship, but fortunately he was satisfied with *la chasse* and made no attempt at a kill. It was, however, a helpful introduction to a great château.

Operational Readiness Inspections were carried out on both the amphibious ships. One was held off the Malaysian coast and the other off the Danish coast. One was well up to standard, but the other put in a poor showing due to the Captain's semi-detached attitude. I was unable to recommend him for another command and as he had been selected for fast-track promotion (of which I was rightly not aware) this caused a stir. However, there was plenty of collateral support for my judgement.

What Next?

I had just completed two years in command of all the most important surface ships in the Fleet which attracted the majority of escorts and support ships. This was to be *Eagle's* last commission, *Hermes* was nearing her end and *Ark Royal* had little more than two years to run.

For the Fleet Air Arm aircrew the future looked uncertain, although morale was immensely high. The growing proportion of RAF officers now appearing in the fixed-wing squadrons heralded the impending handover of all the Phantoms and Buccaneers to the RAF. Nevertheless, I was optimistic about the future, confident the Harrier would arrive and also the new ships in building.

Throughout this period I had been privileged to serve with outstanding officers and men. They were devoting their lives to a task in which they believed and they genuinely seldom bothered to count the cost. They showed tremendous character and steadfastness under pressures which never seemed to ease up either in their ship's programmes or the effect on their families.

My saddest moment came with the news that Admiral Le Fanu had lost his battle with leukaemia. He had completed his time as First Sea Lord and was nominated as Chief of the Defence Staff, an appointment he would never take up as the cancer ran its course. Blood transfusions became more and more frequent ('oil changes' he called them) until the end. Kirstie and I attended his memorial service in Westminster Abbey to say a sad farewell to my old mentor and one of the all-time great naval officers. He had played as important a role in Whitehall as he had at sea.

We had a double blow that day as Kirstie's father died during the morning and we heard the news after we returned from Westminster Abbey.

FLAG OFFICER NAVAL AIR COMMAND (FONAC)

I was delighted to be back in Somerset. The tasks undertaken by the old Flying Training Command and Flag Officer Air (Home) had now been taken over by the Flag Officer Naval Air Command (FONAC) to form a single entity and the Headquarters had moved from Lee-on-Solent to the Royal Naval Air Station at Yeovilton.

The Air Stations at Brawdy and Ford had been closed, but Lossiemouth (Captain Duncan Lang) was still firing on all cylinders despite preparation for the hand-over, including the Buccaneers, to the RAF. Lee-on-Solent would become a technical training establishment.

Yeovilton (Captain Keith Leppard) housed the Vixen and Phantom squadrons and the Commando helicopters and was still a busy and thriving air station which allowed the staff to stay in close touch with day-to-day operations. The staff now included the whole engineering team, headed by Rear Admiral Rennie Cruddas, who was responsible for the Air Repair Yards at Lee-on-Solent and Belfast (Sydenham) and the Fleet Air Arm Air Accident Investigation Group.

The Air Station at Culdrose, (Captain John Robathan) near Helston in Cornwall, was the home of all the Anti-Submarine helicopter training, the parent station for the front-line squadrons and everything to do with AEW. It was extremely busy and its future secure, as was the helicopter station at Portland which trained and parented the small ship flights.

The Air Repair Yards were civilian establishments, but, unlike the dockyards, the executive management was in uniform. When I made my first visit to the Repair Yard at Sydenham (Captain Monk) the

144

problems in Northern Ireland were in their infancy, but the tension was evident. It happened that at this time my soldier godson, Jamie Balfour, was stationed in Belfast. He invited me to accompany him on one of his night patrols. I did not volunteer for another.

The Fleet Air Arm Museum

Very early on I was faced with a crisis at the FAA Museum. Funds were running out and aircraft which should have been on display were deteriorating on open hard standings outside the single hangar. I called a meeting of the trustees. Urgent action was required. We could either go on letting things fall apart or commit ourselves, and our successors, to creating something of which the FAA could really be proud.

There was no hesitation; unanimously we agreed to do whatever was necessary and in doing so we fully understood that nothing could be done without money. How to start? Commander White, on my staff and with many other duties, was the nominal 'museum' man and said he knew someone who was reputed to be a professional fund raiser. This was Hereward Philips, who soon appeared before us and accepted the task. His fee would be seven hundred pounds and we had just over a thousand pounds in the kitty. We made a deal.

Philips was quick to make it clear money cannot be raised from charitable foundations unless there are assets. We had assets, some in the hangar, some in the open. 'Do you own the hangar?' he asked. Of course we didn't, it belonged to the Admiralty, or, more accurately, it is used by the Admiralty but it is owned by the Property Services Agency (PSA) like the Royal Palaces. 'Can you get a lease?' was his next question. 'You will need twenty-one years at least.'

I called the Permanent Secretary at the PSA anticipating a mild rebuff if not outright disbelief, to be greeted with every understanding of my problem and a proposal for the inclusion of more than one hangar as 'I am sure you will want to expand the Museum in due course'. I was not surprised to learn that the civil servant concerned was none other than John Cuckney, now Lord Cuckney, a Lazard Brothers Director on secondment to the Ministry.

So much for the lease. Now for the money. Who would be the Patron of the appeal. Prince Philip perhaps? I called Rupert Nevill, his Private Secretary, who explained that members of the Royal Family do not

145

lend their names to fund raising, the one exception having been when Her Majesty sponsored the appeal for the restoration of Westminster Abbey.

'But,' he said, 'Prince Philip might well agree to be Patron of the Museum itself during the appeal period, say for two years. Then you can put his name on your letter head.' And so he did.

Admiral of the Fleet Sir Caspar John became Patron of the Appeal, having commented that this (1973, the height of the oil crisis, soaring prices and financial uncertainty) was a 'bloody stupid time to try and raise money'. We enlisted a string of well known if only temporary ex-FAA pilots such as Ralph Richardson and Laurence Olivier, and many others who had served in the Navy during the war, like Kenneth Moore, to add to the sponsoring list, and Hereward Philips went on the hunt.

This activity coincided with my closer involvement with the White Ensign Association which had been formed by Commander Charles Lamb, a distinguished ex-FAA pilot, when the Navy had to face its first real reductions in the aftermath of the Korean War. This called for the numbers of officers and men to be radically reduced and, if this could not be achieved by voluntary resignations, cuts would have to be imposed: shades of the Geddes Axe. This had been imposed after the First World War by a committee chaired by Lord Geddes and led to large numbers of officers and men leaving the services with small pensions which were in many cases commuted, the cash sums often being squandered on impractical business ventures.

Charles Lamb's vision was that an association should be formed which would advise those forced to leave on how to handle their funds and guide them in any ventures they proposed to undertake. The Navy at this time had a large constituency in the City and financial institutions, and indeed in business on their own account, who had served in the Navy during the war or later and Lamb had little difficulty in recruiting a team to form the backbone of the Association.

Lamb enjoyed the active backing of Lord Mountbatten and the Admiralty Board and he called on me to help in one of his fund-raising ventures. He had been offered the final pre-opening performance of a new play, *The Unknown Soldier and his Wife*, starring Peter Ustinov at the New London Theatre: he had persuaded the great and the good to attend and the entire proceeds would accrue to the Association.

He had confidently expected to be able to open the whole performance with a fanfare and musical introduction by a band of the Royal Marines. What he had not appreciated was that on 4 January, the date of the performance, the whole of the Navy and Marines, other than duty crews, would be on leave, including all the RM bandsmen. As FONAC enjoyed the privilege of having a small RM Band, could I not as a special favour bring the FAA to the rescue? My band rose happily to the occasion.

Kirstie and I were invited to what was a splendid occasion and joined a dinner afterwards given by one of the Association members, Donald Gosling, who had himself served in HMS *Leander* as a signalman in 1946. I took the opportunity to tell him about the Museum and invited him to visit. So began the involvement of the Museum's greatest single benefactor.

We had drawn up plans for the first stage of the development and received permission to incorporate an adjacent hangar. Putting them together and building across the space between would more than double our floor area and accommodate many of the vintage aircraft currently in the open air. Grand plans for a library and research facilities would have to wait.

Funds or promises of funds were slow to come in. These were times of high inflation, and estimates for the work were only valid for a few weeks. We desperately needed enough funds covenanted to allow us to sign up a contractor before his current estimate disappeared off the top of our scale. Fortunately Donald Gosling came to the rescue and arranged for the required amount to be underwritten. This permitted signature of the contract at the current price, while time was taken to raise the permanent funds.

What happened afterwards is history. The Museum is greatly expanded and has gained formal national status. It has some remarkable interactive displays, including a large-scale flight deck, and has prospered financially. It also houses the first development Concorde to be built, flown in at the end of its life by the first Test Pilot, Brian Trubshaw, and 'batted' onto the runway. Donald Gosling continued to make exceptionally generous donations over the years and served as a trustee for more than a quarter of a century.

Michael Cobham, Chairman of Flight Refuelling, lived not far from Yeovil and was a good friend. When staying with us one weekend he showed great interest in the Museum and became a major benefactor and trustee. The land on which the large restoration hanger, now called Cobham Hall, is sited was donated by him.

Fleet Air Arm Field Gun Crew

The Field Gun Competition, almost the only truly competitive activity in the Royal Tournament, was fiercely competed by four crews, originally from the three Naval Barracks at Chatham, Portsmouth and Devonport, and the FAA. The closure of Chatham reduced the participants to three and, while the Royal Marines took part for some years, the numbers were back to three when I arrived on the scene.

Crew training was extremely rigorous and only the very fittest and strongest survived. It was customary for the Admiral to attend training sessions at various stages and at one such occasion I met a Mr Bill Regan, a close follower of the squad. He had been a Marine himself and now ran a highly successful building company in the south-east called Globe Construction. He suggested that a football match between the FAA and his Globe Construction team which played in the local league might be staged as a benefit match. This was played on a field at Littlehampton and at half time Bill had arranged to fly in Bobby Moore by helicopter. He and Moore had both been young players at West Ham many years before.

I subsequently invited Bill and his wife to Yeovilton and introduced them to the Museum. He soon became another enthusiast and generous benefactor over the years, even after he had emigrated to the USA.

RNAS Lossiemouth

Handing over Lossiemouth to the RAF was a particularly painful duty and I invited Admiral of the Fleet Sir Caspar John – he was the Commanding Officer there in 1947-48 – to come with me. It was undoubtedly one of the best bases in the UK and we hated to see it go, but not before we had given a dinner for Sir Caspar and I had rescued 'the' bed and brought it to the residence.

This large silver double bed had come from the old Royal Yacht *Victoria and Albert* and it was said to have hosted the conception of more than a few Royals and half-Royals. Captain Percy Gick, who was commanding Lossiemouth at the time, was determined it should stay with the Navy and was able to arrange for the bed to be 'taken on charge' as a naval store item and loaned to the captain's house. I was equally determined it should not be handed over to the RAF!

I had acquired an attractive property, Eyewell House, as the new Admiral's residence at Yeovilton. The bed always generated comment from guests and they felt it a should have had its own visitors book. Lord Mountbatten particularly appreciated sleeping 'with an old friend!'

Staff and Domestic Issues

No Flag Officer can be effective without an efficient Chief of Staff and I was well supported by the unflappable Captain Don Morison. He played a huge part in helping the FAA to maintain its normal high spirits and exceptionally high operational standards, despite the prevailing climate of retrenchment. Flying trophies were competed for keenly and I was regularly making awards for outstanding performance.

I flew regularly, but always with my Flag Lieutenant, first Miles Freeman and then Neville Featherstone – just in case! Sadly some accidents are inevitable, but the most tragic was the loss of the Commander(Air), Simon Idiens, in a Phantom somewhere over the Bristol Channel. He had been an outstanding Sea Vixen commanding officer, star of the Navy's Cresta team and leader of 'Simon's Circus' aerobatic display team. He had recently married a wonderful girl who had already lost three husbands in air accidents. One of the daughters of these earlier marriages is now an exceptionally successful film star, Kristen Scott Thomas.

There was a small household staff, a well-knit team led by the formidable Chief Cook, Mr Amos, with Acting Petty Officer Rice as the senior steward. Rice had first joined me in *Eagle* as a good steward with a drink problem – probably inevitable in a Scot born on Islay with seven distilleries within its small boundary. Having dried out, he remained with me as a leading steward when I was the carrier admiral, came on all my travels by air, in helicopters, on jackstays and in small boats. He regretted only that he had never made a catapult launch.

My wife was pregnant when we arrived and this was expected to be something of a shock to the staff after my childless and dogless predecessor. However, it happened that not only was the Chief Cook's wife also pregnant but so too were the wives of the assistant cook and the Royal Marine driver. We were to have a complete zoo!

I was sad to leave the command after no more than fifteen months but not unhappy to be returning to the Ministry of Defence. Many officers thoroughly disliked serving in Whitehall, but only there was the future of the Service and its equipment determined. While no one liked exchanging a cockpit for a mahogany desk these had to be driven by those with recent operational experience. That I was elected a Fellow of the Royal Aeronautical Society at that time had no particular relevance.

ADMIRALTY BOARD MEMBER

Vice Chief of the Naval Staff (VCNS)

Before taking up my appointment I was sent to South Africa to represent the United Kingdom at the formal opening of a new Maritime Control Centre for the monitoring of the heavy shipping traffic passing the Cape, a facility which would be particularly valuable should there be further conflict at sea. The political situation being what it was, only five countries accepted the invitation to attend. Apart from the UK, France, Portugal, Iran and Israel sent representatives – all naval.

Our Ambassador, Sir James Bottomley, who had a distinguished war as a tank officer and had been badly wounded, kindly gave me a bed and Lady Bottomley was a mine of information about South Africa, which she loved but confessed that her conscience would never have allowed her to visit of her own free will.

The Naval Adviser was Commodore Oz Cecil, a splendid character in the best Salisbury tradition, who entered wholeheartedly into the local scene and owned a half share in a rather good horse which won the Queen's Plate on the biggest racing day of the season. Lady Bottomley was required to make the presentation which she told me she did not enjoy.

It was interesting to talk directly with the Minister of Defence and to meet 'Boozey' Bierman again, who was now the Chief of Naval

Staff, but sad to see their focus entirely directed towards France since the UK's refusal to supply ships and aircraft.

Whitehall

When I took over from Terry Lewin in September 1973 Edward Heath was Prime Minister, Lord Carrington Secretary of State for Defence and Ian Gilmour the Minister of State for Defence Procurement. There was every sign that this administration was in terminal decline.

To deal with the rapidly deteriorating coal and energy situation the Prime Minister had formed a new Department of Energy and asked Peter Carrington to take it on in addition to his duties at Defence. However, much more was required than Carrington's renowned charm to sort this one out; cold steel was needed. There was runaway inflation and no let up on the industrial relations front. In November a state of emergency was declared and the nation went onto a three-day week with electricity cuts. Candles were the order of the day in the Ministry of Defence.

Early in the New Year the miners' union appeared ready for a general strike in a direct challenge to the Government, to which Mr Heath would surely have had to respond by calling an election, giving the electorate another chance to decide who they wanted to govern.

Although a bright spot had been the end of the so-called Cod War, the collapsing economy was a bleak background for the Navy's quest to retain a measure of organic air capability in the fleet by operating Sea Harriers, radar-equipped, in the fighter version, from the new 'Command Ships', previously known as through-deck cruisers.

Field Marshal Sir Michael Carver had just taken over as Chief of the Defence Staff. He had something of a reputation as an intellectual which the military normally appear to avoid effortlessly. General Sir Peter Hunt was Chief of the General Staff and when I called on him confessed he had never served in Whitehall before. He was a breath of fresh air and always hugely supportive of strong inter-service co-operation.

The First Sea Lord and Chief of Naval Staff (CNS) was Admiral Sir Michael Pollock who I knew only by reputation but whose son had served with me in *Eagle* as an acting Sub-Lieutenant and at that time was having doubts about his future. He subsequently became a helicopter pilot and a squadron commander.

A Flag Officer is entitled to ask for a particular officer to serve as his secretary and I had one such officer in mind as soon as I was promoted, but the necessary criteria could not be met until now. Mike Hudson and I had served together on the Controller's staff some ten years earlier when he was the Assistant Secretary. He had moved effortlessly into the Whitehall scene and showed an immediate grasp of all priorities, procedures and mousetraps with which these corridors were strewn. I said to myself then, 'If I ever get to Board level, Mike is the man to be my secretary'. Now a commander, he accepted my invitation and joined in the acting rank of captain.

The Vice Chief, as the name implies, is the First Sea Lord and Chief of Naval Staff's immediate deputy and, although always the most junior naval member of the Board of Admiralty, in the absence of the First Sea Lord, has to represent him at all times. This included attending the Chiefs of Staff Committee meetings and also meetings of the Defence and Overseas Policy Committee (DOPC) of the Cabinet held at No 10 with the Prime Minister in the chair, not to mention waiting for hours on a platform at Victoria station as member of a welcoming party for visiting Heads of State.

In his own right the VCNS was responsible for all naval and joint operations and superintendence of the whole of the naval staff, which included plans and policy as well as ship, weapons and air requirements.

The Commander-in-Chief Fleet, Commandant Royal Marines and the Director of Naval Intelligence were responsible to me and I kept in very close touch with all of them.

I also had an interest in the activities of the Royal Naval Scientific Service (RNSS), headed by the Chief Scientific Adviser, who was also a member of the Admiralty Board. The RNSS were full-time civil servants and had enjoyed considerable success in certain areas, particularly in underwater technology where there was little commercial competition, and in some radar applications. But those who had succeeded in these areas often found it difficult to accept change and work could still be found going on in an area which was no longer required.

As FONAC I had been in close touch with Terry Lewin on the two major issues of the time, the new capital ships which had emerged from the Future Fleet Working Party and the battle to retain some organic air defence by equipping the FAA with a naval version of the Harrier. The ships were under construction and Lewin had kept the Harrier issue alive, but there were still many in Whitehall and in parliament who were determined that the Navy should never again be allowed to compete with the RAF in fixed-wing aircraft. Not everyone appreciated that we were rather good at it and had in fact produced both the aircraft which were now the backbone of the RAF front line.

Lewin had been successful in bringing surface-to-surface missiles into the fleet and working on what became known as the offshore tapestry, protecting the wealth in and under the nation's territorial waters.

My colleagues on the Vice Chief circuit were Lieutenant General David Fraser, with a reputation in the Army as a razor-sharp operator, and Air Marshal Ruthven (Gerry) Wade, a fine pilot who seemed less than happy in Whitehall. His boss, Air Chief Marshal Sir Denis Spotswood (CAS), when I called on him, made it clear the RAF had never recovered from the blow of losing Skybolt and thus handing over to the Navy responsibility for the nation's deterrent.

The Vice Chief, on behalf of the CNS, is responsible for the operational readiness of the Fleet and acts as Co-Chairman, with the Controller of the Navy, of the Fleet Requirements Committee (FRC) where the future shape of the Fleet is hammered out, balancing the dreams of the operational staff and the realities of the development process against the inevitable limitation of funds. Having supported the Controller in this forum some nine years before and been, as head of a Naval Staff division, a member of the committee for two years, I found little had changed in the last five. This cumbersome procurement cycle was as lively and at the same time more tedious than ever.

Rightly, the Naval Staff strived to keep the Fleet able to match the present and projected capability of the Soviet bloc, enthusiastically supported by industry only too keen to develop the next generation of ships, aircraft and weapons. This too often leads to disappointment and delay in delivery times and years of poor serviceability on initial introduction.

Then comes the difficult choice of buying off the shelf or waiting while a new system is developed in the UK with all the emotions which attach to national employment and the need to maintain long-term technical and industrial capability. My immediate task was to procure a submarine-launched anti-surface ship missile while satisfying these conflicting demands.

Very soon I confirmed the feelings I had entertained when DNAW that we were hugely overstaffed in Whitehall and this was due largely to the intensity of the inter-service battle for shares of the overall defence budget. No one seemed to care how much this all cost. Every issue was staffed in the greatest detail and at numerous levels by each service and there were huge economies to be made in Whitehall itself –I thought perhaps 20% – and also reductions outside where there was much nugatory effort and expense in providing support to the Whitehall staffers.

A condition of any reduction was of course that these cuts must be taken equally by each service and that procedures must be simplified. I did not wish to reduce our staff work to the level of our continental partners but I did envy them the small teams they worked with compared with ours. The First Sea Lord, however, made it clear that this was not the time to bring this issue to the fore.

Soon after I arrived the First Sea Lord announced he was off on an official visit to Chile. This had been postponed on a number of occasions and now had to go ahead despite there being a crucial Chief's meeting concerning the Harrier which he would miss. 'Actually VCNS,' he said, 'you are probably better able to handle this than me. Arguing air matters face to face with the CAS.'

I was carefully and rather intensely briefed by a Naval Staff team headed by the Assistant Chief of Naval Staff, at that time Rear Admiral Henry Leach, who seemed surprised at the level of my own knowledge about the whole subject. However, quite rightly, this did not stop him giving me a 'line to take' at the meeting. In thanking him I was able to make one or two light-hearted comments which released some pent-up emotion among those present.

The subsequent Chiefs of Staff meeting was at times somewhat heated and certain remarks concerning the Navy's competence to procure aircraft allowed me to put the historical facts on the table. The need for organic air was again challenged and it was not difficult to deal with those old canards; 'Surely you can rely on shore-based cover or the USN carriers because we will no longer operate outside NATO'. Ian Gilmour, who was in the chair, was not a decision-maker and the matter may have been progressed but it was not closed and the Naval requirement remained firmly on the table.

A New Administration

This turned out to be the last year of the Heath government. The Arab-Israeli war had quadrupled the price of oil and put an end to the low energy costs which had propelled the western economies for the past twenty-five years and was about to change the economic balance for good.

The Government was perceived to be following many policies introduced by Wilson. Indeed by not proceeding with privatization and by nationalizing Upper Clyde Shipbuilders and Rolls Royce it was clearly moving in the opposite direction. The PM appeared to be virtually at war with the miners at a time when coal production could have helped to balance the oil price rise, and the incomes policy was in shreds.

Much energy had been expended on entry to the European Union and the Government had got themselves into a hopeless mess with the Trade Unions and the CBI, both of whom expected to be and often were consulted about policy. It was the start of the 'Who Governs?' question. Heath appealed to the electorate and they showed him the door, but not before he had tried and failed to set up a form of national Government involving the Liberal Party in the mix.

On 17 March 1974 it was Mr Heath who had to respond to the Queen's speech as leader of the Opposition. Divorcing oneself from the collective mismanagement of the nation, in our own Ministry of Defence we could always depend on being well served and so we were by the incoming team. Roy Mason was appointed Secretary of State for Defence and John Gilbert Minister of State. Healey went to the Treasury. Unsurprisingly a new round of Defence Studies was announced.

In 1974 Admiral Sir Edward Ashmore, a communications specialist and Russian linguist with a reputation for being the Navy's answer to Carver, replaced Michael Pollock as First Sea Lord and Rear Admiral Peter Berger replaced Leach as ACNS. A veteran of the *Amethyst* on the Yangtze, he still carried bits of Chinese gunmetal in various parts of his anatomy.

Henry Leach, who had been replaced by Berger, was to have a relatively short run at sea and then come back as Vice-Chief of the Defence Staff. When he came to see me, he said he considered he had been sidelined. I could not agree. I told him the Vice-Chiefs were failing as a team, but they could, if properly led, take a huge load off the shoulders of their respective Chiefs. This should be a splendid chance to make a real name for himself. As a passing remark I said, 'Who knows? I might fall under a bus'. Little did we both know!

It was indeed a privilege to be a member of the Board of Admiralty and, although the Naval staff now worked in the main building of the Ministry of Defence, board meetings were still held in the Board Room of the Old Admiralty building. The room itself was much as it had been in Nelson's day, still equipped with the wind direction indicator (how fares the wind for France?) and decorated with a number of beautiful carvings by Grinling Gibbons. We sat at the original large table with a semi-circle cut out at one end allegedly to accommodate the ample form of a board member long ago. He must have been not only huge but sufficiently important to merit this carpentry. The atmosphere was such that our discussions were conducted with appropriate solemnity but never without good humour.

The Offshore Tapestry

Security of oil rigs in the North Sea and their protection against the possibility of hijack or even interference from the Soviet Union had become a live issue and, taken with the needs for fishery protection, Terry Lewin's early work on the 'offshore tapestry' was coming into sharp focus. These tasks could soon make heavy demands on scarce Fleet resources and the need for a specialized vessel to undertake them was gaining currency, but there was no money in the budget to provide them.

It was not long before Sir Eric Drake, Chairman of British Petroleum, appeared in Admiral Ashmore's office to demand that the Navy escort the latest and greatest BP oil rig on its journey from the builder's yard, under tow by tugs, to its chosen location in one of the more remote offshore oil fields in the North Sea. The First Sea Lord declined this 'request' on the grounds that it was not the duty of the Navy to escort a civil craft of whatever nature, a task which, if justified at all, should be carried out by a appropriate commercial craft.

Sir Eric hotly contested this, saying that Soviet electronic surveillance craft were constantly in the area and fully capable of interfering with the radio signals which activated the flooding valves which in turn righted the platform (platforms were always towed on their side) and then sank the legs to the seabed. Interference with this delicate operation would prove disastrous. The temperature was rising and an impasse appeared inevitable.

I was asked to join the meeting and the question was put to me. I suggested that the problem needed to be discussed by me and BP's Deputy Chairman, David Steel, and we would propose a solution within days. This was accepted.

It did not prove difficult. I said that while I entirely supported the First Sea Lord's position, I would try to ensure that there was a naval vessel in the vicinity at the critical time should a Soviet vessel be in the area and in a position to interfere. David happily agreed.

I discovered later that Sir Eric had come to this meeting fresh from three rounds with the Prime Minister who had tried to order Drake to give priority to the UK in distributing the reduced oil now available, (the Government still owning 51% of BP at that time) Drake having refused Heath's earlier request on the grounds that BP was a major international company, indeed supplying more fuel to Germany than the UK. Not to be, and be seen to be, allocating the rationed oil in strict proportion to normal consumption levels would do irreparable damage to BP's commercial standing in the world. Drake said he would comply with Heath's order only if he received a written instruction which he would make public immediately. Heath withdrew.

This incident focused my attention again on the question of an offshore protection vessel for the Navy and as the financial year was coming to a close I spotted a significant sum of money underspent. Monies are allocated to specific procurement projects over the term of the contract and allowance is made for some underspend which for one reason or another occurs almost always and the amount is a matter of judgement. The MoD was still financed at that time by money being voted on an annual basis and if not spent in the relevant year the money was forfeited.

157

The Permanent Under Secretary, who is responsible to the Treasury for the overall result, will always err on the side of caution in making this judgement so that his accounts never go into the red. This leads to some 'underspend' every year. This year it was more than most.

I called for ACNS and his planning team and put to them the proposal that we buy 'off the shelf' – essential to ensure the contract fell into the financial year – as many North Sea trawlers of about 600 tons for the money available. We could be sure of excellent sea-keeping capability, long endurance and low running costs. Trawling equipment would not be installed and the weight saved would be ample for fitting a Bofors gun and sophisticated communications. A splendid command for a young lieutenant, I enthused. The staff supported the concept and in all eight trawlers were purchased, named after famous castles, and served the North Sea Tapestry for over twenty years.

Another Defence Review

Within days of taking over, the new Labour administration demanded another 'root and branch' review of defence expenditure and the roles of the three services. The magic roundabout was to be started up yet again. Once more I found myself sitting on a number of single and tri-service working groups and a committee whose representative from the Treasury was one of the Assistant Permanent Secretaries, Leo Pliatzky.

I got to know Pliatzky quite well and we had a number of informal meetings when he gave me an important insight into Healey as Chancellor instead of Healey as Defence Minister. Pliatzky was a first generation immigrant from Eastern Europe and confessed to strong socialist views while disliking the lack of discipline which appeared to be part of the socialist culture in this country.

On the issue of budget cuts I said the Navy would not oppose cuts as such, but would try to take the fat out of the support and administrative structure and leave the fighting units alone. Also that there must be equality across the three services. I then went on to suggest the next steps which should see the adoption of a policy calling for weapon systems to be developed for theatre use rather than to meet single service needs.

Pliatzky complained that in the Treasury short-termism was

158

rampant. 'Let's reduce the budget today, no matter what it costs to-morrow.' He said he would welcome programme funding rather than annual allocations and agreed that instead of another defence review with the same limited objective of saving money by yet more cuts – more salami slicing – we should be looking at how to spend what we have more wisely and in terms of defence as a whole and not three apparently independent services. Healey would support this and Pliatzky assured me he still kept a beady eye on defence and personal contact with the new CDS, Field Marshal Carver.

Among the proposals made during this latest Defence Review were severe cuts in the size of the Army, who in turn suggested that instead it would be more economical to disband the Royal Marines. This was not one of the Army's initiatives but clearly driven by the Central Staff. There was some resentment at the high profile the Marines always appeared to achieve when they were often the first choice to respond to any emergency, while Army loyalties were stretched to breaking point by the disbanding or amalgamating of many famous and heroic regiments.

We felt keenly for them, but, as General Sir Ian Gourley, Commandant General, pointed out, the Marines were highly trained infantrymen who took their full share of duty in Northern Ireland, the Army was having trouble recruiting and disbanding the RM would produce no benefit to the Army. Men joined the Marines and if there were no Marines they wouldn't join at all. Furthermore, jointly with the Royal Netherlands Marines, with whom they had formed a close working relationship through many joint amphibious exercises, they provided the only European operational amphibious forces in NATO. The Navy view was that, if the Army wanted to save money and thus save some regiments, this should come from reducing the vast cost of stationing units in Germany.

Within the Navy all sorts of suggestions were made. The First Sea Lord claimed – he was right of course – that the Naval College at Greenwich cost as much to run as a frigate. Close it down – save one frigate. I happened to think that if the Navy was to be forced to give up Greenwich it would have to be very carefully handled, and a suit-able alternative use found which would prevent it becoming a office for the DHSS or falling into decay. Admiral Ashmore was not persuaded. I countered with a proposal to lay up the Royal Yacht – much the same cost. We agreed to abandon both ideas.

⋆   ⋆   ⋆

Apart from maintaining a realistic number of frigates and submarines at a building rate to sustain the Fleet at a size capable of meeting its commitments, and including completion of the Invincible class helicopter carriers, the Harrier was the main new project. Others we were anxious to keep in our budget were the development of a submarine-launched anti-surface ship missile and a reliable torpedo to replace the Mark 8 which had been in service since the First World War and without which the attack nuclear submarines were largely toothless. Further ahead was the replacement of the Sea King helicopter.

In the end the Navy retained its ship-building programme and received authority to maintain an attack submarine completion rate of about one every eighteen months and for the purchase of the US Navy's Sub-Harpoon missile for our submarines. There was no decision on the Sea King or the Sea Harrier. And no one liked the idea of bringing the Army back from Germany nor making an attack on the exorbitant cost of inter-service rivalry. The other services fared much the same, but all in all we felt our new Secretary of State had done well in the face of the formidable opposition of Denis Healey.

The Harrier saga ran on and on. We brought British Aerospace in and they gave an impressive display for the Secretary of State, and Admiral Ashmore was particularly persuasive with the new Chief of the Air Staff. The Vice Chief of the Air Staff, Ruthven Wade, and I had reached agreement that the RAF would not actively oppose the Navy over the Harrier at this point, but when Neil Cameron took over from Wade attitudes hardened.

Nevertheless CAS was a good as his word and refrained from objecting, while the Army came out strongly in support. Thus the Chiefs were finally able to agree and recommend to the Secretary of State that the Sea Harrier should be procured for the Royal Navy. Carver, although he had always considered the Harrier just another toy for the Navy, accepted the verdict and played his cards well so that finally the project was agreed.

Mr Mason insisted that he should personally announce the Government's decision and, so that there should be no visible conflict about the matter within the services, that he should be flanked by the two Vice-Chiefs at the press briefing. Neil Cameron found this a most uncomfortable situation. It was an historic moment for the Navy and

160

in the long term turned out to have been as good for the RAF as for anyone.

There remained the problem of AEW. Without AEW, which had been in service since 1952, the Fleet would be more naked than it had been for over twenty years. Technically it was feasible to put it in a helicopter, but it would be 'yet another project for the Navy' and at a time when the RAF were feeling particularly bruised. I was unhappy with the First Sea Lord's decision not to press an issue on which he judged he would not only lose (a judgement with which I sadly had to agree) but generate ill will at the time when he had played a splendid hand in the Harrier game and depended on much good will from his colleagues.

The Navy paid a big price for not having AEW in the Falklands war, regardless of the special pleading which attempted to play this down. Had the Argentine Air Force known they would have to penetrate an AEW screen their tactical advantage would have been much diminished. So strongly was the lack of radar cover felt that a crash programme was instituted to fit radar to the Sea Kings and a prototype was flying within weeks.

A New SACEUR

In late 1974 the US President decided to replace General Andrew Goodpaster as Supreme Allied Commander Europe [SACEUR]. His chosen candidate was General Alexander Haig and, as was customary in NATO, each of the appointments of the three Major NATO Commanders, SACEUR, SACLANT and ACCHAN, had to be approved by all nations. When the proposal reached the MoD there was more than a growl of disapproval. The Chief of Defence, Carver, who happened to be away on leave, felt that Haig, with no field experience above brigadier, was more politician than soldier, a general consensus of the military.

Admiral Ashmore, who was acting Chief in Carver's absence, remarked, 'I can't see why the soldiers are making such a fuss – he's not only called Haig but Alexander as well. What more do they want?'

Only General Sir John Mogg, Deputy SACEUR, got it right. He immediately flew to Washington to assure Haig that he would do all he could to ease the transition and this was the start of an enduring and effective partnership which served NATO extremely well.

As Haig modestly recalled, 'My nomination encountered some initial difficulty in the alliance from a small element who looked askance at my White House experience and wondered about my military experience'. Haig's appointment became effective on 15 December 1974.

In due course, when it was known that I would become Allied Commander-in-Chief Channel [ACCHAN], Vice Admiral Bush Bringle, the Commander-in-Chief US Naval Forces Europe, invited Kirstie and me to an informal dinner at his country home on the Wentworth Golf course estate at which the only other guests were Pat and Al Haig. It was a kind and thoughtful gesture and we both found the Haigs very easy and relaxed. He perhaps rather more than her.

Al was well into his stride and making a great impact in NATO where his well-honed political skills were much in evidence and Admiral Bringle told me that his impact on the US forces under his command had been even more timely. US forces in Europe had become barrack-bound, unfit and unprepared and Al was shaking them all to their foundations. This was having a ripple effect on the other continentals.

In the meantime we continued to work closely operationally with the USN in and outside the NATO area and not infrequently were able to support USN units with fuelling facilities at sea in distant waters. We also held operational staff talks chaired jointly by the VCNS and the VCNO, the Vice Chief of Naval Operations and my opposite number in the Pentagon, which helped to keep us mutually well informed in the many areas where we had particular interests.

Extramural Activities

As Vice-Chief one was essentially minding the shop for the First Sea Lord who, quite rightly, not only needed to represent the Navy but to been seen to do so and opportunities to get out and about were few. One of these occurred when Earl Mountbatten was invited to open a new wing at the National Maritime Museum at Greenwich. I was asked by the First Sea Lord to represent the Admiralty Board and Mountbatten asked me before the ceremony if I would give him a lift back to London after it was all over as he wanted to talk about a forthcoming Admiralty Board meeting.

As an Admiral of the Fleet, Mountbatten was not retired but on 'half pay' and entitled to see Admiralty Board papers but not to attend meetings. An item about uniform on the forthcoming agenda had caught his eye. The subject was the proposed introduction of a full dress uniform with tail coat for wear by Flag officers on ceremonial occasions. He asked me to inform the Board that in his view it was essential to extend the privilege of wearing this uniform to include Princes of the Royal Blood. Sensing my slight hesitation he asked, 'Do you want the Prince of Wales to be married in naval uniform or that of the Royal Regiment of Wales?'

I also represented the MoD on the Shipping Defence Advisory Committee and met most of the Chairmen of the major shipping lines and others who support the industry. This resulted in the first of my invitations to speak at major dinners in the Great Room at Grosvenor House, where the President of the General Council of British Shipping asked me to reply on behalf of the guests. The principal speaker having dealt with all the serious business, it was possible in reply to be rather more light-hearted. I found my splendid Mike Hudson always ready with a few well-drafted remarks and useful bon mots.

While facing more than a thousand diners in penguin suits may seem daunting, the amount of daunt depends on how well they have dined and particularly wined. Their mood also depends on how they have appreciated, or not, the words that have gone before. At the Oil Industry dinner I was warned that the mood could be very uncertain. The speaker, Mr Varley, Minister for Energy, who I thought was rather a good guy putting over a not very palatable message, was really savaged. Perhaps as a reaction they behaved well for me and fell about with delight at the jokes Mike Hudson had produced.

These two years had been demanding and rewarding in about equal measure. The hours were exceptionally long, but we lived in Dulwich and so family life could co-exist. I had celebrated a fiftieth birthday, the arrival of another daughter, Mhairi, and received a Knighthood from the Queen all in one year.

COMMANDER-IN-CHIEF FLEET

In September 1975, almost to the day two years after taking over from him as VCNS, I took over as Commander-in-Chief Fleet from

Admiral Lewin. The occupant of the post wore four 'hats', two national and two NATO. The principal national hat was as Commander of the whole of the seagoing Royal Navy worldwide and the other as the Polaris Force Commander comprising the national independent strategic nuclear deterrent submarines.

On the NATO side one hat was as the Allied Commander-in-Chief Channel (ACCHAN)which ranked as one of the three Major NATO Commanders (MNCs) alongside SACEUR and SACLANT, and the other hat as C-in-C Eastern Atlantic (CINCEASTLANT), a Major Subordinate Commander (MSC) under SACLANT.

There was a good deal of symmetry in these joint appointments because our naval forces were all committed to NATO in time of war and hence our national war plans were NATO war plans, and while NATO had war plans it had no assets of its own until assigned for war or for major NATO exercises.

The staffs were all co-located at Northwood which by comparison with other major NATO headquarters was of modest size. Nine of the fifteen NATO nations were represented and many of the Royal Naval officers were dual-'hatted' for sensible economic and efficiency reasons. Also alongside was the Air Officer Commanding 18 Group, (the old Coastal Command) Air Marshal Bob Freer, and his staff, who, while part of Strike Command of the RAF, were under my operational control. This worked well at all levels and proved very effective.

The whole NATO staff and the Fleet operations staff were accommodated in underground offices, the 'bunker', while the rest of the Fleet staff and the staff of 18 Group worked above ground. When at Northwood I spent the mornings in the bunker on NATO business but with an operational and intelligence briefing from Fleet staff to start off with. This took about an hour unless there were unusual events in train.

My personal staff was again headed by the redoubtable Mike Hudson, supported by two juniors, splitting the national from the NATO papers, and I had a Second Officer WRNS, Sue Winter, as my Personal Assistant. Amongst other duties she made up the guest lists for lunches at Admiralty House which were always given when I was in the Headquarters. The Flag Lieutenant, Jamie Miller, travelled everywhere with me, and usually Petty Officer Rice with all the kit. They were unfailing and I could not have operated without them.

Major Nato Commander

The ACCHAN Chief of Staff was always a Rear Admiral in the Royal Netherlands Navy, Pierre Besnard when I arrived, making ACCLANT the only fully European command in NATO, the others being United States appointees both as to the top men and their respective Chiefs of Staff.

There was also a small EASTLANT staff headed by an RN Commodore which handled this subordinate command's responsibility, one of which was the operational command of the Standing Naval Force Atlantic (STANAVFORLANT) which was continuously deployed on NATO affairs. The US, Canada, Holland, Germany, Norway and the UK were regular and permanent contributors of ships and occasionally joined by Portugal. Command rotated among the 'permanent' nations and in general the standard of operating was extremely high.

On a smaller scale the Channel command operated a multinational minesweeper flotilla run on the same lines which had been formed in 1973. These Standing Naval Forces were not just excellent for maintaining operational readiness but they ensured that common operating procedures became well known in every navy.

While I was very well acquainted with the national organization, settling into the NATO command involved several days' familiarization in Belgium at the NATO headquarters outside Brussels. Member nations were represented at ambassador level and had military and civilian staff officers up to four-star level on all of whom one was expected to call and get to know. Most important were the Secretary General (SecGen) and the Chairman of the Military Committee (CMC), Admiral of the Fleet Lord Hill-Norton, who was kind enough to have me to stay in his elegant quarters on most of my visits to Belgium.

As SecGen Joseph Luns was by this time almost an institution, having come to the appointment after serving as Foreign Secretary of the Netherlands for seventeen years. He was fluent in all the NATO languages and enjoyed talking to the troops of whichever country he might be visiting in their native tongue. He was perceptive, courteous and a great consensus builder. On the language front his only challenger was Sir John Killick, the British Ambassador, who spoke five languages, including Dutch and Russian, and could sing songs and crack jokes in all of them.

The SecGen, the CMC and the three MNCs formed an executive group which in fact drove the NATO alliance. We met once a month, taking it in turns to play host and when it was ACCHAN's turn the meeting was usually held in a ship positioned in Antwerp or once when Terry Lewin provided a nuclear submarine. I also held one at Northwood. This was at a time when terrorist threats were very real and about six months before the bomb attack on Al Haig. It was essential to have the Headquarters and Admiralty House heavily protected by Royal Marines inside and outside the perimeter which resulted in my Labrador flushing some two-legged game from the bushes. The meeting room had to be electronically swept and permanently manned before use.

In addition to calls at NATO, as ACCHAN I called on the King of Belgium and the Queen of the Netherlands. King Baudouin was much preoccupied with the problems facing a constitutional monarch, the predominance of the US at the higher levels of NATO and the importance of the Channel command in maintaining a truly European presence. He was very conscious of the frailty of Belgium, with its deep political and language divisions and six parliaments. I am sure I proved of little comfort to him.

In the Hague Queen Juliana was altogether more jolly and relaxed. She had invited Kirstie to accompany me and, a serious smoker herself, was delighted to discover that Kirstie also smoked. They both puffed contentedly while she assured me that NATO was the most wonderful peacekeeping organization ever devised and the Netherlands could not be a more staunch supporter. I was happy to inform her how much we appreciated the very close relations between our two navies and in particular that between our respective Royal Marines and the singular interest taken in them by Prince Bernhard who had visited his Marines in my flagship during a number of NATO amphibious exercises.

The French Navy was not committed to NATO but was still keen to participate in exercises. They were usually welcome, although, once de Gaulle had pulled France out of the Alliance in 1966, expelled all NATO staff from France and refused to commit forces, there seemed limited value in training those who could not be relied upon when needed.

Having surrendered to Germany in June 1940 and the Vichy Government thereafter becoming virtual collaborators, the French

166

had somehow managed to be treated as one of the victorious allies. They were enthusiastic members of NATO on formation but were not successful when it came to bidding for high positions in the NATO command structure where qualification required actual proven war experience. It was no great surprise when the French decided to pull out.

NATO became the longest lasting and most successful military alliance in history and fully achieved its aim of deterring another world war. For the fifteen countries to work together throughout this period called for patience, tolerance and huge doses of good will. Looking back, I am convinced it could not have accommodated the French.

I was fortunate to have as SACLANT a great character, Admiral Isaac Kidd, who I had known before when he was Chief of Naval Matériel in Washington. Ike was a big man in every way; a champion boxer in the Navy, the father of six and the husband of a delightfully trim blonde, he was a wonderful support and good friend.

As the national Commander-in-Chief Ike balanced his priorities with great skill and was a splendid team player in the NATO context both as provider of an enormously important strike capability to SACEUR and even more importantly of keeping the lines of reinforcement across the Atlantic open. We were very conscious that it was only by maintaining the ability to re-supply the ground forces in Europe rapidly and reliably that the use of tactical nuclear weapons could be avoided. It was clear that the quickest way to end up having to use nuclear weapons would be to run out of conventional ones. Hence the critical role of Channel Command in ensuring access to mainland Europe.

The most frequently asked question from visiting United States Senators and Congressmen was, 'Admiral, can you guarantee to keep the sea lines of communication open so we can re-enforce our boys?'

The answer was always the same. 'First, it is not whether I think it can be done but whether we, NATO collectively, have convinced the Soviets that we have the capability and that you gentleman have the political will to back us'.

Another question was, 'As some sort of balance in MAD (Mutual Assured Destruction) seems to have been achieved, how long do we have to keep this up?' We were in NATO's twenty-seventh year and my answer was, 'About another twenty-three years after which we think it will become impossible to hide a whole nation behind a wall.'

Indeed much of the focus of our forward planning in NATO was based on making reinforcement as rapid and secure as possible. This extended from special measures to unload ships in the event of destruction or blocking of major ports and even to the possibility of strengthening the floors of commercial aircraft in peacetime to provide a massive airlift for tanks and other very heavy equipment in time of emergency.

Haig was a very different character from Ike. Considered by many more a politician than a general, Al was a huge success in every capital, his close connections with the White House and Henry Kissinger being potent factors. Whenever I was in his office or he in mine, a long telephone call from Henry Kissinger was to be expected, seldom without some personal gossip tagged on the end.

As SACEUR Al generated a large number of initiatives to the extent that resistance to this perceived US push built up within the Brussels bureaucracy and he was astute enough to see the value of using my command as the 'lead' MNC. This gave my Dutch Chief of Staff the opportunity to 'corridor' the proposal in advance, give it a European flavour and collect support from a large proportion of the members before putting the case to the plenary session. Throughout, Haig paid the highest tribute to General Sir John Mogg, Deputy SACEUR, whose experience and ability were profoundly important.

Full NATO meetings were the most significant gatherings on the NATO calendar where the SecGen, Chairman of the Military Committee and the three MNCs headed the table with the Ministers of Defence, Chiefs of Defence, Ambassadors and Military Representatives of the nations seated in alphabetical order below.

Often issues became very lively and much time was devoted to encouraging nations to spend more on defence or at least to spend up to their promised levels. Joseph Luns was a master of this task, but on one occasion Denmark, while being cajoled into increasing its current minute proportion of government spending on defence by no more than a quarter per cent, protested that costs were rising to the point where it would be better to be red than dead. Mr Weber, the German Minister of Defence, came to Luns's support.

Weber, a loyal ex-miner from the Ruhr, and good buddy of our new Minister, Roy Mason, an equally loyal ex-miner from Yorkshire, admonished the Danish Minister with the words, 'You will always have to pay for an army. If you don't pay for your own army you will have to pay for the army of occupation. I know. We are doing it now!' he announced, no doubt with Berlin in mind.

On one occasion we had a visit from the President of the United States, Gerald Ford, who was accompanied by his Secretary of Defence, a young Donald Rumsfeld. They made the right noises but left no footprint.

Fleet C-in-C

In my national capacity I was equally fortunate to have as my Chief-of-Staff Vice Admiral Peter Berger who had been with me in Whitehall and was a deputy in whom I had complete confidence. He ran the show when I was away and never put a foot wrong.

With my fellow national Commanders-in-Chief, Air Chief Marshal Denis Smallwood, followed by Andrew Humphrey at Strike Command and General Roly Gibbs and then Edwin 'Dwin' Bramall at Land Forces UK, we formed a committee charged with defence of the UK itself. This met infrequently but had to make sure that plans for emergency evacuation of British nationals from various countries and countering civil unrest or clandestine infiltration and dealing with civil defence were kept up to date. The country had been woefully unprepared in 1938.

By this time the RN was sharing the task of maintaining a highly equipped nuclear submarine permanently off the Russian northern coast, tracking and identifying the noise and electronic profiles of all new Soviet surface and subsurface vessels. This involved a fifty-six-day patrol submerged in enemy waters and had a high stress rating. All our nuclears and those of the USN operated from west of Scotland bases and were escorted outbound through the narrow approaches to the open Atlantic waters where they could then 'lose' themselves. It was essential that they should not be detected and trailed on this outward passage and were screened astern by helicopters throughout this critical stage.

When my programme allowed I would join the returning patrol submarine as it approached the Clyde by being lowered in a strop from

169

a helicopter onto the upper casing and then go below to hear the captain's report at first hand and for my operation staff to make an initial tract chart inspection. There was then usually time to meet some of the crew and often someone who had served with me in surface ships.

Reporting to the C-in-C were three operational sea-going Flag Officers, one commanding all the big ships (FOCAS) and two surface flotilla admirals commanding the remainder of the national assets. In addition the Flag Officer Submarines (FOSM) ashore at Gosport and the Flag Officer Sea Training (FOST) at Portland completed the team. All these Flag Officers were rightly close to their units, while the Commander-in-Chief, many miles from the sea in his HQ at Northwood, suffered significantly from this separation.

On the domestic side we had as a family moved into Admiralty House, the official Residence, situated less than a mile from the headquarters. This was a change for the household staff as Terry Lewin before and Henry Leach after both ran the house as a mess, unaccompanied by family. This I felt was to under-utilize a great asset for bringing the large and diverse NATO and National staff more together and one which we were determined to exploit and enjoy.

We arrived with two very young children and had taken on a qualified and uniformed nanny, Caroline Denham-Smith, to make sure a nursery was run on appropriate lines and the children not spoilt by over-attentive sailors, however well-meaning. She was a splendid twenty-year-old straight out of training, daughter of a prosperous Norfolk farmer and ready for anything, but she needed her uniform to ensure her authority was respected. This worked well. She had an easy relationship with all the staff; some were in their first posting and no more than seventeen years old, often with much younger brothers and sisters and they found it very hard not to sneak into the nursery now and again. To this day there are those who still keep in touch with her.

Apart from the regular visits by commanding officers there were seemingly endless numbers of visitors of sufficient status to warrant a lunch, which became a daily fixture. Also we tried to ensure that all staff officers of the eight nations represented, and their wives, came to at least one function during their tour of duty. This may have seemed like a chore at times but in fact it was important and useful to be able to talk to more junior officers informally and away from the protocol which defined most operational meetings. Dinners were almost weekly events. The Chief Cook, Mr Amos, and Petty Officer Rice, who had both been with us in Somerset, re-joined us at Northwood and, with Petty Officer Welsh, set a fine example to the younger members of the household.

All officers appointed to command ships of the fleet were required to visit the HQ to meet the operations staff personally and to meet the C-in-C himself. This was something to which I attached great importance and whenever possible encouraged re-visits mid-appointment and required them to call on being relieved at the end of their command.

If married, their wives were included in the invitation, spending the day with my wife at Admiralty House and of course joining us for lunch. My PA would pass the names of lunch guests to the house by mid-morning and the list was sometimes enlivened by the occasional VIP or a new young commanding officer such as the Prince of Wales.

When officers about to take up their first command visited I would offer them a few words of wisdom but in the case of Prince Charles I suggested this would be unnecessary as I assumed his father and great uncle would have said more than enough.

'Absolutely not, sir,' he replied. 'They told me to listen to you.'

Many major exercises were carried out under NATO command but it was essential to carry out national exercises at every level in order to maintain basic standards. The most important of these was the major fleet exercise carried out in the Western Mediterranean every spring. Starting from Gibraltar, all available fleet units took part in exercises carefully planned to test and to stretch capabilities to the greatest possible extent. Tactical command was placed with two of the fleet Flag Officers and I spent much time in various ships.

It is never the number of exercises put in that matters, only what is put in to the exercises, and my staff ensured that the pressure was kept on in all the important areas. Inspections were stringent and I made my presence felt at all levels. It was not until many years later that I read in his memoirs that Admiral Ashmore had appointed me to the Fleet Command, describing me as a 'martinet' needed after the more emollient style of my predecessor. Was that my reputation? I was aware I drove hard and demanded high standards but I like to think there was lots of fun too.

RAF 18 Group were always involved in the major exercises, deploying Nimrod aircraft from the UK and I usually took passage with one of them to their forward airfields, Gibraltar in the case of the Spring Exercise. These exercises also offered the chance to take important civilians as well as senior politicians and civil servants to see the fleet in action. One of these, who was to become probably the greatest personal benefactor of naval charities, was Donald Gosling, who had helped me so much with the Fleet Air Arm Museum. On one occasion he came with me to the Mediterranean and returned to the UK from Gibraltar in a RAF Nimrod of 18 Group.

The aircraft captain invited me to join him in the cockpit for the last part of the journey and to make the landing at RAF St Mawgan in Cornwall. As we came in to land, the displaced co-pilot was sitting next to Don Gosling in the passenger compartment and was asked what he thought about having an admiral take his place. He did not know what to say and Don suggested 'Out fenders!'

I also tried to see at least part of important overseas deployments and took advantage of joining one of the amphibious ships, *Fearless*, working with the US Marines in the Guantanamo Bay area. I then took passage to Corpus Christi in Texas where so many of our FAA pilots had completed advanced flying training during both the Second World War and the Korean War. It was a pleasure to entertain the local US Naval Admiral on board but I asked to be excused from accepting return hospitality because great friends had extended an invitation to spend the weekend on their considerable ranch.

My wife had flown out for this visit and as it happened our hosts had left their ranch for their condominium in Vail, Colorado, for some skiing but had thoughtfully positioned their private jet at the Naval Air Station so that we could join them. My Flag Lieutenant and his US counterpart saw us off and Jamie reported a fantastic weekend; never before had a visiting foreign admiral been whisked off in a private jet. We returned by the same aircraft forty-eight hours later, not saddle sore but with different muscles well tested.

I was able to combine this visit with the arrival in San Diego of a flotilla under the command of Rear Admiral John Fieldhouse which was nearing the end of a nine-month round-the-world deployment.

Exercises with foreign and Commonwealth navies were carried out all the way, including a major joint RN/USN exercise off Hawaii, and terminating with exercises off the Californian coast. What made this deployment unique was the addition of a nuclear-powered submarine which gave a completely new dimension to all operations.

As there was a weekend in hand before being due in San Diego on the Monday morning we joined Ken and Kitty Wallace (Ken had now retired from the USN and was working near Huntingdon Beach) who had sailed their boat round through the Panama Canal from Florida. We were quickly signed on as crew and headed for Catalina Island, ending up the second night in a small bay at the northern end of the island. I admit I was somewhat concerned about meeting my arrival time in San Diego where I was aware I would be greeted with an honour guard by Admiral Bob Baldwin, a fellow CarDivCommander in the Strike Fleet and now Commander Naval Air Forces Pacific Fleet.

I need not have worried. Just as it was getting light I donned my full uniform and was rowed ashore by Ken in an eight-foot dinghy. As we neared the tiny jetty all I could see ashore was an enormous herd of buffalo grazing contentedly. Then I heard the familiar beat of a big Navy helicopter which swept down and skilfully manoeuvred its downwash to blow a path through the great beasts from the jetty to a point for a pick-up. I was soon on my way the the US Naval Base at San Diego where we touched down right on time. Bob Baldwin greeted me with, 'Congratulations John, you've managed to avoid getting buffalo shit on your shoes.'

Fieldhouse and his flotilla had clearly had a splendid deployment and performed impressively throughout. The USN particularly appreciated having a RN nuclear submarine with them and was generous in its praise. The week of shore leave was hugely enjoyed by the visitors.

When making a formal visit to the Commander-in-Chief of the German Fleet I decided to go by car from Brussels where I had been attending a full NATO meeting ending on a Friday and with a long weekend before I was due to arrive in Wilhelmshaven, flying my flag in HMS *Kent*. This allowed time for a private visit to Berlin where godson Balfour was now serving. My Royal Marine driver, Sergeant Shuttleworth, was quite excited at the prospect of driving up the corridor through East Germany and exchanging salutes with the Russian sentries.

Despite this being a private visit the General commanding in Berlin, Robin Redgrave, insisted on entertaining us at his spectacular Villa Lem on the Havel. With a huge orangery right at the water's edge and a swimming pool between it and the main house the whole atmosphere was 'Great Gatsby'. The General was a charming host and the absolute opposite of a grenade-touting field commander, but one of the few who spoke fluent German and was much respected.

My godson was a qualified East Zone guide and gave us a conducted tour through the checkpoint. The only condition imposed was that all service personnel had to be in uniform and the Russian guards seemed somewhat bemused by the presence of a full admiral.

The rest of the programme proceeded to time: the helicopter from *Kent* collected me from shore while the ship was still well out to sea and *Kent* secured alongside after the exchange of gun salutes. Admiral Zimmerman was an excellent host and was keen to show me how the German Navy managed to keep up its standards with such a high proportion of conscript sailors limited to twelve months' service.

Getting the Message Across

At Northwood I was endeavouring to spread the NATO and defence message more widely and decided to approach first the movers and shakers in a wide range of civilian activities, starting with major industries and professions. My method was to begin the evening with briefings in the underground NATO headquarters given by my Chief of Staff (Dutch), supported by Operations (US Navy), and land-based Air (RAF) to Chairmen and Chief Executives of industries and Director Generals or equivalent in professional bodies, legal, medical and accounting.

I would open the proceedings and handle questions at the end before we all retired to Admiralty House for dinner. There were twenty guests with me and the other three presenters as hosts and a lively debate ensued during the meal. The first guests came from my own friends who, having concluded the idea was sound, undertook to provide the guests for future dinners which subsequently took place about every six weeks. We all agreed that politicians and union leaders should be excluded.

After several dinners some of the wives asked if they could sit in on the presentation to which I was only too happy to agree and Kirstie would have a girls' dinner for them afterwards.

One of my original guests, the late Peter Simonis of Burmah Castrol, accepting that no politicians were invited, suggested I should meet the Leader of the Opposition privately. His company had employed Denis Thatcher for seventeen years and he had known Margaret as a company wife just as long. As it was a private occasion I drove my own car and pulled up at their house in Chelsea just before the Thatchers arrived in her official car.

Margaret and I shared a sofa and each chose a whisky before dinner. As our host came round with a refresher Margaret declined and when I accepted she rounded on me. 'One is quite enough for me before dinner,' she declared, 'and so it should be for you, Admiral, particularly as you are driving.' Well and truly hand-bagged!

Things loosened up over the meal and Margaret confided that her real problem lay in finding MPs in her party of the right calibre to become ministers. 'A company chairman can select from the whole world, I am limited to three hundred MPs none of whom I have selected in the first place.' It was an enjoyable evening, although Margaret was somewhat pre-occupied by having to make a speech in the House the next day as Anthony Eden had just died. She left soon after eleven and Denis stayed to put his feet up with the rest of the whisky into the early hours.

Later on I was persuaded to relent in regard to MPs and Harold Wilson, having handed the Premiership over to Jim Callaghan, was invited and a form of balance was struck by including a Tory backbencher and good supporter, Neville Trotter.

Wilson arrived straight from recording an interview with David Frost and well refreshed. When he attempted to lay the law down about the Soviets he met his match in the President of the International Rubber (as in making car tyres) Federation who not only spoke fluent Russian but knew a good deal more about the country than any politician could hope to.

As usual Kirstie was in the hall to greet all the guests on their way to dinner, but Wilson swept past her without so much as a nod. He made amends on departure by apologizing profusely and graciously, and she even found him easy to forgive. However, we did revert to the no politicians rule thereafter.

Gas Turbine Propulsion

When HMS *Sheffield*, the first of a new class of ship and propelled solely by Rolls Royce gas turbines, was on sea trials I invited the Chairman, then Sir Kenneth Keith, to spend a day at sea in her. He had an extremely tight schedule but by flying him down to Portsmouth in the evening by helicopter, spending a night in HMS *Kent* which was alongside in the dockyard and joining *Sheffield* in the Solent by fast motor boat the next morning, we were able to show him just what a revolution in marine propulsion had been achieved.

Keith was accompanied throughout by Don Pepper whom I had first met when he was running Rolls Royce and Associates making the vital cores for our submarine nuclear power plants in 1962. He had trained as an engineer in the Navy but had been invalided out soon after the war when TB swept through the fleet. In *Kent* I gave a dinner and then Keith turned in, using the admiral's cabin. About 0300 the ship burst into life with a serious fire in the sonar compartment about four decks below where we were sleeping. Access was through a hatch just outside our cabins. Keith emerged, all six foot four, in white silk pyjamas to enjoy some real live fire-fighting and dined out on the story for years to come.

The next day we had a rough boat ride out to *Sheffield* in the Solent, but she put on an impressive performance in quite heavy seas. The return to Portsmouth was by helicopter, each of us winched up from a lively deck.

HMS *Glasgow*

One of the happier occasions and quite different from the usual routines was an invitation from the Board of Admiralty addressed to my wife to launch a new missile ship, HMS *Glasgow*, building at Swan Hunters yard on the Tyne. This was particularly pleasing in that not only had I served in the previous *Glasgow* but Kirstie is a Scot.

At the same time the Controller asked me if I would stand in for him as the representative of the Admiralty, the 'owner'. So the assembled throng were treated to a double dose of the Treachers. Kirstie gave the traditional bottle of champagne a good thump and the ship slipped gently into the river.

This was the last ship to be built by Swan Hunter before the industry was nationalized and was a particularly emotional moment for Sir John Hunter himself. He was a charming host and made a very appropriate speech, followed by Kirstie and then by me. That is normally the limit of the speeches at launches but the Provost of Glasgow during the lunch asked John Hunter if he could say a few words and I was asked to agree.

The Provost was stocky and hunched, but gifted with the most powerful and sonorous voice, and a strong accent. He referred to my speech in which I had reflected on what a splendid thing it was that here within the shadow of Hadrian's Wall, built to keep out the dreaded Scots, the English had built another superb ship to carry the name of a great city and he went on to say how proud was his city and what a reception the city would provide to the ship and her crew on their first and all subsequent visits. He was true to his word.

It is customary for the lady who launches a ship to make a gift to the ship and Kirstie made a few suggestions to the first Captain, Robin Doe, who chose a pair of ship's decanters, one with an engraving of the first HMS *Glasgow* of the 17th century and the other of the last ship of the name. She had found drawings of the first ship at the Maritime Museum and of course there was no shortage of material on the last ship. Peter Dreiser, at that time the top copper wheel engraver in Europe, had agreed to do the work and she had chosen as the model for the decanters two splendid eighteenth century heavy cut-glass examples which she asked Cumbrian Glass to copy.

Sadly Cumbrian Glass failed to produce and Kirstie had to buy direct from Thomas Goode, only to have Peter Dreiser stumble and fall when delivering the finished engravings. With only weeks to go before commissioning the whole process had to be repeated, and completed, just in time.

Looking Ahead

By the end of 1976 I had served fifteen months as C-in-C in the best appointment in the Navy. It was time to think about the future. Should I go on until my services were no longer required or I should I now take pre-emptive action and put my new family first? In my current appointment I was barely able to make ends meet with the substantial overheads of running Admiralty House and paying for a full-time nanny.

I was fifty-two years old and could look forward to perhaps one more appointment in the Navy, although, unlike the other services, the Navy had no obligation to employ senior officers to the age of fifty-five. Captains after ten years and admirals remain in the service only so long as they are required for specific appointments. All the financial indications were that I should leave as soon as possible.

I, of course, discussed this fully with Kirstie and also took Mike Hudson into my confidence. When I first broached the subject with him he confessed that his thoughts were heading him in the same direction and he was actively studying by correspondence course to pass the qualifying examination for Company Secretary.

I finally made up my mind when I was in Colorado with the NATO Nuclear Power Group visiting the USAF Academy at Colorado Springs early in the new year. The USAF had put on a formation aerobatic display for our benefit and I felt a serious attack of déjà vu coming on. Could I even count up the number of these displays I had witnessed?

I had enjoyed every single appointment in the Navy, but did I really want to go back to Whitehall to play politics? Did I owe it to the Service to go on until it sent me packing?

Mike Hudson and I debated this long and often. My early departure would certainly shuffle the small pack of senior admirals, probably bring Henry Leach back in from the cold and perhaps upset some others. Certainly there was no shortage of talent. There wasn't a war on. Decision made. I would write to the First Sea Lord and say I did not wish to be considered for a further appointment.

There remained only the matter of when. I had been deeply involved with the staff in planning for the Queen's Silver Jubilee review of the Fleet to take place in the Solent in May. All the major decisions had been taken and the Admiralty Board had accepted my proposals as they stood. Should I now delay my departure until after the event? Surely that would be wrong; to host the great naval occasion and leave the next day.

The First Sea Lord was understanding, but tried to persuade me to wait until mid-year to see 'my' review through. I felt that now the decision had been made there should be no delay in its execution. I held to my request to go at the end of March and so it was. Little could any of us have imagined that twenty-five years later there would be no review to celebrate a Royal fifty years.

I attended the review as the guest of the White Ensign Association of which I was now a council member and was delighted to see all the well-laid plans being executed with the precision which was their due. It was a proud moment. Did I have regrets? Of course, but not for long.

Mike Hudson wanted to leave with me but agreed to stay on to see Henry Leach, who relieved me, through his time at Northwood. Afterwards Henry tried to take him to Whitehall, but Mike had, like me, made up his mind and quickly found a job with one of the major industry associations as their Secretary, only to be killed within a year on a street crossing. He was hit by an Army lorry with a learner driver at the wheel. A family tragedy and a terrible waste of a great talent.

I had been in naval uniform for nearly 35 years. It was time for a change.

7

CHANGE OF COURSE

THE FIRST OPPORTUNITY

While mulling over my decision to resign I knew I wanted to go into industry. I had been involved with research, development, contracting, the latest business management techniques and I was numerate. It was not my intention to sit behind a big mahogany desk with a fine job description and no authority. I wanted to find a hot seat and a hands-on position. I knew I did not want to work for the Government or any nationalized industry. I had sounded out a number of close friends with the hypothetical question about 'what if' and they were not encouraging.

They felt I was a bit too grand: difficult to place: would need a large supporting cast. I did not accept any of this but it made me realize that I might have left it too late. However, Sir Donald Gosling offered me a job at National Car Parks (NCP) as a Director and, more importantly, also as an executive. He was not entirely happy with the way the operational side of the company was being run and I was invited to study the organization and propose changes.

NCP was a quite remarkable joint partnership between Sir Donald and Mr Ronald Hobson. Throughout their business life they maintained complete trust in each other and differences of opinion were resolved quietly and quickly. Truly part of a diminishing group whose word was always their bond, they were supported by two devoted deputies, John Flack and Gordon Layton, the latter always being very helpful to me. I could not have asked for more.

My first weeks with the company took me all over the country and to nearly all the five hundred or so sites. I met the new employees and the old timers, including many who had served almost from the start:

180

some claimed never to have taken a holiday. What a giveaway in a cash business! I was escorted by the bright new young Operations Manager, Peter Bewsey, who was trying to get a handle on this sprawling enterprise and not finding it easy.

NCP is essentially a property company, the majority of whose properties are car parks either wholly owned, leased or managed and comparatively labour-intensive. The rest are commercial properties with long-term contracts needing only a small management staff. The car parks generated a high cash flow by engaging in very short-term contracts with car drivers. This demanded twenty-four-hour, three-hundred-and-sixty-five-days a year on-site management and cash control, the latter requiring both computer tracking and actual monitoring by security staff. It was not surprising that some of the younger, and one could say more enterprising, staff had plenty of time working out how a proportion of the cash coming into their pay booth could be diverted to other destinations.

The company had achieved a major success at Heathrow airport when the British Airports Authority (BAA)was being systematically cheated by its existing contractor who apparently had direct links with the Richardson gang, at that time running the Kray brothers a close second. The smooth operation of the car parks in the central area at Heathrow is essential to preserve the free flow of traffic without which all air operations would ultimately grind to a halt. For this reason the Airport Director felt unable to sack the existing operator.

NCP had recently engaged an ex-chief of the Metropolitan Police fraud squad as head of security and he had in turn recruited an excellent team of ex-CID men and women. Armed with this support for the NCP operations staff, an offer was made to the Chief Executive of BAA, Norman Payne, that from the moment the existing contractor was fired NCP would take over the operation with their own staff and there would be absolutely no interruption to the traffic flow. Having achieved this without a hitch, NCP remained as the operator at Heathrow for many years.

To maintain the growing off-airport parking operations at Heathrow I was able to have a local coach company acquired by NCP. This brought with it a licence to operate on the air side of the terminals together with contracts from a number of airlines. The operation was expanded rapidly to cover over thirty airlines and planning permission was won to convert an unused site near the Post House

Hotel into a fully fledged operating base, but only after going to appeal.

However, the operation of a number of car parks in close proximity is not the same as working with widely dispersed locations and there was plenty of room for improvement. Largely this was a case of upgrading the quality of regional and district managers and devolving greater responsibility to them. This was not something the existing top management was initially prepared to do. However, the improvement in results soon showed the way and by the time a Regional Manager was invited to sit on the local bench as a magistrate the status of the company in the community also enjoyed a revival.

This was a period when the Government, in attempting to control inflation, had introduced price and wage controls through the establishment of a Prices and Incomes Board with wide-ranging powers to examine business pricing and to impose limits. NCP, as a high-profile company, perceived by some to be taking advantage of a near monopoly position, was an obvious target. This resulted in being called to account before the Chairman, Ian Hay Davidson, a senior partner in the accountants, Arthur Andersen, seconded by them to run this quango.

John Pragnel, NCP's excellent Finance Director, and I were duly summoned and faced an aggressive attack on our pricing policy. However, Davidson and his staff had not done their homework and had failed to appreciate that, while NCP was the owner of many car parks, many more were managed on behalf of local authorities, who themselves set the tariffs. Indeed where NCP did own a location, it was careful to maintain parity. Davidson was attacking the wrong target and had to back off.

There were in addition a few car parks on the continent, mainly in Germany, owned by a joint venture company with Belgian partners, the De Clerq family, with whom I worked happily. The share in this venture was later sold to a company based in Holland.

Further afield, developers, keen to build and operate car parks over-seas, attempted to draw on the NCP name and experience. They came mostly from the Middle East and South America and all claimed to have access to funding and to possess the necessary government permits. It did not take long to discover the frailty of all these claims and realize that it was the NCP name which was needed to gain the

182

permits in the first place. The imposition of up-front fees soon put a stop to this waste of company time.

There was, however, an apparently bona-fide opportunity in Mexico City whence I was dispatched to investigate. The city certainly had a problem with all eight-lane approach roads turning into virtual car parks every morning as the traffic ground to a halt. If there was space on the street a fee had to be negotiated with the local 'bandito' guarding his patch and protecting cars from vandals.

There were a few multi-storey car parks, but customer parking was not allowed. In Mexico cars are either Detroit monsters or European compacts and no parking space was the right size, so jockeys were used to cram the cars in, usually two compacts to a space. The jockeys were all smartly dressed in khaki overalls, but received no pay, only tips from customers whose cars they retrieved.

Mexico was no place for NCP any more than New York City, where we flirted with taking over one operator. Examination of the books revealed a substantial levy off the gross revenue with no apparent return and in answer to our questions came the laconic reply, 'That's what you pay for operating in New York'. So much for protection.

Before leaving Mexico I received a message from London asking me to head for Hawaii. 'As you are so close' it began – I was in fact seven hours' flight time from Los Angeles and another five from Hawaii – 'Please have a look at a joint venture we were involved in with Bernard Delfont. He has pulled out but our man in Las Vegas thinks we could go it alone.'

Our man in Las Vegas turned out to be Charles Mather, an ex-Royal Marine Physical Training Instructor turned New Zealand night club bouncer, Maori blood brother and now Music Artist Agent in Las Vegas currently managing a successful Maori singer performing in Honolulu. I ran him to earth in Los Angeles and we flew together to Hawaii. He explained that the project was to build and operate a dinner theatre on the top level of the last development to be allowed in the heart of Honolulu and owned by the most prominent Hawaiian family.

Mather was hugely enthusiastic and already had in mind the show which he would bring over from Las Vegas – bigger and better than anything before. I was very doubtful, but with the help of family contacts in a major local corporation I was able to get a handle on the practicality of the whole project and an order of costs. Following detailed discussions with travel agents (this was very much a Japanese market) I was able to put together a business plan which looked workable. But who, I wondered, would run the show? Not Charles. Super agent he might be, but not chief executive material.

I reported to London. What did they have in mind? They came up with the name of someone who had managed a hotel for them in London and gone on to better things in the USA. They trusted him, which was vital. I got him on the phone.

'Sounds fantastic! When do I start?' he asked. I breathed a sigh of relief.

'Tomorrow,' I replied. There was a pause.

'There's one problem,' he said. 'I don't fly.'

London's reaction? 'We thought you might like to take it on.' I put the phone down slowly, made apologies and gave my thanks to all those who had spared me so much of their time and knowledge over the past weeks and flew home.

Press Council and Others

Both chairmen had made it clear that it would be useful experience for me to have directorships in other companies. My first offer came not from industry but from Lord Shawcross, Chairman of the Press Council. He invited me to replace Captain George Baldwin as one of the eighteen lay members of the council, the other eighteen coming from the press, owners, staff and unions.

The Press Council at that time was a non-statutory body to which members of the public could address complaints about the manner in which issues had been treated by the press. Legal costs would not be incurred by either side, the plaintiff agreeing not to litigate and the newspaper agreeing to answer questions openly. If the Council adjudicated against the newspaper, then the newspaper was bound to publish the findings in a prominent position the next day. This was an example of self-regulation which would be unworkable without good faith on both sides.

Complaints were initially heard by one of two sub-committees and their recommendation put to the full council for adjudication. The work (unpaid) took about one day a month and gave a fascinating and in many ways disturbing insight into the workings of the press.

184

There were a number of golden rules, not always respected. One was that a reporter should always keep notes of an interview, but, sadly, the reporter almost always had some feeble excuse for having lost the record. Another was that whoever was being interviewed should be informed of the name of the paper being represented but with one important exception. This was if the reporter judged that access and interview would not be given if press involvement was admitted, and if the matter under investigation was considered by the editor to be in the public interest as opposed to being of interest to the public, i.e. salacious or simply gossip.

This was a perfect recipe for disagreement. Let me give an example. A girl reporter penetrates a lesbian commune where female children are brought up in ignorance of there being an opposite sex. Is this in the public interest or only of interest to the public ?

On a different tack, the unhappy daughter of an establishment family, and one without a high profile, committed suicide in a foreign capital. The bare fact was clearly newsworthy, but one tabloid printed a full-page photograph of the body. A friend of the family complained that this had caused great distress to the family and added nothing to the story. The Council unanimously found for the family. The tabloid duly printed the adjudication, but accompanied it with a banner headline inviting readers to give their views and published the photograph once again. 'Were We Right Or The Press Council?' So much for self-regulation. The Editor was John Junor. His reward, a knighthood.

Junor's inelegant behaviour was matched by his opposite number at the *Daily Mail*, David English (also to be knighted), who chose to interpret being censured by the Press Council as 'Censorship', and ran a banner headline to that effect.

On the other hand the *Daily Telegraph*, which was taken to task for indulging in cheque-book journalism during the Jeremy Thorpe trial, not only printed the adjudication on the front page but the Editor, Bill Deedes (now Lord Deedes), wrote a first leader headed 'We Got it Wrong'. Sadly few editors reacted this way.

Hartley Shawcross handed the Chairmanship to Patrick Neill (now Lord Neill) who invited me to stay on for a second three years, but by this time I had begun to share the late Jimmy Goldsmith's view that the Press Council was indeed a paper tiger. The failure of the Press to honour the code of self-regulation meant most of our work was worthless.

185

$\star$ $\star$ $\star$

There followed invitations to join the Boards of British Airways and of Westlands from their respective chairmen. I was minded to accept both nominations and accordingly sought the agreement of my joint chairmen. In the light of the sentiments expressed earlier I was taken aback when they both objected.

After some discussion it was agreed that I should take up Lord Aldington's invitation to join Westlands, but not the offer from BA. I think there lurked in their minds the thought that I might be tempted to join one of them full time and to some extent they were right.

Much as I appreciated the experience I was gaining in a job that really was 'hands on' I could not see myself staying with NCP for the longer term. This was a close-knit, essentially family company for which I was too new and too old and certainly not a perfect fit. Moreover, I was regularly receiving offers from headhunters and in 1979 Spencer Stuart approached me as a candidate for taking on the task of leading a joint venture between Ericsson and Philips which had just won the contract to install a telephone system throughout Saudi Arabia. It involved a four-year contract to manage a team of 400 engineers from both countries and a mainly Pakistani workforce of about 2000.

The Chief Executive would be required to live in Riyadh but would have to travel widely, for which a fleet of six company aircraft would be provided. As I had left the Navy in order to secure the financial future of my family and the terms being offered were generous, I allowed my name to go forward, although the domestic problems, with two small children and the nearest English language school being in Jeddah some 500 miles from Riyadh, would be formidable.

When I was informed, after a number of interviews, that I was one of two final candidates and the last steps in the selection process would be personal interviews with the Chief Executives of both companies at their offices in Eindhoven and Stockholm, and, furthermore, if I was selected then I was committed to go, Kirstie and I really had to face the hard domestic questions. On balance we decided it was an opportunity that had to be grasped. The visits duly took place. I lost. We went out and celebrated!

I continued to receive invitations from headhunters, none of which appealed to me. However, two years later Kit Power at Spencer Stuart came back to me with another proposal. I did not initially respond but they persisted and finally caught me on a bad day at the office and I decided to hear more about it.

THE HEADHUNTER'S TARGET

A new Chairman and Chief Executive were required by the Playboy Corporation to run their casino operations in the UK, the Bahamas and one just started in Atlantic City. The present boss, Victor Lowndes, had lost the confidence of the Gaming Commission and Playboy was deemed to be no longer 'fit and proper' and hence in danger of losing its licence to operate in the two major London casinos which represented ninety per cent of the business. The package presented was again financially attractive and by now I had been with NCP for four years without seeing a clear path ahead. I listened.

There were some huge regulatory obstacles to be overcome and no guarantee that the job would last a year. Two top executives had been parachuted in from Los Angeles to hold the fort, as the immediate removal of the current Chairman and Finance Director had been demanded. Long-term replacements were being sought with sufficient experience and gravitas to persuade the Chairman of the Gaming Board, Lord Allan, that the company was again 'fit and proper' and thereby win the case which was due for a court hearing in the autumn.

A formidable legal team had been assembled, headed by the top commercial silk at the time, Robert (now Lord) Alexander. supported by two other silks, Gavin Lightman and Michael Sherrard, plus two juniors. Clifford Chance were the solicitors and Perry Simpson the designated partner.

I was persuaded that there was a better than even chance that, properly presented and with a completely new and demonstrably clean and responsible management in place, the licences could be retained. I also needed to see the accounts which clearly showed substantial profits on a healthy turnover. Not until later did I discover that these were also the major profits of the whole Playboy operation.

I needed to know who else was in the running for the job and they were reluctant to discuss this until we were down to the short strokes. They then said they were considering splitting the roles of Chairman and CEO with which I would normally have totally agreed. However, in the tight compliance regime which would be essential, overall responsibility could only rest with one man, in my opinion. If they wanted me it had to be me alone doing both jobs. It was Richard (now Lord) Marsh, ex-Labour MP and Chairman of British Rail and now very conservative, that they had in mind. I knew Richard and liked him, but could never have worked with or for him.

But first came a visit to the Playboy Mansion West (to distinguish it from the original mansion in Chicago) to meet Hugh Hefner and the rest of the team. Apart from the two temporary London executives who by this time I had got to know quite well, Frank DiPrima and Marvin Huston, this included Derick Daniels, the President and Chief Operating Officer, (whose grandfather, Josephus Daniels, when Secretary of the US Navy, introduced prohibition to ships at sea) and Hefner's attractive daughter, Christie, a graduate lawyer as well as an accountant and well able to fight her corner. Hefner's P.A., Don Parker, also a lawyer and one-time student monk, who proved a useful guide through the half office, half love-nest which was the mansion, completed the group.

A huge hunk of mock Tudor-Breton-Gothic set in five acres of Beverley Hills and pretending to be a Cotswold Manor, the mansion was the corporate headquarters as well as the setting for many of Hollywood's grandest charity shindigs. The boardroom was more like a panelled dining room. Here Hefner presided at the top of a very large table clad in his trademark black silk pyjamas and cradling a can of Coke. The members sat in a half-circle around him. There was no sign of any Playmates, only a smooth young man providing glasses with water or – coke.

Hefner was brief and to the point. He said his team wanted me for the job. I had asked for a six-figure salary and a three-year contract, the right to choose my own team and an assurance that he, Hefner, really wanted to win the case and would not give up if we lost at the first round. To this end I needed his assurance that I would have full authority to carry out a comprehensive investigation of the matters raised by the Police and Gaming Board and to implement all the necessary remedial action that might be required to achieve the proper running of the casino operations. Furthermore, I sought his agreement that, whether or not the current action against the company succeeded, Playboy was committed to maintaining and expanding its operations in the UK. He agreed.

*　　*　　*

I returned to London and broke the news to my bosses at NCP. I knew they were aware I was restless and I had in fact broached the subject the year before. This time I did not want to raise the matter with them until I had a done deal. They took it well, appreciated what I had achieved and were confident that the new management structure was now up to the task. I am happy to say I have remained good friends with them both.

In June 1981 I took up my duties at the Playboy offices in Park Lane as

Chairman and CEO of Playboy Corporation Inc., the parent company of Playboy Clubs of London Ltd., comprising a number of subordinate companies which covered the three London casinos, one in Manchester and one in Portsmouth and about 25 betting shops.

The crisis facing Playboy had arisen from a feud between Stein at Ladbrokes and Lowndes at Playboy apparently sparked by alleged stealing of members by one from the other and retaliation alleging breaches of the gaming regulations. Both men were openly antagonistic at a meeting of the Casino Operators Association chaired by the wonderful Field Marshal Lord Harding, who, with a Group Captain as his assistant, had welcomed a sailor to make the party tri-service! How the gallant Field Marshal became involved I never discovered, but he was a brilliant chairman of a very unmilitary group.

The press had a field day with

189

my appointment. They had already written copiously about the problems at the company and were well versed in the life style of the previous chairman. My initial press conference gave me the chance to put my views over and attempt to deal with the 'not only is he a Sir but he's an Admiral as well' attitude in the context of recruiting a Mr Clean. The dailies in Chicago, Los Angeles and New York picked up on the story.

There were plenty of cartoons, some of which played on the problems the then Secretary of Defence, John Nott, was having with the Admiralty, and at a slightly higher level there was some interest that here was an admiral who had not ended up behind a boring desk. Indeed, a good friend and contemporary, son of a distinguished naval family dating back to Nelson, who was currently a Bursar of a well-known College, broke into verse and I quote it here.

Lines Inspired by Report in *The Times* of 9 July 1981

Is it true that Johnny T
Stole a march on you and me,
And acquired a job that brings both jam and honey?
Will *he* take the centre-spread
To his king-size oval bed,
And pretend he only does it for the honey?

When they sewed that tempting scut
On a Bunny's jiggling butt
Which would make a hare apparent to a beagle
Did they have the least idea
That this ornamental rear
Would attract the erstwhile Captain of the *Eagle?*

When they added extra thrust
To the proudly nubile bust
She'd been given by a generous Creator,
Do you think that they could see
That by overcoming 'g'
They would fascinate a naval aviator?

You may ask – but have no doubt
That despite the charms they flout
As they minister demurely to the thirsty,

190

The non-gambling Mr Clean
Will dismiss them from the scene
When the time arrives for going home to Kirstie

This was also the summer of the marriage of the Prince of Wales and Lady Diana Spencer and the media gave full coverage to the news that Kirstie and I had been invited to attend. Facing the daunting task of who she should place on her list of guests at the Cathedral and to the ball which was held at Buckingham Palace the night before, Diana took the sensible line that this should be limited to those who had been guests at the marriages of both her sisters: old friends only and not those now seeking to move in on her new status.

In the receiving line at the Palace, the Prince said, 'I am delighted to hear about your new job,' and, as I turned and embraced his bride to be added, 'I didn't know you two knew each other.' I began to reply, ' I have known her since . . .' but she stopped me right there.

Gaming in the United Kingdom is exceptionally well regulated, safe and entirely free from intimidation or mafia-style involvement. In central London the casinos are elegant, understated and smoothly managed. The Playboy flagship was the Clermont in Berkeley Square, housing Annabel's nightclub in the basement. Here there were only six tables, attracting the pick of the girls from the Playboy Club on Park Lane. Picked not just for their looks but for their ability and poise, having traded their Bunny outfits for *haute couture* evening gowns they had to be able to handle the really big players and not be overawed by single bets of many thousand pounds. Small numbers played for very big money. Losses and gains could run into several million pounds in an evening.

At the Victoria Sporting Club in the Edgware Road near Marble Arch the situation was reversed. The big gaming floor catered for large numbers playing for relatively small money and at the Playboy Club itself in Park Lane there was something for everyone and a private floor reserved for big punters. All the clubs were open from two o'clock in the afternoon to four in the morning, the staff working two seven-hour shifts.

It was not easy for the UK to come to terms with legalized gaming and when this finally took place it was under regulations most of which were designed to prevent a gambler becoming addicted. The casinos had to be clubs where only members could play. Joining involved a

forty-eight-hour delay between application and membership, a cooling-off period during which prospective members were presumably expected to drop this foolish idea. The casinos themselves were not allowed to offer incentives. Again very much unlike the USA where free flights and other inducements were commonplace.

Furthermore, gambling was for cash only, aimed at ensuring that punters could only lose the money in their pocket and not raid the family savings account. This soon proved impracticable when the Commissioner of the Metropolitan Police stated that he could not protect important visitors moving about the city with suitcases containing millions of pounds.

Cheques then became accepted but on strict conditions. A record had to be maintained of all cheques passed and they had to be redeemed by noon the following day. This was treated as a serious insult by the millionaire players and on some occasions these rules were breached. Mr Stein saw fit to pay two Playboy employees to report to the Commission that this practice was in fact prevalent at Playboy clubs and a raid on the premises of the Playboy and Clermont Clubs in February 1981 gave rise to Police and Gaming Board objections to the renewal of the licences at these two premises.

The case against the Company when the licences came up for renewal before the Westminster Magistrates in September was to be that the clubs were both 'habitually used for unlawful purposes' and that 'the Licencee Company is not a fit and proper person to hold a licence under the Gaming Act'.

It was felt at Playboy that there had always been resentment at American ownership, active dislike of the flamboyant life style of the Chief Executive and that the Commission was enjoying this opportunity to 'sort them out'. I had to make it clear that any feelings of this nature were out of order. Mr Hefner had in any case accepted that the future management should be all-British and that the case against the company should be vigorously defended. Ownership by a US parent company is commonplace and here there was no case to answer.

For the Americans the British system of lay justices was a total mystery and they were in shock at the idea that the case would be heard in front of five justices, none of whom was legally trained. However, they accepted that preparation for the case had to be as thorough as if it was to be heard in the High Court.

*   *   *

In the meantime the casino operation had to continue and I had to recruit a new team to whom I could make no promises for the future. Their contracts needed careful structuring. I was lucky to find an able accountant with a strong background in the entertainment industry and, with compliance a key issue, was fortunate to recruit as a non-executive Director, Anthony Beeley, a senior partner at Binder Hamlyn and at that time Chairman of Boodle's. When challenged about taking on the job he said that gaming and the pursuit of beautiful women had been the favoured pastime of the English gentleman for centuries and he was happy to continue. Welcome!

On joining, I had issued a personal letter to all staff making clear my determination, and that of all the new executives, to ensure that all our gaming operations should be properly and lawfully conducted and that I expected total commitment to this end by everyone.

A root and branch examination of the previous management's business practices revealed an appalling lack of attention in every department. Staff were gravely ignorant of the essential details of the Gaming Act and there was no published in-house guidance to assist them. I therefore took immediate steps for the legal experts to produce a readable and easily understood summary of the Gaming Act for distribution to all employees and instituted a parallel training course.

Essentially Playboy was a business requiring normal financial management with specific attention to cash control with large sums having to be accounted for every morning at 4 am when gaming ceased. While this latter area was generally well covered, the broader financial management was lax. Mr Gerhauser (deputy to Lowndes and previous chief financial officer but with no formal qualification) appeared to have tolerated Lowndes's creative accounting which no doubt sustained his generous life style, attempting to mirror the Playboy Mansion at a country house where he arranged for training of croupiers to be undertaken on a residential course. That alone invited immense speculation.

Playboy Enterprises (the parent company) was at the time not a prosperous venture and the success of the UK operation was such that Los Angeles appeared to be only too happy to accept the crucial financial contribution it made and apparently were not prepared to question the management. Lowndes was very much left to do what he liked and that did not include any form of internal audit.

There were strict rules that senior executives and their families should never take part in gaming, but there were some who had imprecise positions, such as non-executives and trustees, and staff who found difficulty in handling their participation. Also it was essential to watch for any collusion between croupier and punter and there were firm rules about socializing after hours. This was as important in the case of the young male croupiers as much as it was with the girls.

The 'Bunnies' were in general cheerful, attractive and, in the case of the croupiers, extremely numerate, quick and authoritative. Quite a few of them had graduated to positions of Pit Boss and while I was there one became a floor manager and one in charge of training. The croupiers worked hard: seven-hour shifts with 20 to 30 minute spells at the tables (stressful and demanding complete concentration) and similar time in pleasant rest rooms. They were well paid, appeared to enjoy the buzz associated with the club and felt well looked after by the 'Bunny Mother' who ran their personnel side. She had a sensible attitude to life and her approach that being a Bunny was no big deal worked well with the issues which frequently arose in a company with a majority of female staff.

I had inherited an excellent gaming manager, Brian McMullen, who, as manager of the Victoria Club at the time, had not been implicated in the problems at the Playboy and Clermont Clubs and had been cleared by our legal team after exhaustive cross-examination. The major complaints against the company rose from Section 16 of the Gaming Act which concerned the acceptance of cheques. Among other requirements it stipulated that cheques could only be accepted if drawn on accounts known to be held by the drawer and to be in sufficient funds. In practical terms these conditions could not be fulfilled. Many of the players had numerous accounts at different banks, were men of great wealth and accepted at all London casinos. To have hesitated to accept a cheque would result in the loss of a valued customer and probably a job by the cashier concerned.

To receive cheques which are not honoured at once is not infrequent in many businesses and appropriate steps are taken to deal with each in turn, bearing in mind all relevant factors. No such procedures were in place at Playboy where even more stringent action was required under the Gaming Act.

The irony was of course that these stringent rules concerning cheques were imposed to protect the 'innocent' from gambling beyond their means and had no relevance when those concerned were mostly oil multi-millionaires for whom this hugely expensive legal action was now being undertaken.

There was also a Casino Managers Committee in existence which had become all but dormant. I brought it back to life and expanded it to include not only the gaming director and casino general managers but also the new Finance Director, the Credit Manager and those responsible for security and compliance.

Another area of concern was membership and reception procedures. Those in place were hopelessly inadequate and had resulted in what became known as the Hall Porter's Scheme whereby a hall porter 'member' introduced guests to the clubs but was not responsible for their subsequent behaviour. New procedures and computer systems were introduced to prevent this and frustrate attempts to gain access with a borrowed card. By the same token, those being refused entry at any club would be known and treated similarly by the others. All very simple and obvious.

Finally, but certainly not last in importance, I instituted a strong internal audit team headed by Anthony Beeley, resourced sufficiently to ensure not only financial probity but ongoing and constant compliance with the Gaming Act. All these new initiatives were in place by the time the case came to court but had not yet been able to prove their worth in the longer term. It was our job to convince the magistrates that they would.

Playboy International

During all this preparation I made time to visit our Playboy casino in the Bahamas which was in need of reassurance as well as attention. This was a low-key affair compared with the competition which was a Las Vegas-style building on Paradise Island. The casino was situated in one of the top beach hotels, put on a modest floor show and induced its players, who mainly came from Florida, by providing free charter flights to the island. Staff then ensured that those using these free flights did some serious playing to secure a seat home on the return flight.

The Minister of Tourism was taking a keen interest in the problems Playboy was facing in London and concerned that our management in the Bahamas was not tarred with the same brush. I did my best to convince him that the alleged misdemeanours in London were quite outside the regulations as applicable to the Bahamas, that we were defending the case vigourously and had a complete new management structure in place.

He remained sceptical but said that the wife of the Prime Minister, Mr Pindling, would be in London in the near future and I said I would be happy to give a dinner for her. She duly arrived, accompanied by a close friend, the daughter of the Governor General, the first Bahamian to hold the position. We got off to rather a stiff start as Mrs Pindling did not touch the glass of Dom Perignon which had been poured out for her. I asked her companion if there was a problem. 'Yes, she only drinks Krug.'

A bottle was soon produced and we started again. I had invited Peter Shand Kydd to join us and balance the party and he opened the conversation by asking the companion how she had such a light skin. She laughed and replied happily, 'That's quite easy, my father was a Scot.' She went on to tell us that when the Queen and Prince Philip came to the Bahamas for the handover at the time of their independence, Prince Philip asked her father how many children he had. The answer was thirteen, six inside and seven outside. Philip looked nonplussed until her father explained.

The ice was broken and we were then given a vivid insight by both of them into the new emancipation of women in the Bahamas which appeared to focus on their right to have toyboys as much as their husbands enjoyed their extra-curricular activities. Neither of the ladies showed the slightest inclination to gamble and I heard later that Mrs (now Lady) Pindling dined out on having sat next to Princess Diana's stepfather.

The Hearing

When the hearing eventually began in the Caxton Hall, with Mr Godfrey QC leading for the Gaming Commission, much time was spent initially in establishing the acceptability of the evidence of the two 'paid' witnesses for the prosecution. After this the case developed upon predictable lines. I was a principal witness for the Company, detailing what had been done to prevent any repetition of the acts which we accepted were against the spirit of the Gaming Act, but, while ill-considered and misjudged, they did not amount to deliberate and orchestrated attempts to subvert the Gaming Act.

I was on the stand for the best part of two days. Godfrey focused on what he considered as fraud when cheques, which a cashier might have known to have been written on a non-existent or closed account, were accepted because he, the cashier, was satisfied they would be honoured without delay. He reworded his contention repeatedly as he attempted to have me accept this as fraud and I countered that it might be against the spirit of the Gaming Act but it certainly did not amount to fraud. After several repetitions Robert Alexander rose to intervene.

'If both parties are aware of the circumstances, please tell me who you consider is being defrauded.'

Having failed to score with this line of questioning, the attack returned to an attempt to prove premeditation versus our defence that, while errors had been made and penalties had been applied, there were really no grounds for withholding a renewal of the licence. The changes that had been introduced were much greater than those demanded in previous gaming cases in which nearly all the other major clubs had been involved at one time or another.

Robert Alexander summed up superbly on those lines and the court adjourned. The court were unable to come to a decision that day or the next and the verdict was held over until the following Monday. DiPrima nearly had a breakdown and took off for Paris. I felt that we had made our case well against a predicted guilty verdict and that the magistrates were persuaded. However, the delay in announcing a decision indicated some division in their opinions and hence the need to take further advice over the weekend.

When they finally gave a guilty verdict after an unprecedented delay our advisers were outraged and convinced we would win on appeal. To the press I simply said we were considering one and decided to take Robert Alexander to Los Angeles to explain the situation face to face with Hefner.

At the subsequent meeting – same place, same cast with the addition of Alexander – Hefner asked him to start by explaining how we could spend over a million pounds (this is what we had run up) on legal fees appearing before lay justices, whatever they were. Robert did his best. Then came the question.

'If we go to appeal who hears the case?'

'Then there is a judge.'

'OK. So the judge is legally trained.' This was a question rather than a statement by Hefner, to which Robert replied, 'Yes, but he is flanked by two lay justices.'

'Yeah – OK, but they don't get to vote?'

'Well, yes they do,' said Robert.

It was at this point that Hefner clearly gave up on UK law and, despite the assurances he had given me, decided to sell up.

James (Lord) Hanson, on behalf of Yorkshire Television, made a bid which Hefner accepted. It was so low that I almost felt like making a bid myself and must have said so in an unguarded moment as there were a number of backers about. 'Treacher to make bid' made an immediate headline. It was far from reality.

I handed over to Ward Thomas, chairman of Yorkshire Television, and told Hefner I did not wish to stay on. He asked me to have another look at the Bahamas and take an interest in the new Casino they had opened in Atlantic City which belonged to Playboy Clubs International, part of my parish. After some time there, and appearing as a witness for Playboy in a case which was brought by a competitor in the USA challenging Playboy's fitness in the light of the London decision, I decided to call it a day.

8

ROTATING THE WORLD

THE WESTLAND STORY

When I joined the board of Westland as a non-executive director in 1978 the company was the only prime contractor in the aerospace industry to have escaped nationalization by the Labour Government, as it was perceived to be financially sound and capable of survival on its own. This was only partially true.

Founded in 1915 as the aircraft branch of a small west-country engineer, Petters Ltd, and called the Westland Aircraft Works, it did not have a separate identity until nearly twenty years later when it became registered as Westland Aircraft Ltd. During the First World War the company built a number of Short, Sopwith and de Havilland aircraft and gained a reputation for high quality, no doubt enhanced by the inclusion of a barrel of Somerset cider strapped into the second seat when an aircraft was delivered direct from the factory to squadrons in France.

The Air Ministry encouraged the company to produce its own designs and the Wallace in 1933 was the first aircraft to fly over Mount Everest. At the same time the Government sought to strengthen some of the smaller British companies by encouraging participation from major engineering firms. Thus began the long association between Westland and John Brown. In 1978 two of the directors, Lord Aberconway and Sir Eric Mensforth, had between them served on the boards of both companies for more than a hundred years!

The company's reconnaissance aircraft, the Lysander, with a very short take-off and landing capability, was an immediate success. It served with particular distinction ferrying agents in and out of occupied Europe during the Second World War. Thirteen hundred machines were produced.

The company also built 2,267 Spitfires, and was involved in the design of the folding wings for the Seafire, of which well over a hundred were delivered to the Navy.

After the War Westland found itself with a turbine-engined attack aircaft, the Wyvern, coming into production for the Royal Navy essentially as a torpedo bomber to replace the Blackburn Firebrand, the last of the piston-engined genre. Both had short and relatively undistinguished careers in operational squadrons. Beyond that the future appeared very uncertain and a bold decision was made to turn from fixed wing design and construction to rotary wing. The company had some early experience, having built a Cierva autogiro in 1934, but helicopters had long overtaken the autogiro and had seen service during the war, such as the Sikorsky S 54 with the Royal Navy during the last year.

Igor Sikorsky, who built his first rotary-wing vehicle in Russia in 1909, also designed fixed-wing aircraft and, after leaving Russia for the US during the revolution, he established his reputation by producing the famous Flying Clipper flying boats before returning to his first love, the helicopter. Backed by the famous Jack Horner of United Technologies Corporation (UTC), by 1939 he had proved the dynamics in a tethered rig and some four years later had received the first commercial certification for the four-seater S 51.

The Westland board were smart enough to realize that the quickest way to become a helicopter manufacturer was to take a licence, and particularly one from the most successful designer in the world at the time. This was negotiated in 1946 and the S 51 was put into production.

Designated the 'Dragonfly', the first flight took place in 1948 and two years later the first RN Squadron No 705 was formed. In February 1953, when the sea defences in Holland were overwhelmed by high wind and tides, the nine Dragonflies of 705 Squadron imme- diately crossed the channel and airlifted 810 people to safety, a dramatic demonstration of the helicopter's unique capabilities.

The Company had recruited as Chief Test Pilot an ex-Fleet Air Arm officer called Alan Bristow who was described by the Chairman as very hard-working but exceptionally difficult. He did sterling work but had to leave after disagreements with management and went on to form his own helicopter company. This enjoyed much good will and support from Westland for many years.

*   *   *

Westland consolidated its commercial position by acquiring all the other companies in the field: Saunders Roe in 1959, and the helicopter divisions of Bristol Aircraft and Fairey Aviation the following year. Saunders Roe was based on the water's edge and their primary interest was, not unnaturally, in float-planes and flying-boats. This culminated in the development of the only fighter aircraft with a flying-boat hull and the massive Princess, the largest flying-boat in the world, which appeared with stunning effect at the Farnborough Air Display in 1952. Neither proved a success.

At the same time Saunders Roe were working on a rocket-powered fighter in response to an RAF requirement for a very high-level operational ceiling. Designated the SR 53, it was capable of reaching 80,000 feet in one minute and flew at Farnborough in 1957. At the other end of the altitude spectrum Saunders Roe, in association with the National Research and Development Corporation (NRDC), was pioneering the development of hovercraft.

Their chief test pilot at that time was Peter Lamb with whom I had served and shared a cabin in the carrier *Triumph* in Korea when we were both in 800 Squadron and where, as Senior Pilot, he won a well-deserved DSC. At Saunders Roe he rightly claimed to be the highest and lowest test pilot in the world!

Westland set about rationalizing its product line, choosing to concentrate on military helicopters to meet specific military requirements. This was substantiated by the decision of the Royal Navy to make the helicopter the prime weapon system in anti-submarine warfare and embark them in every ship in the fleet.

By 1977 the Westland Lynx was coming into service to replace the Wasp and the Sikorsky S 61, anglicized and equipped with an autonomous anti-submarine system, was about to appear as the Sea King. Together with the prospect of the work share on the Anglo-French helicopter programme, the company could look forward to a comfortable order book.

In addition, the large hovercraft, the SRN4, had established itself as the preferred car ferry for cross-channel traffic and its performance was being enhanced by the introduction of a stretched version with more speed, better rough-sea performance and larger capacity, its future threatened only by the prospect of a channel tunnel.

*   *   *

Much can happen in a year. The optimism at Westland had turned almost to despair and, at my first board meeting in 1978 the stark facts emerged that provision in the accounts had to be made for losses of nearly £20 million on the Lynx programme for the Navy and over £5 million on the 'stretch' of the Hovercraft. The company was plunged into loss and the share price collapsed.

Management failure was only too evident and a new Finance Director had already been recruited. The jobs of the Managing Directors of both the Helicopter Company and British Hovercraft were on the line and confidence in the Chief Executive badly shaken. So much so that he was relieved of his position as Deputy Chairman which was assumed by Lord Aberconway pro tem.

John Brown were also in trouble. Sir John Cuckney was appointed to the board by the institutions and their 30% holding in Westland was sold. It was a sad occasion. The boards knew each other well and met frequently. Indeed it was at one of these meetings that John Cuckney sought my advice about India where his people from International Military Services (IMS – another company of which he was chairman) were having trouble finding their way.

Westland had been run for many years by two remarkable Managing Directors, Edward (Ted) Wheeldon and David Collins. Both were strong on people, which befitted what was still in many ways a family company. They had recruited a Chief Executive, Basil Blackwell,from Rolls Royce, but there continued to be an evident lack of up-to-date financial information available to the board.

David Collins had handed over the chairmanship to Lord Aldington by the time I arrived and I very quickly appreciated that being a non-executive was no way to find out what really lies behind the information fed to the board. I had reservations about the new policy now being put forward which was aimed at entering the civil helicopter market to balance the cyclical nature of military procurement and was convinced that the company was ill equipped to do so. I put this to the Chairman who said he understood my concerns but felt that the company could rise to the challenge.

The concept was that the 'running gear' – the expensive rotor head and blades developed for the Lynx – could be used with an enlarged fuselage to produce a sixteen-passenger civil helicopter at a comparatively low development cost. This was to become the W30 programme.

★   ★   ★

This, however, would do nothing to load the factory floor in the short term and the company desperately needed additional orders for the Sea King. The Indian Navy, already the operator of an early mark, was in the market for another twenty aircraft with a much enhanced anti-submarine performance. Now, however, Aérospatiale, with the Puma, developed under the Anglo-French joint programme, were aggressively marketing it as a more modern and capable Sea King replacement.

I was planning a visit to the Far East in 1980 and was asked to adjust my itinerary to take in India. This would allow me to renew many of my old contacts in the Indian Navy and provide the chance to make some discreet soundings about the local attitude to Westland. I was also able to spend time with the Westland team on the ground and hear about their problems at first hand. They were led by Don Berrington, one of Westland's very best engineers, now running the company's military division.

On my return to England I made a report to the Chairman, clearly stating that without a complete re-casting of the marketing and commercial approach to the Indian Navy they would buy French.

A year or so later, following my time at Playboy, I took Kirstie on a farewell visit to Beverly Hills and then continued on to Australia and home via India. On two occasions I suffered acute angina. First, when piloting the de Havilland (Australia) company aircraft, a Beech King Air, the pain came on during a bad weather approach to landing at the Australian Navy's air station at Nowra. The second attack happened when swimming off the beach in Goa.

On return to England it was clear that something had to be done and I ended up with open heart surgery on Grand National Day 1982, joining Al Haig and Henry Kissinger, who had already become members of the triple bypass club.

I had been taken in for an angiogram from which the cardiologist, Lawson McDonald, who had been a Surgeon Lieutenant in HMS *Glasgow* with me, predicted a massive and possibly fatal heart attack within six months. I was operated on by Donald Ross the next morning.

This was also the start of the Falklands War and the night before, having been fully prepared for surgery, I received a telephone call from Peter Snow, the presenter of *Newsnight*, a programme on which I had recently appeared at the request of the First Sea Lord to support the Navy's position on warship design.

'Admiral,' he almost shouted, 'thank God I've found you at last. Can you be at the studio in an hour?'

'Do you know where I am?' I replied.

'No, but my team have taken ages to locate you.'

'They did well. I am in the Harley Street Clinic, shaved from head to toe and awaiting open heart surgery in less than 12 hours.' There was a moment's pause. 'Oh my God,' he said and hung up.

While convalescing in France, Lord Aldington invited me to become an executive director of Westland with wide-ranging responsibility for marketing. The Chief Executive was keen to involve me in all markets worldwide, but my immediate task lay in India where the situation was becoming serious. I was happy to accept.

The Indian Navy

The top civil service officer in the Indian Ministry of Defence, Mr Bhatnagar, said, 'After Lord Mountbatten you are the best known British naval officer', and indeed many of those who served in *Vikrant* with me were now in senior positions in the Indian Navy. However, these contacts counted for little in finding where the real power lay in the decision-making process. The Westland staff in India were constantly being approached by plausible intermediaries purporting to have the entrée to this or that man of influence, sometimes a senior politician but more often someone closely connected with the Prime Minister, Mrs Indira Gandhi.

Westland had misguidedly dispensed with the services of its long-term agent who had not only served on Mountbatten's staff, when the Admiral was Viceroy of India, but had also been Naval Adviser to the Indian High Commissioner in London. He was much trusted and admired by his contemporaries, many of whom were still serving, and I found a distinct shortage of goodwill towards the company.

Currently the Chief of Naval Staff was Oscar Dawson, who had been the navigating officer in *Vikrant* with me and I knew him well. Over many months spent in New Delhi I was able to mend fences and restore goodwill while our technical team, led by Richard Case (later to rise to the top of the company), and test pilots were able to prove that in fact the performance of the Sea King was still equal to the Puma and, given its thoroughly proven sea-worthiness, we could argue it deserved to be the chosen vehicle. The same applied to the highly sophisticated sonar and electronic equipment specified, which should have less development risk given Westland's past experience.

Having secured our position with the Navy, only the political hurdle remained. The importance of this contract was such that the Westland board expressed their collective anxiety regarding the sensitive question of engaging an agent to assist in negotiations and went so far as to propose points of contact. Fortunately, during the many months I had spent in Delhi, I had established clear views on the acceptability and effectiveness of the various players and was able to deflect suggestions put forward, with the best of intentions, via my Chairman. I knew those they had in mind to be suspect and one subsequently became the subject of a very high profile bribery scandal. Beware of wealthy expatriates!

Throughout this period I could not have asked for more understanding and co-operation from the High Commissioner, Sir Robert Wade-Gery, and his Defence and Naval Advisers.

Happily, with the unfailing efforts of Berrington and his team, I was able to plot a safe course to the final negotiating table where a decision was made in Westland's favour. This was an order which, in financial terms, was greater than the total market capitalization of the company and highlighted its vulnerability as a prime contractor.

South America – Chile

Westland had supplied helicopters to the Brazilian Navy since the early fifties and the Lynx was currently in service. At the same time Chile, which had traditionally acquired most of its warships from the UK, had supported the UK during the Falklands conflict and had recently negotiated the purchase of several County Class destroyers from the Royal Navy, required helicopters to complete their armament. The Sea King looked like the natural choice for this role, although some modifications to the hangar arrangements would have to be made before they could be embarked. These were all designed and agreed, the work to be undertaken in the naval dockyard at Talcahuano.

I had regular meetings with Admiral 'Peppi' Merino, the number two in the Junta and who had been the Chief of Naval Staff since the start of the Pinochet regime in 1973. He used to enjoy introducing me as a Chileno who had spent some time in the Royal Navy. He lived in an unguarded house in the suburbs of Santiago with his wife and family and would happily accept an invitation to dinner, arriving without escort or bodyguard.

All Sea Kings, although much developed and enhanced from the original Sikorsky S 61, derived from the original licence and we were aware that this needed to be extended to cover Chile. Our preliminary enquiries led us to believe this would not be a problem, but as contract discussions began in earnest the US State Department informed Sikorsky that, so long as the Pinochet régime remained in power, permission would be withheld. The best efforts of Ambassadors, particularly John Hickman in Santiago, and Trade Ministers proved of no avail and eventually we had to withdraw. A sad end to a long marketing campaign.

However, Kirstie had joined me on some visits and I managed to re-establish contact with a few of the families we had known when we lived in Valparaiso and Concepción. In the former were the Hardy family, headed by Graham, who had joined the Gurkhas during the war, using our home in London as his base, and his sister Moira, who I had seen often when she came to England in the fifties with her mother. She was now a key member of the staff at the British Consulate and received an MBE in 1989.

In Concepción we found Bunny Everard, the head of the family and a godfather of my sister. He was a sprightly ninety-two years old and his daughter, Mary, showed us the house in which my parents had lived when my sister and I were born.

Brazil

In Brazil the Navy was in the market for more helicopters, but was having technical problems with its Lynx helicopters and, as usual, we faced strong competition from the French, particularly over funding. An accord had been entered into in Paris which prevented Government-assisted funding of defence contracts, but Aérospatiale was paying scant attention, continuing to offer easy terms through their government agency, COFAS.

Through our own channels and supported by the Ambassador we were able to provide proof of this activity and I took the matter up with Alan Clark, then working for Norman Tebbit in the DTI. He was full of enthusiasm for a fight and confident that, with the evidence available, he could ensure the playing field was levelled.

Off he went to the Treasury, who may have been impressed but were giving nothing away. 'Leave it to us,' they said and confronted their opposite numbers in Paris, who feigned horror that this could happen and promised immediate action to bring it to a stop. Not what was wanted at all and, predictably, I was met on my return to Brazil by our agent who had managed to obtain a copy of the latest offer by the French. This began by stating quite bluntly that the perfidious Brits had intervened to prevent them making the very good offer currently on the table but assuring the Brazilians that they would be able to provide equally attractive terms from other sources. And we knew what these were. So much for Alan Clark.

Fortunately I enjoyed very good relations with the Brazilian Navy, whose aircraft carrier, the *Menas Gerias*, had been in service with the RN as HMS *Vengeance* and they were particularly delighted to learn that it was the ship in which I had made my first deck landing in a jet aircraft thirty years earlier. Admiral Daldegan, the head of their naval aviation, appreciated the efforts we were making on their behalf to improve technical support and accepted that procurement of sophisticated equipment by overseas countries often created problems with maintenance.

A Westland engineer was assigned permanently to their only shore base at San Pedro d'Aldeia, on the coast some twenty miles north of Rio, but this was not enough. Graham Cole, the excellent Westland manager in Rio, then came up with an idea which immediately gained the support of Admiral Daldegan.

Some of the senior Brazilian technicians were highly competent but were never in post long enough to become fully effective. Many were close to retirement and facing the prospect of having to move themselves and their families from the comparatively idyllic coastal area of the base at San Pedro to the urban jungle of greater Rio de Janiero, there to battle for employment among the other eight million inhabitants. The solution was for Westland to train some of them in depth and give them long-term employment at the base as support engineers.

When this plan was implemented, the serviceability of the Lynx flights rose to over 80%, all aircraft embarked in excellent condition and immediate back-up available when required. After a very long haul Wesland was rewarded ultimately with an order for more Lynx helicopters and the up-grading of their original ones.

★ ★ ★

Throughout this period we enjoyed the strong support of our agent in Brazil, a major commercial company, Mesbla, owned by the de Botton family. Henrique de Botton and his wife Jacqueline presided over the family from their beautiful home overlooking the bay at Rio de Janiero. They were widely connected with the senior politicians and military personnel and hugely respected. Their old-fashioned honesty and loyalty, combined with a genuine affection for things British, had profited UK industry over many years and earned Henrique a well-deserved CBE.

Sadly, these very qualities did not count in the ever more demanding days of cut-throat competition and a currency devalued massively on an almost daily basis. Nor did the more unattractive entertainment widely available in Brazil, and offered by some agents to entice customers, find any place in their inventory. Inevitably the company fortunes declined and, following the death of Henrique, none of his four sons was able to ensure the company's survival.

Good support also came from our ambassadors, first John Ure, who I had known when he was our ambassador in Portugal, a great traveller and travel writer, and then Michael Newington, who took a more personal interest in our problems There was equally strong support from the commercial attaché and two naval attachés, Captains John Ashton and then Richard Duffield. However, isolated as they were in Brasilia, much reliance had to be placed on our Consul General in Rio, the stalwart Roger Hart, who never let us down.

Over these years Kirstie and I were lucky enough to visit the more remote areas of the Mato Grosso, where André de Botton owned a huge tract of the Pantanal, and to travel up the Rio Negro, north-west of Manaus in the Amazonas. Not exactly in the wake of the great explorers but quite testing at times.

Australia and New Zealand

The Royal Australian Navy (RAN) was also equipped with Sea Kings and the Royal New Zealand Navy (RNZN) with Wasp helicopters. The RAN, with the Army, were in the market for many more of all types. I tried hard to persuade their Government to expand their existing capability to at least assemble aircraft in country. David Gardner, Westland's man for the area, worked with me to convince

208

the Industry Minister, Senator John Button, that Australia should not leave all the running in that part of the world to Dr Habbibi (an ex-director of the German helicopter company MBB) in Indonesia, but we failed to generate support. In the longer term Australia looked to the USA for its equipment.

The Civil Market

Westland had built in the early sixties a helicopter landing platform reaching out into the Thames near Battersea. Over the years it became an important facility for nearly all civil helicopter traffic to and from the city of London. It was sited in the borough of Wandsworth and the number of flights was limited, for environmental reasons, to a maximum for the year at a maximum rate per month, with exceptions for such events as Ascot and Epsom racing and the Farnborough Air Show. The lease was relatively short and had to be renewed, always against local opposition, every few years.

For a short time there was also a platform moored in the Thames near Cannon Street and we looked, with British Airways and BAA, at a platform forming part of a major property development in that area, but demand did not last.

The approach to the Westland Battersea facility was by a short road which tended to attract rubbish but not the attention of the council, whose responsibility it was to keep it clean. At one Farnborough Show Mrs Thatcher charged onto our stand and proclaimed, 'Admiral, your heliport is a disgrace. It needs to be thoroughly smartened up'.

She did not wait for a reply, but I drew Denis Thatcher aside and said, 'I thought she was going to thank me for providing her with a helicopter facility. But, more to the point, I am sure it is the approach road she was unhappy about. This belongs to her favourite Borough [Wandsworth was very Tory and had the lowest rates in the country] and, even more important, they are being very difficult about renewing our operating licence which is about to expire.'

I am sure this resulted in some pillow talk, for within a week I received a letter from the Private Office informing me that I would soon be hearing from Wandsworth Borough Council that our licence would be extended for a further ten years.

The Civil Lynx

While much engineering effort was devoted to production, research into all aspects of helicopter development continued and in 1983 the Westland engineers produced an advanced design of rotor blade, made entirely of composite material. Fitted to a Lynx helicopter this provided the opportunity to attack the helicopter world speed record.

On 6 August 1986, under the watchful eye of, and across a course instrumented by the International Aviation Federation, run in both directions, the Lynx, piloted by the Chief Test Pilot at the time, John Egginton, broke the world speed record by a generous margin.

This powerful demonstration of leading-edge technology earned very positive publicity and an award ceremony when the presentation was made by Prince Andrew.

Meanwhile the civil W30 had completed development and was now in service with British Airways Helicopters (BAH) on short-haul work among the gas fields off East Anglia, and between Cornwall and the Scillies.

Interest was again being shown by certain American airlines in providing helicopter services from city centres to hub airports in New York (Pan Am), Chicago (Midway) and Los Angeles (American) and we managed to get the W30 into service with two of them.

None of these opportunities would have been realized without the expert financial engineering of Finance Director Hugh Stewart and the outstanding performance of the Chief Test Pilot Roy Moxam, who demonstrated the helicopter all over the USA, often in extremely poor weather and with minimal technical support.

As the US market developed I had formed a US subsidiary company, Westland Inc., and poached Robert Gladwell from Rolls Royce as President. Gladwell had been a British Aircraft Corporation (BAC) engineer who arrived in the US with the first BAC 111 jet airliners delivered to Mohawk Airlines in 1960. He stayed and prospered, serving in senior positions in BAC and Rolls Royce.

To enter the civil market Westland had to readjust its culture from one of serving military customers, whose in-house engineering and spares support could almost invariably make good any shortcomings on the part of the Company, to supporting commercial customers whose revenue depended on the performance of the aircraft and its supplier, and failure could lead to litigation. On top of this, when the Westland board came fully to understand just what the liability would amount to in the event that sixteen first-class passengers went for an involuntary swim in the East River, I felt a shiver run through their collective spine!

Sadly the company could not meet the challenge and this led to a number of heated exchanges between me and Blackwell. It was a constant battle, with endless serviceability problems and equipment failure bad enough for the aircrew to lose confidence. Despite this, Pan American continued to operate the New York service until the airline itself collapsed, following its expensive acquisition of National Airlines, and at Los Angeles until the losses incurred by the operators could no longer be tolerated.

It was perhaps surprising that only one accident occurred during these operations when a helicopter from Los Angeles to Orange County lost tail rotor control at about four thousand feet at night and hit power cables on its descent. Happily this cushioned the impact and the most serious casualty suffered a broken arm, but the city of Long Beach was plunged into darkness. Gladwell carried out a brilliant damage control exercise and, after a brief grounding by the Federal Aviation Authority (FAA), the helicopters were soon back on schedule. Nevertheless, it was a losing battle.

Gladwell was not only a most capable President and CEO for Westland Inc. during the W30 period but subsequently in both the USA and Canada worked with me to promote the EH101. He also widened his sphere of influence in Washington, holding the Chairmanship of the British American Chamber of Commerce for many years and his work was rightly recognized with the award of an OBE.

At this time in India, apart from the Navy's Sea Kings, interest was expressed by the Oil and Natural Gas Corporation (ONGC) in acquiring twenty W30 civil helicopters to service their offshore oil rigs. The Indian Government had in mind the funding of this programme from part of the annual aid provided by Her Majesty's Government and this was agreed after excellent work by the Overseas Trade Division headed by Chris Benjamin.

The ONGC had expressed anxiety that the helicopters should be provided as soon as possible and Westland was equally anxious to book the order. A letter of intent to place the order was received from

211

the Indian Government and, while normally no funds would be committed by the company before receipt of the signed order itself, in this case, with the financing provided and agreed by HMG, the company decided to proceed with the order for long-lead materials. A substantial financial commitment was involved but orders placed early and in bulk meant that a keen price could be negotiated.

Very soon after this commitment Indira Gandhi was assassinated and her role as Prime Minister assumed by her son Rajiv. The immediate reaction of the new administration was to put all outstanding contracts on hold pending either re-negotiation or cancellation. This came at a very delicate time for Westland whose finances were now over-stretched and the loss of the W30 order would have provoked an immediate crisis. In due course the inevitable delays to this contract, ultimately honoured but only after the personal intervention of the Prime Minister in discussion with Rajiv, contributed to the problems which subsequently arose.

Ministry of Defence

As our major customer, the Ministry of Defence played a dominant part in the life of the company and it was with the Chief of Defence Procurement that we were most closely concerned. This post normally rotated between a senior service officer of at least three-star rank and a civil servant of equivalent status. The Secretary of State, Michael Heseltine, was to change all this with the appointment of Peter (now Lord) Levene.

Levene had built up a small defence contractor by a series of acquisitions and this rapid growth had caught the eye of the city where, as United Scientific Holdings (USH), it was floated on the Stock Exchange. My first direct contact with him came when he telephoned me in 1983 to ask if Westland would be prepared to refurbish the twenty Westland Sea Kings, supplied some years previously to the Egyptian Air Force, as the Egyptians now wished to dispose of them. This was news to me and I was confident that if it was more than speculation I would have been the first to hear. I assured him refurbishment could be undertaken but that the request must come from Egypt. No more was heard.

Peter Levene next appeared on Westland's radar when our Merchant Bank alerted us to a build-up in holdings of our shares by a series of Swiss nominee companies and unearthed that USH was the purchaser of over two million shares. This was just after Levene had joined Mr Heseltine as an unpaid adviser for a period of six months in 1984.

The Chairman alerted the board to these developments and Sir Frank Cooper, who had recently joined the board after retiring on completion of his career in the Civil Service as the Permanent Under-Secretary at Defence, admitted that he had been responsible for recommending Levene to Heseltine and that he had had dinner with Levene the previous evening, but Westland had not been discussed.

The Chairman then confronted Heseltine, saying it was wholly unacceptable for an 'insider' to be acquiring shares in a defence company while serving on the Minister's staff. Levene was ordered to desist and Aldington agreed that talks between top executives from both companies should take place to determine the real reasons for their interest.

During this meeting, which took place on 24 May 1985 and was attended by Blackwell, Stewart and myself, Levene stated that his intention had been to achieve an agreed take-over or merger because he considered Westland to be weak on marketing and that USH had much to offer in that respect. After long discussions it was mutually agreed that neither side was likely to gain from joining up.

The Board consulted their Bankers, J. Henry Schroder Wagg, on the matter of disclosure and it was concluded that, as the discussions with USH had been terminated and there having been no significant movement in the price of the Company's shares, there was no requirement to make a public statement. However, this whole episode coloured the company's relations with Levene from then on.

Levene duly became part of the Defence Department on a five-year contract with the rank of Second Permanent Under-Secretary as Chief of Defence Procurement (CDP) at a salary nearly twice that paid to the senior civil servant he was displacing. The appointment was driven through by Heseltine and generated much ill will both in the Department and beyond.

Peter Levene's arrival in the MOD was akin to putting the proverbial fox in the hen house. Heseltine knew what he was doing and was delighted. While the Controller of the Navy had introduced the disciplines of competition to the ship-building industry in 1963 Levene would be attempting to do the same to the aviation and electronics industries and this was long overdue. The task had to be done, but the style would be very different.

I was to see a lot of Levene over the years. He had been impressed by what John Lehman had achieved when Secretary of the US Navy in using the Intellectual Property Rights (IPR), which accrued to Government agencies from fully funded research and development, to force competition for the subsequent production contracts carried out by industry. The results were not always to prove successful.

Overall, there can be little doubt that the impact Levene had on the MoD was long overdue and, while the sclerotic procurement procedures changed little, he was able to introduce a much-needed measure of competition in dealing with the aircraft and weapons industry.

Collaboration

The Royal Navy had expressed the need in 1975 for a vehicle whose physical dimensions should not exceed those of the Sea King, with enhanced range and endurance and fitted with an ASW capability superior to that in service with the RAF Nimrod patrol aircraft, while the Ministry of Defence had decreed that all future new aircraft would have to be developed in partnership with one or more other countries whose armed forces had a similar requirement.

Meeting both was no easy task. Eventually the search for a partner ended when the Italian government indicated that such a helicopter would meet their need for both shore-based operations and those from their new cruisers. Westland sought to be the majority shareholder in the joint-venture company on grounds of experience and the number of helicopters to which the UK was committed in comparison with the much smaller Italian requirement. The Italians, however, made it clear that their participation would be as a full 50% partner, through their Agusta Company, or not at all and Westland had no alternative but to agree, despite serious misgivings.

At the same time both companies identified a need in the civil market for a new helicopter of this size and this was provided for fully in development.

The Chief Executive of Westland (Basil Blackwell) and Count Corrado Agusta became Joint Chairmen of the new company, European Helicopter Industries (EHI). While there were many teething troubles caused not least by the collapse of the Agusta Company which saw its immediate nationalization, the departure of the good Count Corrado and his replacement by the government nominee Rafaello Teti, sometime Vice-Chairman of Alitalia, the two companies set to at working level and the shared design work proceeded. It was at this time that I became a member of the EHI board of directors and later replaced Blackwell as a joint Chairman.

Peter Levene had little time for collaborative projects, but did his best to keep the Italian government side up to their responsibilities and worked hard on his opposite number, Admiral Mario Porta. It was uphill all the way. The same applied to my relations with Teti, as Agusta were always late with their stage payments and I made some light-hearted jokes about their connections. It was not so funny when Teti absconded with his attractive P.A. to Brazil where he ended up in Manaus. He was replaced by Roberto D'Allesandro who had made a name for himself when, appointed by the government, he success-fully dealt with the terrible problems in the port of Genoa.

The relatively small EHI management structure, with an Italian Managing Director and a head of Administration and Finance, the worthy Andy Moorhead, who had held the fort since the start, depended on the two companies working together with complete devotion to the task. In practice competing priorities within the two companies prevented this occurring, despite the best efforts of existing managers.

Beyond this there were funding problems on the Italian side which did not escape the attentions of the Italian fiscal authorities when they were attempting to crack down on senior executives in industry. Cesare Rommiti of Fiat, as well as some top men in Agusta, spent time as guests of their government. After I had left Westland I had occa-sion to telephone Enrico Striano, the ebullient MD of EHI and he came straight on the line.

'Enrico,' I said, ' I did not expect to get you so quickly. I thought you would be in prison.'

'Oh no, I am not important enough,' he replied. 'Now, in Italy we have a new meaning for VIP – Visto In Prigione'. (Seen in prison.)

Our relationship with Agusta was not made any easier when we found them offering a so-called militarized version of their light civil A109 helicopter to the Belgian Army in competition with our battlefield Lynx. NATO found it wholly unacceptable as a weapon system and were horrified when Agusta won the contract. This generated such deep feeling, even inside the Belgian forces, that serious investigations were put in hand. These led to the early suicide of a Belgian General and, much later, the forced resignation of Willie Claes from the prestigious post of Secretary General of NATO. He had been head of his political party when it had been involved in the chicanery.

At this time the Royal Canadian Navy submitted a requirement for a replacement to the S 61 helicopters which they were operating from their frigates. Their ASW philosophy matched that of the RN with regard to autonomous operation and the EHI appeared to fit their requirement closely. The Canadian Ministry of Defence issued tenders and EHI, Sikorsky and Aérospatiale responded.

Bob Gladwell, from Washington, was my man quickest on the scene and EHI (Canada) was set up. We assembled a strong team with a CEO acceptable to the Canadian Government and recruited William Boggs, a doyen of the Canadian Aviation industry and past Chairman of de Havilland (Canada), to our board as a non-executive director.

In the event we persuaded Sikorsky that their Sea Hawk helicopter had no chance as a competitor and that they should support the EH10I. We were thus able to put in a proposal backed by the personal endorsement of the Presidents of Sikorsky as well as Bell Helicopter and Canadian Marconi. We won, but the final contract was not to be awarded until we had achieved certain critical milestones. The dependable Don Berrington was drafted in from Westlands to pull the whole programme together and the contract was signed some years later.

The EH101, named the Merlin, is now serving in the Royal Navy after a very protracted development of fifteen years, which made heavy demands on the test pilots led by Colin Hague. Of the nine development aircraft two were lost, the first in Italy which cost the life of Agusta's Chief Test Pilot, the second at Yeovil where the crew were able to escape.

Hostile Bid

In 1983 I became a member of the Council of the Society of British Aerospace Companies (SBAC) and in May 1984 I was appointed Vice-Chairman in place of Basil Blackwell who had been reinstated as Deputy Chairman on the retirement of Lord Aberconway. I was not entirely happy with this decision as I was at odds with Blackwell over his management style and his lack of control over some of his senior appointees. However, as long as Lord Aldington remained Chairman I was prepared to carry on.

At the end of the year Lord Aldington announced his intention to retire and I informed him that I would go at the same time. In the nicest possible way he made it clear that he considered it my duty to the company to stay and support Blackwell. I stayed.

In February 1985 Blackwell was duly appointed Chairman and within a few weeks I found it necessary to write at length detailing management changes which I considered essential. Blackwell accepted them, but much more needed to be done and little had been achieved before Alan Bristow launched a bid for the company. I had warned the board during the past year that Bristow, who I met regularly when shooting, was constantly referring to how poorly he thought the company was being managed and that he was minded to do it himself. I said I did not think this was just idle talk.

An emergency board meeting was called, attended by the company's brokers, Rowe and Pitman, and merchant bank, Schroder Wagg in the person of Nicholas Jones, who was to become the architect of Westland's defence. He started badly. Supported by Blackwell, he proposed a letter to shareholders advising outright rejection of the bid and assuring them that the board would find a more suitable alternative. I disagreed. The bid was pitched high enough to be attractive to shareholders and, in my view, we would be hard-pressed to find a better one. Thus shareholders should be advised to take no action at this time and await the considered advice of the board who were exploring all possible alternatives. This was agreed.

In the ensuing weeks Bristow's advisers carried out 'due diligence' while Westland openly courted investment from other sources. This did not bear fruit and it became clear that finding a convincing alternative was proving impossible. At a board Meeting on 21 June Blackwell accepted that the Bristow bid would have to be recommended and placed his resignation at the disposal of the board. He then departed for a week in the Channel Islands.

Meanwhile in the Bristow camp all was not well. Realization was dawning that the bid had been pitched too high, probably disastrously so. On the grounds that there had not been acceptances of the offer by more than 90% of the shareholders by the due date, the offer was withdrawn. The chairmen of our two banks, Barclays and NatWest, then demanded the replacement of Blackwell and I sought the advice of Kit Farrow, at the Bank of England, who kept a file of potential candidates. Within twenty-four hours he came up with the name of Sir John Cuckney. We met the next day and I took Hugh Stewart, whom he did not know, with me, as he would be a key player in any new structure.

John Cuckney's conditions were that he would not take on an executive role and he would only stay for three years. Hugh Stewart became the key. Would he take on the role of Chief Executive? He was clearly the man for the moment. John Cuckney and I did our best to convince him and he rose splendidly to the occasion. I called a Board Meeting at which John Cuckney was elected Chairman. Blackwell was still on holiday.

THE HESELTINE CONUNDRUM

The Westland Affair, as it became known, has featured in most of the books written by ministers who were involved to a greater or lesser extent. Their accounts are inevitably coloured by the way they would wish their readers to remember their role, and their recall of events differs. Michael Heseltine refers to it as the most powerful storm in his political life.

The parts played by two Departments of State were also centre stage. While the Department of Trade and Industry is the sponsor of industry in general, those companies who are major or prime contractors to the Ministry of Defence have a particular interest in maintaining good relations with their principal customer, who disposes of something in the region of 3% of the nation's Gross Domestic Product. In the case of the Westland group of companies this represented 95% of their turnover.

The so-called affair lasted from October 1985 to March 1986. The foundation had been laid nearly a year earlier when the company, in hot pursuit of export sales, found its financial resources overstretched. It was without its long-term 30% shareholder John Brown, and then became the target for a hostile bid from Alan Bristow.

*   *   *

The genesis of the crisis can be traced to the original decision to enter the commercial helicopter market with a civil version of the Lynx, designated the W30. Unprofitable in the UK and USA, a perceived breakthrough came when twenty W30 helicopters were chosen by the Indian Oil and Natural Gas Corporation (ONGC) for oil rig service.

The ONGC was pressing for early delivery and the company was committed to advance payments for long-lead materials. The cancellation of the order in the wake of the assassination of Indira Gandhi precipitated the financial crisis which could have made the company technically insolvent.

As the affair developed, it quickly took on a political dimension, generated widespread comment and much, mostly ill-informed, speculation. In some of the more lurid reports the affair nearly reached scandal status as ministerial behaviour was questioned.

After it was all over there began a steady flow of reports by political and financial commentators, while constitutional lawyers and historians picked over every aspect of its handling by the Prime Minister, the Cabinet, Secretaries of State, civil servants and the company. There were rich seams to be mined. Individual and collective responsibility within the Cabinet and the part played by the Select Committees of the House of Commons did not escape notice, nor the use of selective leaking of information.

The first book-length report, under the title *Not With Honour*, was produced by two young journalists, Martin Linklater and David Leigh. As ever with 'instant' or 'inside' stories, facts are few, assertions widespread and authenticity is claimed by the liberal use of quotations. Balance is sacrificed to speed and inaccuracies planted in the first pages grow into rampant distortions as the narrative expands.

Ministers most closely involved published memoirs over the years, giving their recollection of events and the respective parts they played. *The Financial Times* printed a resumé of these writings on the fifth anniversary of the affair, highlighting the often completely opposing views of what actually happened at the same meeting. Pity the poor minute writer should he come into contact with the diarist!

The Search for a Partner

When Sir John(Lord) Cuckney became chairman in June 1985 he was fully aware of the situation and that a complete financial reconstruction was inevitable unless an alternative customer could be found at once for the helicopters ordered by the ONGC.

He immediately set about restructuring the Westland board of directors and proposed a change of merchant bank from Schroder Wagg to Lazard Brothers. He had been a director of Lazards in the past and I had become disenchanted with Schroders during the Bristow bid and was happy to support the change. In addition I had not been comfortable with a partner in our merchant bank sitting on our board as a non-executive director. Chinese walls are not sufficiently thick.

This was an important change welcomed by the whole board, as was the appointment of two new non-executive directors, Sir Maldwyn Thomas and Lord Fanshawe, who between them brought strong business and government experience to bear on board deliberations.

Attempts to fend off the Bristow bid had revealed that there were no 'White Knights' prepared to support the company against a take-over and the withdrawal of the bid left the company free to find a major industrial partner to assist in a complete financial reconstruc-tion. Finding a strategic partner prepared to take an equity stake in the company of up to but not over 29.9 % was central to this task.

The company had alerted the DTI and the MOD early in 1985 to the potential crisis and Michael Heseltine professed complete indifference to the situation, showing no inclination to support an indigenous helicopter industry on military grounds. We were aware that Heseltine had been mauled by his colleagues over his arrogant and inept handling of the appointment of Peter Levene and may well have been stung by Lord Aldington's intervention, but in view of the MoD's involvement with the DTI and Westland in the EH101 project for the Navy, his cavalier attitude was unexpected.

Sir John met Heseltine in mid-July to press the case for some alterna-tive assistance to Westland in the form of advancing the date of programmed orders for existing aircraft and I called on Norman Tebbit with whose department I had been working so closely on the ONGC contract for India. While showing considerable interest in Westland's position, he was careful to emphasize that he did not wish to see his Department in any way involved in what could be repre-sented as a rescue attempt.

I then had a long meeting with Clive Whitmore, the Permanent

220

Under-Secretary at the MoD. No one else was present. I had known Clive over many years and he had been a bright Assistant Secretary in the Admiralty when I was Vice-Chief. In the meantime he had served the PM with distinction and was perceived as a strong contender for heading the Civil Service in due course. Unfortunately his close association with Heseltine during this difficult time did not appear to help.

Dr Rafaello Teti, Chairman of Agusta, met John Cuckney in early September to explore the possibility of the two companies taking cross shareholdings or forming closer collaboration or even partnership. This was not something Westland would have welcomed as Agusta, a private company when the EHI joint venture was set up, had in 1983 become bankrupt and was now owned by the Italian Government, which was not proving an easy partner. However, it was necessary to show that every avenue was being explored. Teti said he was not prepared to help unilaterally, but might if Aérospatiale (France) and MBB (Germany) also participated.

Westland's problems had not escaped the notice of Sikorsky, with whom the company still enjoyed a harmonious design and manufacturing relationship which had endured for nearly forty years. Sikorsky had declined to become involved at the time of the Bristow bid, but Westland was already in discussions regarding a licence to manufacture the new Blackhawk battlefield helicopter and their parent company, United Technologies (UTC), now indicated they would be prepared to assist in the financial reconstruction. This led to a meeting between UTC and Lazards and, a couple of weeks later, with Michael Heseltine.

Although this was a very attractive option, the board did not want this to be the only one. There were two major corporations in the UK which could have become industrial partners, British Aerospace and General Electric, and John Cuckney approached both chairmen. At BAe, Sir Austin Pearce made it clear he did not wish his company to participate and when I met his Chief Executive, my old colleague Ray Lygo, he confessed that his group was already carrying more risk than was prudent and he would certainly not support the further exposure which any association with Westland would bring. At GEC both the chairman, Lord Prior, and the Managing Director, Lord Weinstock, declined an invitation to talk.

Approaches to the three other European helicopter manufacturers were made at a meeting on 8 October attended by John Cuckney and me. Not unexpectedly, there were general mutterings of support, but underlying it all we perceived an awareness that Europe could not in the long term support four national helicopter manufacturers and that this might be the time to let one sink rather than helping to keep a competitor afloat. Moreover, they showed no grasp of what in commercial terms would be required to effect support of a publicly quoted company, even if they had been so minded.

At this stage Peter Levene was taking a pragmatic view of the situation and buttonholed me at the Army Equipment Exhibition at Aldershot in September to say, 'You, Westland, will have to go with Sikorsky. It's the only realistic solution.' I said it certainly looked like it, but we were not comfortable with a one-horse race.

At a lengthy meeting on 17 October with Leon Brittan, who had taken over from Tebbit at the DTI, John Cuckney brought him fully up to date on the current situation and Brittan repeated almost word for word Tebbit's caution to me that it was the company's sole responsibility to find a solution. There would be no support for a lame duck from this government.

The Sikorsky option had now taken on a European dimension by including Fiat as an equal partner in the proposed 29.9% shareholding, a move on which we had been consulted and agreed. UTC, however, had difficulty with their own Government because Fiat was not permitted to bid for any contracts in the USA due to the fact that Libya – Colonel Gadaffi –held 15% of their shares. He had acquired these some years earlier when the company was in dire financial straits.

It was made clear that unless these shares were redeemed the deal could not go through. The shareholding, now immensely valuable as Fiat was Italy's largest company, was promptly taken up without recourse to raising funds in the market.

John Cuckney and I then flew to Turin to meet our new shareholder, and for meetings with Cesare Rommiti, the Fiat Chief Executive, and other senior executives. This was followed by lunch with the Chairman, Gianni Agnelli, at his home overlooking the city. His splendid residence lay behind high walls and was closely guarded. We were offered drinks in an elegant salon, over-crowded with furniture, which opened onto a terrace where lunch was served.

The salon was policed by two large white chow dogs who then

stationed themselves under the lunch table and were somewhat obtrusive. Agnelli instructed his major-domo to remove them. They failed to respond to several calls before the major-domo put his hand in to grab them. This was greeted by savage growls, the rapid withdrawal of the major-domo and a blunt riposte to Agnelli which even my limited Italian easily translated as a common oath followed by, 'If you want your dogs removed, do it yourself'. The dogs remained under the table.

Europe or USA?

Bill Paul, President of Sikorsky, had now taken direct charge of his company's interests, had called on Heseltine and had lined up the necessary financial resources.

Heseltine then broke cover. He began by attempting to persuade the government to declare their preference for a 'European' solution and plugged to the press the line that what was about to happen was an American 'takeover' of Westland with the result that the 'UK would become dependent on the USA as its sole supplier of military helicopters because Westland would lose her own independent manufacturing capability'.

This travesty of the real situation was fed into the data bases of the teenage scribblers, the mantra being repeated every time the word Westland appeared in copy. Sadly the word 'takeover' also stuck, so much so that even many who should have known better came to use the word for years afterwards. To my dismay even John Nott, one-time Secretary of State for Defence and Chairman of Westland's merchant bankers, Lazards, repeats the canard in his memoirs *Here Today, Gone Tomorrow*.

As far as the company was concerned, a realistic alternative proposal was to be welcomed and John Cuckney made no secret of this in discussion with both Secretaries of State. However, the European companies had failed to make progress and the Westland board now harboured grave doubts that any European group could put together a credible offer in terms that the financial markets would accept and in the timescale demanded by the need to service the company's bank debt.

Heseltine, nevertheless, was determined to bring about a European solution and, in a step well beyond exploration, called an extraordinary meeting of the National Armament Directors (NADs) of the UK, France, Germany and Italy, seeking their agreement that the future need for military helicopters in Europe would be met solely by European-designed and built machines.

While this agreement could not be held as binding on the signatories, the implication was that, should Westland choose the support of a strong shareholder from the USA, there would be no market for their helicopters in Europe. The signal was quite clear. The DTI was maintaining a neutral stance, but the MOD was putting on political pressure in favour of a European solution.

Heseltine states in his memoirs that Westland was invited to attend, but that was not so. He telephoned John Cuckney immediately after the all-day meeting and concluded by giving him their recommendation. This was so clearly a blatant attempt to threaten the company's future that a letter was immediately sent to Leon Brittan seeking confirmation that the UK would not be bound by the NAD's recommendation. Brittan expressed outrage at this breach of the agreed policy of no direct interference and said he would confirm that the NAD decision would not be binding on UK.

Despite Heseltine's action, the need to find a realistic alternative to the Sikorsky proposal was always at the forefront of the company's strategy and, while our preference was to find a UK solution with quoted companies fully versed in the complexity of completing a financial reconstruction acceptable to the banks, we persevered with effots to find a European solution.

During November it was arranged for the European manufacturers to meet Lazards who would explain what was required, particularly regarding the appointment of a banker. This was reinforced by me at a meeting with MBB and Aérospatiale on 22 November and Lloyds Merchant Bank (LMB) were subsequently appointed, Mr David Horne being nominated to lead. This resulted in the first non-specific proposals being received from LMB on 2 December.

Cabinet Meeting

On 9 December the Economic Affairs Committee of the Cabinet met at No 10 Downing Street. Those attending included the Home Secretary, Foreign Secretary, Minister for Trade and Industry, Chancellor, Norman Tebbit, now Chairman of the Party, and

Heseltine. John Cuckney and I had been invited by the Prime Minister to attend and on arrival were welcomed by Charles Powell and ushered into a waiting room where he explained that, when seated, we would be on the left of the PM. Shortly afterwards Mrs Thatcher entered, shook hands and said it would be about twenty minutes before she would be ready for us. My role was as technical advisor and corporate memory.

When called upon, John Cuckney stated the company's position with his usual clarity and emphasized the lack of substance in the so-called European Consortium's proposals which in their present form did not in fact constitute an offer as such. While he remained open and indeed valued an alternative to the Sikorsky proposal he had to meet crucial financial deadlines and must continue discussions with them.

Heseltine then waxed lyrical about European co-operation and quoted previous Anglo-French experience. I was invited to comment. This gave me the opportunity to expose the reality of these so-called joint programmes which in the past had generally, and particularly in Westland's case, resulted in cost overruns and failure of partners to fulfil their obligations.

We withdrew before the end of the meeting, but not before we had heard a robust performance by Nigel Lawson telling the PM that Heseltine had already been given more than adequate time to get his act together, which he had clearly failed to do, and the company should now be allowed to get on with its own solution without inter-ference. We were later informed that it had been decided that the European consortium would be given until 13 December to produce a firm proposal.

On 10 December John Cuckney and I, together with Michael Boughan of Lazards, met Heseltine, supported by John Bourne (later, as Sir John, to become Auditor-General) and Norman Lamont. This was Heseltine at his most assured: a leader still on his chosen path to the top, scenting success. It was quite a performance and left us convinced that he now had backing for a full bid, the only possible trump card. We reported to the board accordingly, but nothing happened.

Heseltine, while drumming up support from Europe, encountered a challenge from the German Minister of Defence, who, not sur-prisingly, asked why help was being sought from Europe for an ailing

English company while British industry was doing nothing. Heseltine tried to explain that he could not coerce privately owned companies, only to meet the response that as a massive customer he could surely demand participation. Our German colleagues shortly reported with glee that Heseltine had taken the hint. BAe announced they had joined the consortium, with GEC following shortly thereafter.

In subsequent meetings with the Chairmen and CEOs of the two companies who had previously so steadfastly refused, on good commercial grounds, to become involved we listened with some amusement as they struggled to explain their new role as poodles under pressure. Arnold Weinstock privately never ceased to be embarrassed at having given in, telling me it was something he would regret for ever.

Meanwhile, David Horne was putting together an offer from his consortium which was presented on 20 December and passed on to shareholders for information. Heseltine claimed very publicly that 'the offer was widely described as superior to the Sikorsky-Fiat alternative'. Yet another example of deliberate misinformation. Indeed the Westland board considered every offer from the consortium with great care but were truly disappointed and concerned that these so-called 'offers' did not deserve to be treated seriously.

Media interest was intense and our private office team of Susan Jessop, my PA, and Anne MacDonald coped brilliantly on top of their other workload, which had more than doubled. Our company PR men, John Teague and Ian Wodward, were now anchored by the heavyweight and well established Bob Gregory. There were never less than a dozen correspondents and photographers at the entrance to our offices in Carlton Gardens where every morning at 10 am John Cuckney held a press briefing and both the BBC and ITV were always represented. He invariably dealt with questions in a masterly fashion and his grasp of the financial issues was such that he was never at a loss. Occasionally John Nott, as Chairman of our merchant bankers, attended and usually perched on the edge of a table in the background.

On one memorable morning the Defence Correspondent of *The Times* fired a largely political question at John Cuckney who refused to be drawn. The questioner then wheeled round to look at John Nott and said, 'Perhaps the ex-Secretary of State for Defence would like to give me an answer'. By this time Nott was already heading for the door in a crouched run with the TV cameras in hot pursuit.

There was no let-up over Christmas and we were constantly in meet-ings with the various parties except on Christmas Day. Shortly after Christmas Heseltine, in a letter to John Cuckney, implied that should Westland proceed with a solution involving US shareholdings the company might not be considered suitable for participation in European projects. This was yet another attempt by Heseltine to put pressure on the company and it was essential to clarify the position. John Cuckney wrote immediately to the Prime Minister to ask if a link with UTC/Fiat would result in Westland being considered non-European.

This clearly called for an equally swift reply, which was neutral in tone and was made public at once. This did not satisfy Heseltine who reacted by arranging for a letter to be sent by David Horne seeking clarification which provided the opportunity to restate all the points Heseltine had wished to be accepted and which had not been agreed by colleagues, including the words that 'HMG had received indica-tions from the other governments and companies that a Westland link with UTC would be incompatible with participation in future European ventures'.

Heseltine sent a copy of this letter to John Cuckney which was leaked and printed in *The Times* the next morning. The board, which was in almost continuous session, was becoming deeply concerned at the apparent determination of Heseltine to defy the Government's stated policy of neutrality and bemused by his obsession with Westland, to which, when asked to assist earlier in the year, he had expressed active hostility, and the failure of the PM to control this maverick member of her Cabinet.

The leaking of letters and claims that some contained material in-accuracies quickly led to the involvement of the Solicitor General, Paddy Mayhew, and the Attorney General, Sir Michael Havers. Press officers were accused. The PM's office was implicated. The media feasted.

By this time an offer from the consortium had been topped by a revised figure from UTC/Fiat. Heseltine admits that soon after this he was beginning to doubt whether his efforts would prevail and that resignation could be one outcome.

Then came Heseltine's well-publicized resignation on 9 January. He admitted later that at first he was optimistic about the way the

Cabinet meeting was going until the Prime Minister took the opportunity to announce that all future public statements on Westland should be cleared with her office in advance. Heseltine declared he could not accept that condition and walked out of the meeting. His announcement to an astonished press corps outside No 10 as he strode away, 'I have resigned from the Cabinet and shall be making a full statement later on', was repeated constantly on TV and radio as analysts attempted to assess the implications.

There had been many cabinet resignations over the years but never one quite so humiliating for the PM or so ill-judged by the minister concerned. That Heseltine was able to deliver a statement to the assembled media running to over three thousand words, only a few hours after walking out of Cabinet, convinced even most of his friends that the speech had already been written, that he had been determined to challenge the PM and waited only for a suitable moment at which to mount it. He sought to justify his action by his view that the Prime Minister was not respecting Cabinet government and that he felt the European solution should have been imposed on Westland.

At the same time as the fateful Cabinet meeting the Chiefs of Staff were themselves meeting under the chairmanship of Admiral of the Fleet Sir John Fieldhouse. On return to his office Heseltine sent a hand-written note to Fieldhouse saying, 'I have resigned. I would like to see you'. Fieldhouse disclosed its contents to his colleagues and said, 'Either we now close the meeting and reconvene later or we adjourn until after my meeting with the ex-Secretary of State.' They unanimously decided to adjourn.

It was a brief meeting. Heseltine said what he had done and that he felt he had no alternative. Fieldhouse responded, 'I hope you know what you are doing.'

As far as the Chiefs were concerned it would be business as usual. Heseltine had all but deserted the Ministry for the past six weeks and his continued absence would not be felt. Indeed they looked forward to a new Secretary of State who would be less shy about making decisions which might be politically risky.

Backbencher

Freed from his ministerial responsibility, Heseltine threw himself into promoting the so-called European solution, and the media, feverish with excitement, loved every moment. To counter this the Westland board decided that John Cuckney should continue to deal exclusively with the direct interviews with city and financial correspondents and I should deal with the operational and industry aspects.

Inevitably there were requests for live debates on television and by this time we had the invaluable advice of the late (Sir)Gordon Reece, one-time adviser to the Prime Minister, who recommended we agree to appear, that I should do so but should avoid direct confrontation, all questions being put through the presenter. My first appearance was on the *Panorama* programme on 13 January 1986, to which we had agreed on the condition that it would be devoted entirely to Westland.

Peter Emery was the presenter and the programme began with some lengthy footage of Heseltine at home on his estate and in his beloved arboretum, taking up a full fifteen minutes, before turning to the subject at hand. This began with the cameras going live in the factory canteen at Yeovil where a very substantial gathering of employees were asked their views.

Feelings had always run high at the factory because the French were perceived, quite rightly, as gaining an unfair share of the work on the joint programmes. They were keenly aware that, while the UK actually ordered the number of helicopters on which the design and work share was based, the French fell well short. The work force enjoyed the chance to speak their minds and gave the interviewer a hard time. This resulted in this part of the programme being cut and we were back on air in the studio.

Heseltine brushed the workforce reaction aside as emotional and typically anti-European. I said it was natural and accurate and quoted some figures. Emery then turned back to Michael who quickly took the opportunity to reiterate the canard that Sikorsky would take over Westland and reduce the company to metal-bashing status.

This gave me the opportunity to express surprise that someone who claimed to have had a successful business career was unable to distinguish between a takeover bid and a financial reconstruction. I explained that what the company wished to achieve required a robust financial partner prepared to invest in the company to the extent of 29.9%: preferably a company with industrial synergy and to that end we had sought the interest of the other helicopter manufacturers in Europe. Because they were Government-owned they did not understand the structure of financial markets or Stock Exchange rules. They continued to address correspondence to the DTI or the MoD. I ended

229

by saying that our attempts to interest the two major UK corporations were equally unsuccessful for good commercial reasons which we fully accepted.

Heseltine made no attempt to address these facts and blustered on about the spectre of an American 'takeover', generating a lot of heat and no light. That he was permitted to maintain this charade throughout the remainder of the programme fully illustrated the financial illiteracy of most of the media and Peter Emery in particular.

Gordon Reece agreed with me that the main thrust of the programme was more about Heseltine than Westland and hence contrary to the basis on which we had accepted the invitation to appear. A strong letter was written to the Director General of the BBC, who acknowledged that 'the balance of the programme was not as good as it should have been.' Nothing new there.

ITV were not to be left out and selected 27 January for a special *News at Seven*. Michael Heseltine and I were both given a camera crew and invited to make a seven-minute film putting over our respective positions. These would be screened at the start of the programme.

Peter Sissons was the presenter and, after introducing Michael and me, he announced that later in the programme, to put the civil service view, we would be joined by Clive Ponting. Michael immediately leapt to his feet, tore off his microphone and stormed out of the studio. Ponting had been a senior official in the Ministry of Defence, who, having been sacked by Heseltine for a gross breech of security by leaking a secret document to *The Guardian*, challenged this in court and lost. He then appealed to the European Court and won.

There was a moment of confusion while Heseltine talked to the producer who agreed to remove Ponting from the programme. Heseltine returned to his seat and Sissons announced that the time which had been allotted to Ponting would now be split between Michael and me, both of us being invited to put three questions to the other, through him.

After the programme Heseltine said to me,'John, you and I disagree about many things but you can't disagree with my action'.

'Absolutely,' I replied. 'It was outrageous that they should have programmed Ponting to take part without telling us and we would both have refused to agree. But surely all you needed to do was to say to Sissons, on camera, what you no doubt said to the producer, "Do you want Ponting or me?" What on earth did you achieve by storming out?'

This had been vintage Michael Heseltine but not at his most assured.

Soon after this a bizarre meeting took place between Ray Lygo, apparently self-appointed to lead the consortium effort, and Leon Brittan at the DTI. According to Lygo, Brittan had claimed that the position being adopted by BAe appeared hostile to the USA and was causing him problems in negotiations concerning alleged subsidies by European Governments to Airbus Industries. Lygo said Brittan had told him that 'he should withdraw from his activities'.

Lygo's immediate reaction appeared to be that this was a threat meant personally against him, but, as he recounts in his memoirs, on reflection he came to see this as a wholly unwarranted and deliberate attempt by the Secretary of State to interfere with BAe through its CEO and accordingly called a BAe board meeting to report and seek a corporate response.

He had first sought the views of Geoffrey Pattie, the Minister at the DTI, who was also at the meeting. He cautioned Lygo not to escalate the issue. 'I don't think you should make too much of it. I think you'll find it will all blow over.' Good advice, but not what Lygo wanted to hear. He scented that there might be some advantage in going on the attack when Brittan had clearly been at least unguarded in his remarks and Lygo was a master at extracting the last drop of advantage at every stage of negotiations.

His pursuit of this issue resulted in an ill-judged letter from his Chairman to the Prime Minister which caused this incident to cloud the much more important decisions requiring attention. Lygo was ultimately required by his board to agree a compromise which avoided his company being at loggerheads with two major Departments of State. A face-saving formula using the time-honoured word 'misunderstanding' was brought into play, but this was inevitably portrayed by the press as 'Lygo backing down'. It was clearly a very uncomfortable time for him and he implies in his book that this was at some cost to the confidence felt in him by his board.

The damage to Leon Brittan was more immediate and cost him his parliamentary career. Lygo had sent Heseltine a copy of his Chairman's letter to the P.M. and when Brittan made a statement in the House on the 13 January Heseltine asked him about the arrival of a letter from BAe. Brittan, although he must have known the letter had reached his department, gave the impression that he had not seen it. This caused a number of backbenchers to call for his resignation and in due course this was the result.

The Resolution

Heseltine's assumption of his role as a leading exponent of the European solution coincided with Alan Bristow's reappearance on the scene with a substantial percentage of Westland shares still in his possession. However, from being a total supporter of an association with Sikorsky when he was bidding for the company six months before, he now presented himself as a staunch backer of the European option. There followed a period of feverish acquisition of shares by the competing parties which resulted effectively in a two-tier market, a situation the Stock Exchange was unable to prevent.

Meanwhile an Extraordinary Meeting of shareholders had been called for 14 January in the usual venue of the Connaught Rooms. However, with a limited capacity of 900 and the company having 12,000 shareholders, it was judged necessary to find a larger capacity location. The Albert Hall was booked for the 17th.

During this period Bristow had meetings with certain prominent people who he alleged had tried to entice him to change his allegiance back to the Company with the promise of an honour for having done so. This was hotly denied by those named and caused long-term damage to Bristow's relations with many old friends. There was inevitably huge media cover and some amusing comments, one such was to suggest he had been offered a 'night out' and not a knighthood. This did not stop Bristow threatening libel actions against nearly everyone for months afterwards, but nothing materialized.

When the Extraordinary Meeting took place on 17 January fewer than 500 shareholders attended. There were nearly as many media representatives. As no resolution could be carried by a show of hands, the company's Registrars had to make a headcount on each occasion. As this took up to an hour there was plenty of time for media interviews and, with both the BBC and ITV much in evidence, the young organist who entertained us throughout had excellent exposure and a huge boost to his career.

Bristow played a major part in this meeting and, having been allowed to state his position at length, John Cuckney took little time to demolish both Bristow's position and the credibility of the Consortium.

'This was the Bristow,' he said, 'who last year had tried to buy the Company so that he could become Chairman, re-establish ties with Sikorsky and build the Black Hawk. Now he condemns the Black Hawk and is prepared to see Westland part-nationalized by a sell-out to Europe.'

'And what about the Consortium?' he asked. 'An ill-assorted bunch with Aérospatiale and its poodle MBB, Agusta keen to escape the discipline that might be imposed by the more commercially minded Fiat and then the two British worthies forced into action by their major customer. Who will be in charge? Lygo who had difficulty under-standing a conversation, an ex-Minister fleeing his Department, an anxious banker or now Bristow clearly joining this concert party. Let us have none of this management by five different owners with only a three-year commitment in mind.'

It was all excellent stuff, hugely enjoyed by the large number of employees who had come up from Yeovil to attend, but, under the company's Articles of Association, a 75% vote was required to approve the proposals and this failed to materialize. No more than 65% of the votes were in favour of the company. It now became neces-sary to re-cast the relevant resolutions so that a majority of over 50% votes would be sufficient and this was achieved at a meeting held on 14 February 1986.

However, this was not the end of the matter. At the final count it was established that 20% of the Company's shares had been held by six nominee companies and had changed hands during the previous few days. The company was uncomfortable with this situation, as it did not have the power to disenfranchise shares held by nominees where the ultimate beneficiary is unknown. This view was shared by the Stock Exchange.

John Cuckney and I attended several meetings with the Stock Exchange committee during the following months and later in the year the company proposed that new Articles of Association be drafted, which would allow the automatic disenfranchizing of a share-holding if the identity of the beneficiary had not been disclosed when requested. However, the Stock Exchange blocked the proposal, saying it was not consistent with their listing requirements.

The Trade and Industry Select Committee, with Kenneth Warren in the chair, deliberated for a year and published its conclusions in February 1987. They were suspicious, but had no proof, that concert parties had been in operation, considered the Stock Exchange rules to be inadequate to deal with the matter effectively, and recommended Government action to require prompt disclosure of those holding controlling voting rights. This was very close to the proposals we had put forward nearly a year earlier.

Throughout, Heseltine continued to declare that UTC/Sikorsky/Fiat, by owning 29.9% of Westland, would control the company. A sell-out to America was his constant and strident claim. That John Cuckney and Margaret Thatcher were working to the same agenda against a European solution was also a constant theme and endlessly repeated in his autobiography. Where they were completely in agreement was, of course, that the company should be allowed to find its own solution. In the event it did, but not before four million pounds of shareholder's funds had been expended in dealing with the intervention of Heseltine.

The 'NEW' Westland

Following the restructuring, new board members were appointed to represent the new shareholders. For UTC these were John Lehman, ex-Secretary of the U.S.Navy, and Tom Pownall, former chairman of the Martin Marietta Corporation. I knew them well and they were to be thoughtful and energetic members. Fiat nominated Professor Zanone.

Within the company Hugh Stewart was tightening up on management and cutting costs, while production work on the two contracts for India kept the helicopter floor loaded. John Varde had joined the company as Managing Director of Westland Helicopters and adequate support for helicopters in operation remained a challenge. The main priorities were to get on with the EH101 project and pursue orders for the Sikorsky Blackhawk.

The Blackhawk was acknowledged as the best battlefield helicopter and the UK would need to replace its ageing Wessex and Puma fleets, but we harboured no illusions that it would be purchased for the UK, certainly not in the short term. However, from the start we had been made aware that the Saudi Arabian Army Air Corps were in the market and we were working with the Defence Export Sales team for this order, to be financed as an extension of the Al Yumama project with BAe for the provision of Tornado aircraft.

George Younger, the new Secretary of State, was a breath of fresh air in the MoD and not afraid to face difficult decisions. While Heseltine and Levene were wasting their time on Westland, a far more important project was being neglected. This was the attempt to provide an AWACS system by converting RAF Nimrod patrol aircraft and fitting GEC equipment. Younger lost no time in cancelling the project on which 500 million pounds had already been wasted. At the same time he was very supportive of our approach to Saudi Arabia, including me in talks with Prince Sultan, the Minister of Defence, and ensuring that I attended the dinner at No 10 Downing St, given by the Prime Minister in his honour.

The Saudi order was conditional on the availability of the latest American anti-tank missile, the Hellfire. This required that the associated firing system should be fitted and that the US Government should permit sale of the missiles. A further requirement was that as much work as possible should be carried out in Saudi Arabia. To this end we formed a joint company with Saudi interests in order to fulfil this requirement, while doing all the development required in the UK.

Meanwhile the Saudi Ambassador in Washington, son of the Minister of Defence and very well connected at all levels with the Reagan administration, was confident that the necessary permissions would be granted. I had remained a close friend of Al Haig ever since he left the Army and now, after he had set up his own consultancy, Atlantic Associates, I had regular meetings with him when I was in Washington. He gave me additional confidence that Prince Sultan would carry the day but warned that we should not underestimate the pro-Israel lobby. He was right.

Not only was permission to sell Hellfire withheld but allegations were made against Sikorsky that Westland was being used by them to evade US legislation. A disgruntled Sikorsky employee in Saudi found a lawyer in Washington who backed his claim: lots more work and fees for the lawyers and much time wasted making it clear that US Government approval had always been fundamental to any contract. For Westland it was as big a disappointment as it was for Sikorsky and sowed the seeds for their ultimate disengagement.

★ ★ ★

John Cuckney had only agreed to be chairman for three years and by mid-1988 was thinking about a successor. He had continued to chair and remain a director of other companies and was now sought to chair 3i (Investors In Industry, the venture capital company owned jointly by the main high street banks). I would be reaching my retiring age the following year and Sikorsky were becoming critical of Stewart's management of the company. Meanwhile Fiat exercised their right to sell their shares and these were picked up by GKN who ultimately also took up the Sikorsky holding.

There were a number of people interested in succeeding John Cuckney, who took me into his confidence when making a choice and the chairmanship was finally handed to Sir Leslie Fletcher, who was then Deputy Chairman of Standard and Chartered Bank and well respected in the city. Headhunters introduced Alan Jones, a senior executive with Plessey, as a potential replacement for Stewart. He had excellent credentials and knew his way around Whitehall.

Fletcher said he would continue to base himself in the city and use our offices as Cuckney had. In the event he quickly departed from Standard and Chartered and became a permanent resident in Westland's London office. Jones duly took over from Stewart and I found it as difficult to work with this new team as they did with me. I had been with the company for eleven years; it had been as challenging as it was rewarding and I had enjoyed every minute.

9

WINNERS AND LOSERS

THE EIGHTH DECADE

Immediately following my departure from Westland a number of new opportunities arose and I was in no mood to give up. Quite apart from anything else I had heavy losses at Lloyds of London which would take many years to repay.

I cover most of these ventures in this chapter. Few of them were profitable, most were interesting and some entertaining. However, they all contributed to achieving the aim of not being at home for lunch, perhaps the most important of one's marriage vows.

Throughout this period, when I was no longer tied to an executive's unforgiving schedule, I was increasingly able to work at home in London when not travelling. The lease on our house in Ibiza still had some years to run and the young showed no inclination to spend their holidays elsewhere. With a pool, a beach and toys ranging from windsurfers to serious ski-boats there were plenty of attractions and the night-club scene came into focus in their later teens. Now, with the grandchildren, there is a new bucket and spade generation growing up.

MEGGITT plc

While I had taken on a number of consultancies and was determined to avoid non-executive directorships of publicly quoted companies, I was almost immediately asked to join the board of Meggitt by its Chief Executive, the late Ken Coates, who was a fellow council member of the SBAC, and for him I made an exception. Ken had been Chief Executive of Flight Refuelling and, after some differences with his chairman, left to start his own company, taking the finance director,

Nigel McCorkell, with him. The company had been backed by 3i and one of the senior executives, Donald Driver, became the first non-executive chairman.

A spectacular start had been made and Meggitt grew rapidly as an international group of companies operating on the continent of Europe, in North America and the Far East as well as the UK. Its specialist aerospace engineering skills made it a world leader in a number of high-integrity products and technologies for both civil and military aircraft.

I was delighted to have this opportunity to stay in touch with the industry and to meet up with many old friends and colleagues. Meggitt was a supplier to both Westland and BAe, as well as Boeing, Northrop and many others, and usually found it had a stand next to that of Westland at the Farnborough and Paris air shows, which added to the fun!

Meanwhile I had been retained by Mesbla in Brazil as a consultant after leaving Westland, and Kirstie and I were invited to be present during the visit of the Prince and Princess of Wales. Mesbla were much involved in their programme and had put the use of the company's HS 125 jet at the disposal of the royal couple. We found ourselves staying in the same hotel (there was no other choice in Brasilia) and on their arrival we happened to be in the lobby. Diana ignored the line-up of ambassadors to come over and give us both big hugs. There was no reason for us to have been on their official programme but we attended nearly all their functions and she was always happy to see familiar faces.

It was on our return from this visit that I suffered renewed attacks of angina and a further angiogram revealed that my arteries were again badly blocked. My splendid GP, Mike Bloomer, this time selected Mr Patrick McGee who had now assumed the mantle of top man in the bypass fraternity and there was a wait of a week to get a slot in his programme. However, I was in bad shape and within two days McGee found the time to open me up. It was in fact a surprise to learn that one could have a repeat of this operation, but I was assured even three times was not uncommon.

Nine years on from my past operation, techniques had improved vastly. The operating time was reduced to less than four hours and recovery to two or three weeks. I was just happy it had not hit while I was in Brazil. It did not stop me musing on why neither Al Haig nor

Henry Kissinger, two and one year ahead of me respectively, had been similarly affected, not even to this day.

I remained with Meggitt until another sell-by date arrived in 1994 and this really did mark the end of my direct association with the aerospace industry.

INTEROUTE TELECOMMUNICATIONS plc

During this period I was also involved in Switzerland where, with an old friend, Simon Kimmins, we set about entering the expanding world of telecommunications, attempting to buy the systems subsidiary of the major manufacturer ASCOM. The company was in some trouble and had recently fired its Chief Executive and appointed Felix Wittlin, who we knew, at the time a member of the Supervisory Board, in his place. Unable to raise the necessary funds ourselves, we introduced the opportunity to Cable and Wireless who made the acquisition.

John Mittens, the senior executive at Cable and Wireless who had been responsible for the acquisition, soon left to form his own company, Interoute, one of the first to become a telephone service 'least cost' re-seller. He was anxious for the company to become pan-European and invited Kimmins to set up in Switzerland. Within a year the service was active in France, Germany and Spain, as well as the UK and Switzerland and in need of additional funding. Such was the market enthusiasm that, with James Capel as our brokers, we floated the company on the AIM in 1996.

By this time I had become the non-executive Chairman and was determined to make sure proper accounting was enforced. Mittens was an excellent CEO, but telephony has an insatiable appetite for funds and we had severely underestimated the quantum. The removal of the finance director and his replacement by our senior auditor could not disguise the fact that we would have exhausted the funds we had raised well ahead of budget.

This was at the end of 1997: our original backers were not interested in assisting and James Capel said we would have no chance of raising further funds from investors. There were already a number of major companies taking an interest in us, particularly Americans who wanted to break into the European market. They made generous offers, but all subject to conditions which ruled them out. I was then fortunate to have an introduction to Victor Bishoff, the moving force behind the Sandos Foundation in Switzerland, itself holding about 60% of the original company now renamed Novartis.

Victor said he wanted to take a position in this market and had been impressed by John Mittens and what he had achieved. He made an immediate cash offer which I accepted. This in fact treated our shareholders quite well. I resigned and Victor took over, growing in confidence and investing heavily. Mittens stayed on and Kimmins continued to run the Swiss company until massive competition drove margins down to unsustainable levels and he left the company in 1999.

After acquiring an Internet Service Provider Victor began building a worldwide network. He was not alone. By the time his network was complete at a cost of over a billion pounds so were many others and the industry now had a vast over-capacity. The company failed in 2003.

Meanwhile Kimmins had teamed up with a musician turned internet guru who had been closely involved with the introduction of messaging over mobile telephones. He saw the future going from message data to streaming music and assisting the music industry in its battle to prevent illegal downloading. The aim was to make streaming on demand more attractive than downloading and, more importantly, keeping it legal.

We raised funds for this venture in Holland and for two years developed a programme compatible with the major software companies and designed to work on the third generation mobile networks. These 3G networks encountered long delays; funding from mobile telecom companies had almost dried up in the wake of the huge debts they had incurred acquiring licences and our original plans failed to materialize. The work continues, but it is now limited to internet delivery and I am no longer involved.

LLOYDS of LONDON

I should not fail to mention this financial disaster. Soon after I left the Navy I was introduced to the perceived advantages of becoming a 'name' at Lloyds whereby funds could be pledged without having to be realized. Two for the price of one. The risk of course was that the pledge was unlimited and if funds were 'called' this could include the last cuff-link. However, one was assured that risks never ran more than three years, Lloyds has been a success for over 300 years and, after all, many of my friends had been funding school fees this way. Little did I foresee the possibility that within a few years Lloyds would be sustaining losses which would wipe out the accumulated profits of those 300 years in the next three.

I was encouraged to chair a small maritime underwriting agency, R.L.Glover, by its managing director and major shareholder, and by Murray Lawrence, Deputy Chairman of Lloyds, who was making efforts to bring outside management experience into the market. I could soon see why. It was clear that R.L.Glover had no future.

We achieved a sale to a larger agency headed by Brian Kellet and I remained on his board until he in turn sold on. Soon the worst happened. The catastrophe has been widely analysed and over-reported everywhere, but from my own experience over ten years, I am left with the uncomfortable feeling that the top men had more than a hunch about what was coming. The rush to double membership from fifteen to thirty thousand in the years immediately before these crushing losses may be coincidental, but only an operatic suspension of reality can prevent one from having doubts.

My losses were substantial and I was still 'working for Lloyds' for many years, in the sense that I had yet to clear the loans I raised to pay my debts.

Health Clubs and Substance Abuse

These do not go together as the title may suggest but followed each other. I had become involved in a company setting up a chain of health clubs in Canada and the USA which happily enabled me to make visits to my children over there on a reasonably regular basis.

For her part Kirstie had to give up her partnership in an antique business, where she was jointly and severally liable for almost as much as I was at Lloyds, and had become a trustee of a charity endowed by a close friend, dealing with substance abuse – alcohol and drugs. Most of those involved in this area are themselves 'in recovery' and those who are not need to experience the regime of the treatment centres.

I went along in support on a week spent at Hazelden in Minnesota, the headquarters of the Twelve Step AA programme. We each joined a group of twenty-four (single sex) undergoing a twenty-eight-day course; one came in and one left nearly every day. We both found it a harrowing experience.

New arrivals in the group were required to 'tell their story' to the other members on their first evening. In my group they ranged from a senior captain in North West Airlines reported by his cabin crew to a priest from Wyoming who was seeking to survive a sabbatical without the discipline of having to care for his parish and a teenage messenger boy from Washington DC sent by his employers.

I often found it hard to tell from their stories just how heavy their dosage had become. One mentioned the daily cocaine level he had reached, a figure which meant nothing to me. I asked him later to explain. 'Kill a horse,' he said.

The first step is for each new member to come out of 'denial' – denying they have a problem. There was little humour about, although the Hazelden shop sold T-shirts with DENIAL in huge print across the chest and underneath, in small print 'is not a river in Egypt'.

Maintaining Contact With The Navy

I have been fortunate that, quite apart from business, I have been able to maintain contact with the Navy through various channels and at various levels. The first was through Kirstie's ship, HMS *Glasgow*, which she launched in 1976 and was the central figure at the commissioning ceremony which took place in Portsmouth dockyard in May 1980.

Thereafter Kirstie kept in close touch with the ship, visiting whenever opportunities arose. On these occasions I found myself playing the 'Denis Thatcher' role, bringing up the rear. Kirstie was naturally the guest of honour and while she was getting the VIP treatment I was able to visit the Chief Petty Officers and be brought right up to date on the 'real' issues; always informative and good fun.

Glasgow, under the command of Captain Paul Hoddinot, was one of the first ships to reach the Falklands, having deployed in haste direct from the Mediterranean. Normally all valuable 'trophies' are landed from ships going to war, but there was no chance this time. *Glasgow* was in company with HMS *Sheffield* when the latter was hit by an Exocet missile, but *Glasgow* had detected the missiles coming in and Hoddinot took all the essential defensive measures.

However, the ship was not to escape unscathed and was later hit by a 500lb bomb released at sea level and very short range. It entered the hull just above the water line in the auxiliary machinery room and went straight out the other side without exploding. The Captain liked to tell the story that the stoker on watch in the compartment at the time – a boring task requiring instrument readings at set intervals – had a copy of *Playboy* in hand as the bomb blasted through, snatching the magazine from his hand. He was severely traumatized – by the loss of his favourite reading!

The damage was sufficient to put the ship out of action and she had to return to the UK for repairs before rejoining the fleet. Now she is twenty-eight years old and, having been in very good shape when passing her 20th year (the normal maximum life) she was one of very few to be given a major refit in 1978 and recommissioned for a further ten years' service. Kirstie had the pleasure of doing the honours once again. Sadly, *Glasgow* is now being taken out of commission.

I thoroughly enjoyed ten years as President of the Bromley Sea Cadets, having been invited to take over from an ex-Royal Marine, a contemporary of mine during the war whose brother was killed at Normandy after surviving three gruelling years in the desert, and through the White Ensign Association, of which I was a council member from 1977 to 2001, I have also enjoyed frequent contact with naval events including many fund-raising spectaculars masterminded by Sir Donald Gosling.

Even more enduring is my association with the FAA Museum, doing well under its Director, Graham Mottram, and for the last ten years I have been President of the Swordfish Heritage Trust (SHT), set up to provide support from industry for the Historic Flight. While the flight itself is capable of running repairs, the SHT can undertake complete aircraft and engine re-builds, without which the Flight would not have been able to continue.

While the whole aerospace industry has contributed, it has been British Aerospace to whom the greatest debt is owed. The driving force has been the Chairman and Chief Executive, Dick Evans, and the execution has been due to the dedication of those responsible for apprentice training. They confess that these restorations are splendidly motivating for the apprentices and are a major factor in maintaining long-term interest. So the benefit works both ways.

Plans are now in hand to combine these separate but inter-related parts of the Naval heritage in one Fly Navy Heritage Trust

The US Navy

I have also been able to maintain a link with the USN through the Center for Naval Analysis in Washington. A driving force behind this is a retired Navy captain, Harlan Ullman, who has become a defence analyst, writer and commentator. Harlan is a friend of twenty-five years and on our bi-annual visits to my daughter and grandchildren in Chicago Kirstie and I spend two days in Washington with the Ullmans when I am invited to address members of the Center, the last time being on the day after the invasion of Iraq, 21 March 2003.

It was quite a moment and I was surprised to have the Deputy Commandant of the US Marine Corps at my talk. He came over afterwards to commiserate over the loss of six of our Royal Marines on the first day in one of the Marine Corps helicopters.

Harlan has written a number of books and coined the phrase 'shock and awe' to describe the effect of a massive assault in a book written in 1996. The result was frantic media interest and television interviews throughout our visit.

While serving in the US Navy, Harlan held an exchange posting with the Royal Navy spending a year on the staff at Britannia Royal Naval collage and a year at sea in HMS *Bacchante,* then commanded by Julian Oswald, later to become an Admiral of the Fleet. He married an English girl, also Julian, and during part of his career served on the staff of the War College. Among his students was a Colonel Colin Powell. They became close friends.

At a very large lunch given in Washington to celebrate Colin Powell's sixtieth birthday he had Julian seated on his left. During his speech he paused to put his arm around her shoulders and said, 'I have a confession to make. This beautiful girl and I have slept together.'

This was received in stunned silence by the guests and Powell continued, 'I can see that I owe you an explanation. When I was a student at the War College her husband, Harlan Ullman, was one of the distinguished members of the faculty. As you know the wives of the students and the lecturers may also attend and Julian and I often sat side by side. When her husband was lecturing after lunch we slept together!'

Harlan continues to 'think outside the box' and remains an influential and respected author and commentator.

REFLECTIONS

During my service career in the senior ranks I had never had the good fortune to be part of an administration which had the wholehearted respect of world leaders. The UK still relied on the traditional, understated British presentation, the quiet search for consensus, the assumption that everyone will play by the generally accepted rules.

Harold Macmillan thought that he was preserving free enterprise while ensuring that the lesser well off prospered. 'You've never had it so good'. In fact he presided over the decline of British competitiveness while always searching for consensus.

Trade union power had expanded throughout Wilson's first government and when Ted Heath ultimately decided to challenge the unions Macmillan advised against dividing the 'One Nation' which he felt had been created with such care and pain over the past twenty years. Heath went to the nation in 1974 and the voters deserted him. We had not yet found a leader prepared to fight by the new hard rules which were the order of the day, not until the arrival of Margaret Thatcher.

She carried no ideological baggage and no guilt about the past. Not only did she have a belief in freedom of choice and reward for endeavour, she had the determination to force this change upon a nation set on a path of self-destruction. And she earned for the nation and herself the respect of the whole world. It was no easy path. The majority of the old guard conservatives gave her little hope of success and little support in her attack on the restrictive practices and unbridled union power. The establishment was not prepared for the challenge as made clear in Lord Prior's book *The Balance of Power*, in which he concluded that 'the unions were not ready for it.'

I had two years dealing directly with the unions before the Thatcher administration and it was very hard to make managers realize it was their prime duty to manage. The unions liked to refer to 'their men'. I told them they were mine not theirs. Management provided the work and paid the wages, not the unions.

And so to Europe. I first became involved in Germany in 1978, then Holland, Austria, Italy, Switzerland and Spain. It did not take long to recognize the difference between their culture and ours. We show our concern that the Mayor of Paris may be using city property for his family or mistress and paying for his holidays with cash from special 'funds', but fail to understand that this is tolerated by the populace simply because they are mostly doing something similar, if not on the same scale. Sin regularly, confess and start again. As one French lady put it to me, 'You English must lose your Protestant guilt'. But, more than that, the Anglo-Saxon commitment to competition and private ownership is not to their taste and tax-payer's money continues to support ailing companies.

No realist working in Europe can have any illusions that closer British involvement would result in us being able to influence any decisions. The expressed desire for the British to commit ourselves totally is based on a determination to cut completely our ties with the United States, without whose dedication and overwhelming support we would not have won two Great Wars and saved continental Europe from itself.

Nor should anyone have illusions about the hapless European Parliament, driven by a unelected commission staffed by failed politicians fronting for the shrewd and mainly French graduates of the Écoles Supérieure who preside over an ever-expanding bureaucracy.

I still work with a wide circle of friends and colleagues in continental Europe and am as convinced that we are European as I am that we should never be bound by continental constitutions and codes. We have never faced a land frontier and have never therefore had the chance to start life taking goods illegally across borders, always being sure to keep a sweetener for any guard who might apprehend us. Because we are in general satisfied with our own institutions we are seldom provoked to defy them and hence tend to treat the ever-expanding demands of Brussels with a respect they have seldom earned.

We close down our abattoirs and abandon our cheese makers while the French Préfect makes no attempt to enforce those Brussels edicts which he knows would result in fearsome local reprisals. If our Dutch friends suspect a scam they are likely to negotiate rather than expose. Meanwhile in Brussels the corruption continues, whistle-blowers are sacked and the failure to provide audited accounts for nine years goes unpunished. Groucho Marx famously said he would not join a club which would have him as a member: I don't think we should join a Union which has any continental Europeans in it!

Margaret Thatcher was reviled for saying there was no such thing as society. Quoted in context she was quite right: it is the people that make up 'society' and whatever form it takes. My life has been based on people and I have named many of them in this book. They have all formed part of what is called our society which reflects our culture and broadly, based on a democratically elected parliament, we accept the wishes of the majority. Our weakness is our tolerance and we have now reached what I believe to be the point where we are tolerating the intolerable.

We welcome in our country those seeking a better way of life than that provided by the land of their birth, but they do not give us their allegiance. They continue to pursue the very cultures from which they chose to escape and foster cells of disaffected youths even when they present a direct challenge to the freedoms we have sought to preserve at the cost of thousands of lives. We are in danger of being colonized by cultures, undemocratic, brutal and intolerant, which have contributed nothing to the dramatic changes the world has seen in the last 200 years and remain frozen in a bygone age.

Our Armed Forces today, unquestionably the best in Europe and the only real 'edge' that our Prime Minister enjoys in EU terms, face a totally different and far more insidious enemy buried in sleeping cells of trained fanatics within our own communities, an enemy which attaches no value to any human life. This will place even more emphasis on the need for political will to back actions which will be fiercely opposed by those who believe the need for an identity card is an infringement of their liberty.

Appendix I

Letter written on the occasion of the death of Samuel Treacher

His Majesty's Ship Porcupine Passage
30th January 1814

I am sorry to Inform you of the Loss of
His Majesty's Schooner Holly in the Harbour of
St Sebastian's at 4 OClock Yesterday morning which
I have no doubt but you will be very sorry to hear
especially when I explain the Loss we have sustained
Your dear son Saml Sharp Treacher is no more
we parted our cables & run upon the Rocks under
the Mount of St Sebastian's a heavy sea running at
the Time washed my dear Freind Le Treacher
(with Wm Cram Assistant Surgeon & Two men)
overboard & was never more seen — I with the rest of
the officers most bitterly lament the Loss — I with
the rest of the officers and Men Escaped in our
Shirts. the Tide setting out drifted every thing to sea
No bodies is yet found — If you wish any —

Explanation respecting his accounts I should
find myself pleased to the highest degree in
giving you every Information in my power
We are at present on board His Majesty's Ship
Porcupine expecting to be sent to England in
the first Vessel that goes. —

I am Dr Sir with the greatest
respect your most obedt
Humble Servant
R. Busby Clerk

Appendix II

VISIT OF HER MAJESTY
THE QUEEN
TO THE WESTERN
FLEET AT TORBAY
28th & 29th JULY 1969

Admiral Sir John Bush K.C.B.. D.S.C.★★
Commander-in-Chief Western Fleet

Vice-Admiral Sir Michael Pollack,K.C.B.. M.V.O.. D.S.C.
Flag Officer Submarines

Vice-Admiral A. M. Lewis, C.B.
Flag Officer Flotillas Western Fleet

Rear-Admiral M. F. Fell. C.B.. D.S.O. D.S.C.
Flag Officer Carriers and Amphibious Ships

Rear-Admiral G. S. Ritchie, C.B., D.S.C.
Hydrographer of the Navy

EAGLE   Captain J. D. Treacher
Commander-in-Chief Western Fleet

GLAMORGAN   Captain S. L. McArdle M. V. O., G. M.
Flag Officer Submarines

HAMPSHIRE   Captain R. P. Clayton
Flag Officer Flotillas Western Fleet

BLAKE   Captain R. F. Plugge, D.S.C.
Flag Officer Carriers and Amphibious Ships

HECATE   Captain J. H. S. Osborn, R.A.N.
Hydrographer of the Navy

EASTBOURNE	Captain I. S. S. Mackay
PHOEBE	Captain C. R. P. C. Branson
CHARYBDIS	Captain D. W. Foster
PLYMOUTH	Commander St. J. H. Herbert
WARSPITE	Commander J. B. Hervey
SIRIUS	Commander J. A. de M. Leathes, O.B.E.
VALIANT	Commander G. R. King
TENBY	Commander R. I. T. Hogg
FAWN	Commander C.E.K. Robinson
ABDIEL	Commander T. M. B. Seymour
LLANDAFF	Commander W. H. Stewart
TORQUAY	Commander P. J. Symons
KEPPEL	Commander J. M. S. Ekins
DIANA	Commander E. D. L. Llewellyn
CUZON	Commander B. K. Perrin, V.R.D., R.N.R.
VENTURER	Commander F. A. Williams, R.D., R.N.R.
FOX	Lieutenant Commander R. Dathan
DUNDAS	Lieutenant Commander E. M. England
LEWISTON	Lieutenant Commander R. G. Teasdale
ODIN	Lieutenant Commander N. G. Warneford
DUNCAN	Lieutenant Commander W. M. Forbes
UPTON	Lieutenant Commander G. J. Claydon
BILDESTON	Lieutenant Commander R. J. D. Allan
ACHERON	Lieutenant Commander D. W. Mitchell
AMBUSH	Lieutenant Commander J. P. Speller
OLYMPUS	Lieutenant Commander R. F. Channon
TIPTOE	Lieutenant Commander J. J. S. Daniel
ORACLE	Lieutenant Commander G. T. Swales
SOLENT	Lieutenant Commander G. R. Hill, R.N.R.
SOBERTON	Lieutenant D. T. Ancona
RESOURCE	Captain E. D. J. Evans
OLMEDA	Captain S. C. Dunlop, M.B.E.
LYNESS	Captain C. G. D. Barker
ENGADINE	Captain J. H. McLoughlin

H.M.Y. BRITANNIA Rear-Admiral P. J. MORGAN, C.B., D.S.C.
T.H.V. PATRICA Captain K. Carstens

INDEX

252

Cuckney, Sir (later Lord) John, 145, 202, 218, 219, 221, 223, 224, 225, 226, 227, 229, 232–3, 234, 236
Cunningham, Admiral Sir Andrew, 19
Cunningham, Jock, 104
Cunningham, Mary, 104
Cuxhaven, 107–8

Daily Express, 118
Daily Mail, 185
Daily Telegraph, 185
Daldegan, Admiral, 207
Dalgleish, Surgeon Lieutenant Commander David, 60
D'Allesandro, Roberto, 215
Daniels, Derick, 188
Daniels, Josephus, 188
Dann, Lieutenant Commander Wally, 84, 85
Danskin, Henry, 31
Darwin, SS, 64
Davidson, Ian Hay, 182
Dawson, Lieutenant Commander Oscar, 85, 87, 204
de Botton, André, 208
de Botton, Henrique, 208
de Botton, Jacqueline, 208
de Clerq family, 182
de Gaulle, President Charles, 166
de Valdivia, Pedro, 3
Deane, Donald, 33
Debré, M., 113
Deedes, (Lord) Bill, 185
Delfont, Bernard, 183
Denham-Smith, Caroline, 170
Denman, Charles, 98, 100–1, 102
Dev, Commander Krishnan, 84
Dimbleby, Richard, 74, 107
Dimmock, Lieutenant Roger, 73
DiPrima, Frank, 188
Doe, Captain Robin, 177
Dolore, HMS, 7

Drake, Sir Eric, 156
Dreadnought, HMS, 92, 93, 94, 96
Dreiser, Peter, 177
Dreyer, Vice Admiral Sir Desmond, 91
Driver, Donald, 238
Dry Ginger, 91
Duffield, Captain Richard, 208
Duggal, Lieutenant, 85, 86
Duke of York, HMS, 20
Dunkirk, 11

Eagle Express, 133
Eagle, HMS, 50, 51, 74, 108, 113, 116, 122, 123–34, 135, 140, 143, 149
Eagle, Lieutenant Commander John, 132
Eagles, Lieutenant Commander David, 116
Easthampstead Park, 10
Easton, Commander Ian, 57
Eaton Hall, 16
Eden, Sir Anthony, 89, 175
Egginton, John, 210
Eia, Bjiane, 16
Eisenhower, General Dwight D., 19, 24, 59
Elizabeth II, HM Queen, xii, 128, 129
Emery, Peter, 229, 230
Empson, Air Vice Marshal Reginald, 115
English, David, 185
Enterprise, HMS, 21, 22–3
Erhard, Chancellor Ludwig, 107
Eskimo, HMS, 17
Essex, USS, 77
European Helicopter Industries (EHI), 214, 221
European Parliament, 246
Evans, Rear Admiral Charles 'Crash', 70, 73, 75, 78
Evans, Dick, 243
Evans, Lieutenant John, 61

Everard, Bunny, 206
Everard, Mary, 206
Explorer, HMS, 92
Eyewell House, Yeovilton, 149

Falk, Roly, 50
Falkland Islands, 63–7
Falklands War, 203, 242–3
Fanshawe, Lord, 220
Farley, John, 128
Farmer, Vivien, 6
Farnborough Air Show, 209, 238
Farrow, Kit, 218
Fearless, HMS, 135, 142, 172
Featherstone, Flag Lieutenant Neville, 149
Felixstowe, 5
Fell, Rear Admiral Mike, 128, 135
Fiat, 222, 226, 227, 234
Fieldhouse, Rear Admiral John, 172; Admiral of the Fleet Sir John, 172, 228
Finisterre, HMS, 30
First Canadian Infantry Division, 4
Fisher, Admiral, 54
Flack, John, 180
Fleet Air Arm Museum, 121, 145–8, 172, 243
Flemington Race Course, 6
Fletcher, Sir Leslie, 236
Flying Enterprise, SS, 50
Ford, President Gerald, 169
Fraser, Admiral Sir Bruce, 20
Fraser, Lieutenant General David, 153
Frazer, 'Tubby', 121
Freeman, Flag Lieutenant Miles, 149
Freer, Air Marshal Bob, 164
Frewen, Captain John, 59
Frost, David, 175
Fuchs, Sir Vivian, 60–1

Gadaffi, Colonel, 222

Gandhi, Indira, 204, 212
Gandhi, Rajiv, 212
Gardner, Charles, 50
Gardner, David, 208
Gardyne, Flag Lieutenant
    Patrick Bruce, 136
Gatis, Lieutenant George,
    46
Geddes, Lord, 146
General Electric (GEC),
    221, 226
German Clinic, 1
Gibbs, General Roly, 169
Gibraltar, ix, 17, 81, 108,
    123, 131
Gibson, Commander
    Donald, 45
Gick, Captain Percy, 148
Gilbert, John, 155
Gilmour, Ian, 151, 155
Gladwell, Robert, 210,
    216
Glasgow, HMS, 21, 22, 23,
    24, 26, 176, 177, 203,
    242
Goetz, Lieutenant
    Commander Tim, 124
Gold beach, 22
Goldsmith, Sir James, 185
Goodhart, Commander
    Nick, 54, 56
Goodpaster, General
    Andrew, 161
Gort, John, 104
Gosling, Donald, 147
Gosing, Sir Donald, 172,
    180, 243
Gourley, General Sir Ian,
    159
Gourock, 27
Graf Spee, 22
Gray, Captain Jock, 81
Great Bitter Lakes, 33
Greaves, Lieutenant
    Commander George,
    124
Greece, 33
Gregory, Bob, 226
Gretton, Commodore
    Peter, 57
Griffin, Rear Admiral
    Anthony, 120
Grundisburgh, 4
Grytviken, 65

Guantanamo Bay, 138,
    172

Habbibi, Dr, 209
Hague, Colin, 216
Haida, HMCS, 21
Haig, General Alexander,
    161, 162, 166, 168,
    203, 235, 238
Haig, Pat, 162
Haile Selassie, Emperor, 5,
    9
Hall, Admiral, 22
Hall, Sir Arnold, 111
Halliday, Captain Roy
    'Gus', 121, 135
Hamburg, city of, 107
Hamburg, 107
Hamilton, Lieutenant
    Commander 'Shorty',
    80–1
Handley, Lieutenant
    Thomas, 44
Hanson, (Lord) James,
    198
Harding, Field Marshal
    Lord, 189
Hardy, Graham, 206
Hardy, Moira, 206
Harries, David, 124–5,
    130
Harrison, Ernie, 114
Hart, Roger, 208
Hartwell, Lieutenant
    Barry, 79
Havers, Sir Michael, 227
Hawkins, HMS, 22–3
Hay, Commander Jock
    Petrie, 76
Healey, Denis, 97, 112,
    113–14, 115, 117,
    118, 158, 160
Heath, Edward, 151, 155,
    157, 245
Hefford, Lieutenant, 128
Hefner, Christie, 188
Hefner, Hugh, 188, 192,
    198
Hegaty, Lieutenant
    Commander, 62
Heinemann, Ed, 48, 77
Heinemann, Zel, 77
Hennessy, Graham, 13
Hercules, HMS, 83

*Here Today, Gone
    Tomorrow*, 223
Hermes, HMS, 74, 81,
    113, 135, 143
Herndon, USS, 23
Heseltine, Michael, 212,
    213, 218, 220, 221,
    223, 224–34
Hickman, Devereux
    Henry, 6
Hickman, Florence, 6
Hickman, John, 206
Higgs, Lieutenant
    Commander Geoff,
    76, 80
Higton, Denis, 80
Hiles, Lieutenant Peter,
    46, 47, 48, 49, 52
Hillary, Sir Edmund, 60–1
Hill-Norton, Admiral of
    the Fleet Lord, 165
Hobson, Ronald, 180
Hoddinot, Captain Paul,
    242
Holford, Commander
    Bunny, 57
Holly, HMS, 7
Home Guard, 11–12
Homer, Chief Petty
    Officer Charlie, 46
Hong Kong, 40, 41, 109,
    122
Hood, HMS, 129
Horne, David, 224, 226,
    227
House, Rear Admiral
    William, 137
Howe, Admiral Lord, 123
Hudson Bay Company, 4
Hudson, Lieutenant
    Commander Mike, xii,
    98, 152, 163, 164,
    177–9
Humane Society of
    Kenora, 4
Hunt, Lieutenant
    Commander Geoff,
    124
Hunt, General Sir Peter,
    151
Hunter, Sir John, 176
Hunting Aerosurveys, 60,
    63
Huston, Marvin, 188
Hutton, Captain, 39, 40

255

256

258